LE DUC ET CÉLIE

From edition 1880, Le Hazard du Coin du Feu

FOUR NOVELISTS
OF THE
OLD RÉGIME

❖

Crébillon, Laclos, Diderot,
Restif de la Bretonne

❖

BY

JOHN GARBER PALACHE

LONDON
JONATHAN CAPE 30 BEDFORD SQUARE

FIRST PUBLISHED MCMXXVI

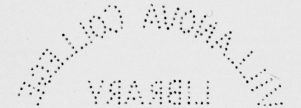

PRINTED IN U. S. A.

Table of Contents

v

V. Les Liaisons Dangereuses
Page 83

The story — Criticisms.

VI. Diderot
Page 99

General character of his fiction — Diderot as critic — His personality — Diderot as playwright.

VII. Diderot's Novels
Page 110

Les Bijoux Indiscrets — Jacques le Fataliste — Le Neveu de Rameau — La Religieuse.

VIII. Restif de la Bretonne
Page 142

Preface — The qualities of Restif as a writer — His character and personality.

IX. La Vie de Mon Père
Page 152

Origin of the Restif family — An Eighteenth-century village — Paternal authority — The Household — The Farm.

The Story of Monsieur Nicolas
(Restif de la Bretonne)

X. Childhood and Youth of Restif
Page 161

Preface — Schoolboy and shepherd — Choirboy at Bicêtre — Seminarist at Courgis.

Illustrations

Foreword

A tale of Crébillon *fils* is the comedy of a corrupt and brilliant society in its last phase.

The novel of Laclos is the tragedy of that society.

There is no protest in the work of Crébillon *fils*. The protest in that of Laclos is against particular persons, not a revolt against an existing social system.

Crébillon *fils* and Laclos belonged to the old France. Diderot and Restif de la Bretonne belonged to the new; as novelists, they had a different point of departure and moved in another direction. Their separate paths were among the many that led to the Revolution.

Four Novelists of the Old Régime

CHAPTER I

Introductory

THE history of the French eighteenth-century novel is a series of contrasts, a natural parallel to the political and social history of the time. Some of its most striking phases are to be found in the works of three novelists, scarcely mentioned in English and American essays, and in the novels of Diderot, who is chiefly known as a philosopher and scientist. Crébillon *fils,* Laclos and Restif de la Bretonne have been usually considered too "shocking," and of little or no literary or historical value.[1] It is true that they are not among the greatest artists in the history of novel-writing. They give, however, an insight into some aspects of the life of the eighteenth century which are not so clearly brought out in the writings of their more illustrious contemporaries.[2] The answer to the charge of licentiousness is, for Crébillon *fils,* Laclos, Restif and Diderot, the fact that they recorded, more frankly than Voltaire and Rousseau, events and manners which they knew and had seen. There is often a tendency to find literary fault with a novel on the ground of its "unclean" subject, as well as to over-state the case for literary praise if the subject be "clean." But an

---

[1] George Saintsbury, in his *History of the French Novel,* is appreciative of Crébillon *fils* and Restif, but he strangely misjudges Laclos—not because of that author's subject-matter, however.

[2] Voltaire and Rousseau are mentioned only incidentally in these pages, for they have been thoroughly discussed in any number of books and articles.

I

imaginary line between "clean" and "unclean" subjects has frequently been drawn with such confident rigour, that the importance of treatment—the manner of handling the subject—and the historical significance of a fact have been forgotten in the cry of protest: "These things are unpleasant, therefore they have no place in a novel."

The usual position of Diderot, in the company of the Encyclopedists, is necessary in any consideration of his work as a whole. But his philosophical and scientific works are far better known than his fiction, and it is for this reason that he has been included in this group of less familiar novelists.

It would be difficult, anywhere, to find an account so intense, so dramatic as that of the cruelty and intrigue observed by Laclos in definite instances, and presented in *Les Liaisons Dangereuses*—the tragic side of a game which, in the stories of Crébillon *fils,* consisted of cleverness, gaiety, and an accepted attitude of easy, unscrupulous freedom. When one compares the *Confessions* of Rousseau with the autobiography of Restif there are many points of sincerity of character, of personality, in favour of the latter. And nowhere in the French novel of the eighteenth century is the realism of later fiction so definitely foreshadowed as in some of the work of Diderot and of Restif.

The first part of the eighteenth century in France was a final phase of the preceding century in the generally accepted philosophy of life and of literature. The latter part, under the influence of "new" ideas, ushered in the Revolution and the nineteenth century. This process, as it is reflected in the history of the novel, is usually regarded as a regrettable series of adventures between the finer productions of the

seventeenth and nineteenth centuries. The majority of
French critics look back with pride at the classic beauty of
the work of Mme. de La Fayette and the distinction of
Lesage, who, though he wrote his most important novel in
the early eighteenth century, has more points in common
with Cervantes than with the French writers of either the
seventeenth or the eighteenth centuries. The peculiarity of
the orthodox critic is that he too often disregards a genius
in which there are supposed or actual blemishes of style and
of taste while he expatiates upon the purity and serenity of
a talent. The typical eighteenth-century critic did not always make a successful effort to understand a writer, but
contented himself with the application of standardized rules
and regulations. One of the chief sources of literary information on the eighteenth century, the correspondence
of Grimm, gives instances of this attitude. Grimm, like
Voltaire, could not appreciate Shakespeare. He warned
young French writers against the dangers of copying Shakespeare rather than Racine, whom he regarded as the inevitable model of all French tragedians. Yet, strangely
enough, Grimm could understand many a genius as inferior
to Racine as Shakespeare was greater than the French
dramatist.

"In the eighteenth century, royalty, nobility, religion
gradually declined, but *l'esprit humain* was on the increase." [3] Unfortunately, literary dogmas did not follow
the example of religion and royalty, nor did they surrender
to *l'esprit humain.*

The influence of eighteenth-century English novelists on

---

[3] Sainte-Beuve, *Portraits Contemporains,* II, p. 275.

those of later eighteenth-century France, follows several curious lines, the more popular of which begins in Spain and leads directly to England, and from there to France, with a branch which reaches England by way of France, in the novels of Lesage, and communicates with the rest of France only after crossing and re-crossing the channel. Meanwhile, French philosophers and thinkers clearly affected the thought of English philosophers, and the social life of Paris attracted men of as different callings as Gibbon, Garrick, Walpole, Hume and Sterne.   Gibbon wrote: [4] "Had I been rich and independent, I should have prolonged and perhaps fixed my residence in Paris."   Horace Walpole remarked that he could make a nation entirely to his taste out of certain qualities of eighteenth-century England and of eighteenth-century France, but that neither nation, as it existed at that time, wholly satisfied him as a place in which to live, so he divided his time between them.   He devoted much of his comfortable leisure to the reading of contemporary French and English fiction, but his literary judgment is not dependable.   He preferred Crébillon *fils* to Fielding—an opinion which was shared by some of his French and English friends.

That the French eighteenth century was essentially a time of literary, personal and political quarrels is no less clear than the fact that the general tone of English literature and conversation was based at this time on good-humour and healthy reasonableness.   England was for letting well enough alone, while France drifted from the

---

[4] 1763.

conservative, "common sense" attitude of the early eighteenth century to the distorted though naturally furious logic which the leaders of an oppressed people thought to be a glorification of reason.

Two of the most famous quarrels are extreme, rather than typical examples of some of the differences between certain important persons of the old and of the new France. When Mme. du Deffand ordered Mlle. de Lespinasse out of her house, the issue was clear. There were clean cuts of jealousy, pride, revenge—no sentimental quibbling. But Rousseau's complaints of all his friends were, for the most part, hysterical, morbid, pitiful, unsound, and undignified. When Rousseau left France, Voisenon [5] said: "He will die of anger if people do not torment him." Rousseau continued to imagine the torture.

London society was less formal and less intellectual than that of Paris, and it had not cultivated an equally polished wit. There was the stimulus of discussion in the English club, which, in this regard, resembled the French salon, although, in the latter, one could never be so much at ease; the bitterest irony must be pronounced with absolute self-possession. This restraint had begun to be established early in the seventeenth century, when the salon expressed a protest in the form of a retreat from the crudity and barbarity to which the religious wars and the reigns of the later Valois had opened the doors of the court. More than a hundred years had done the work of building, adorning, refining. The salons were temples of

[5] Voisenon, *Anecdotes Littéraires,* IV, p. 28.

social art in which women were high-priests. But the
ceremonial, with all its beauty and brilliance, was not without its tedious hours.

On the other hand, "the club in England, corresponding
more or less to the salon in France, differed in the marked
absence of feminine elements. The clubs meant, essentially, a society of bachelors. The Englishman enjoyed
himself over his pipe and bottle, and dismissed his women-
kind to bed." [6] In Paris there were men's clubs, such as
the Caveau, which were as informal as the English clubs,
though not so numerous nor so firmly established as the
English. Diderot and many of his contemporaries would
have enjoyed English freedom of speech, in spite of the
fact that their ideas were too revolutionary to have
appealed to Englishmen in whose clubs "there were no
troublesome people with philanthropic or political or religious nostrums proposing to turn the world upside down
and introduce a millennium. There was no imprisonment
in England for expressing one's opinions, as in France at
this time." [7]

In France there was a closer relation between society
and literature, than in England. Women of social position
helped the writers for whom they cared. Rousseau prof-
ited by the favour of Mme. d'Épinay, and Restif by that of
Mme. de Beauharnais.[8] In Diderot's time it was often
possible to be elected to the Académie Française through

---

[6] Leslie Stephen, *English Literature and Society in the Eighteenth Century*,
p. 44.

[7] Ibid., p. 97.

[8] In the seventeenth century, examples of this kind were comparatively
rare.

the influence of some person of power at court, or of a leader of one of the salons—nor has unaided literary merit always been sufficient at other times.

Again, in the French salons, the tone of conversation had its parallel in some aspects of the traditional French school of writing, from which Diderot and others broke away. There was the insistence on *l'agrément*, a harmony of aim in contributing to a conversation which should never be too emphatic for elegance and proportion. This would have been as intolerable to the majority of Englishmen, as it was to many Frenchmen, though a Horace Walpole could appreciate the art of conversation which, in France, had become an institution.[9]

Of other amusements, Walpole wrote [10] that card-playing took up too much of one's time in Paris, and that "the best diversion is found in some of the theatres that perform comedies. Fashionable people attend only on fashionable nights, and then they go, be the play good or bad, except when Molière's plays are announced. They are weary of him." According to Grimm,[11] the reason for the unpopularity of Molière's plays was that everyone in Paris knew them by heart. In London they were popular in translation, partly because they were not so well known.

The contrast between the two nations is further shown in their novelists. The English writer of fiction sought to

---

[9] La Rochefoucauld said, in the preceding century: "The reason why so few people are agreeable in conversation is that most of them think more of what they wish to say, than of what others are saying." Fielding wrote in his Essay on Conversation: "The art of pleasing or of doing good to one another is the art of conversation."

[10] April 21, 1739.

[11] Grimm, *Correspondance*, I, p. 157.

amuse, or to give lessons in morals and sentiment, and this
tendency to preach invaded the later eighteenth-century
French novel. The French novelists' sermons, however,
were more radical and antagonistic than the English, especially in questions of social or governmental reform.

In an introduction to Smollett's novels, Saintsbury calls
him "almost an incarnation of the [English] eighteenth
century in its merits and defects:—vigour, shrewdness, zest
and relish of life, as it understood life—of the things that
are *seen*—combined with an astonishing blindness as to the
things that are not seen." The complete contrast to
Smollett which Richardson presented, provoked Walpole's
disgust at his tedious lamentations, and Fielding's laughter
at his timid scruples. It is remarkable that *Pamela* should
have served as the object of Fielding's debut as a satirical
novelist, while the works of Richardson aroused the excessive admiration of Rousseau and Diderot, who would
have asked nothing better than to write as he wrote.

Richardson knew very little of French literature, and
Fielding's knowledge of it was not extensive, though he
mentions Montaigne and Voltaire, and was probably influenced, in *Joseph Andrews,* by Lesage, Marivaux and
Scarron. Fielding's chief foreign influence was the work
of Cervantes. In the eighteenth century, Fielding was less
popular, in France, than Richardson, and some explanation
of this may be found in the "so-called translations, which
were paraphrases in which Fielding appears as a facetious
story-teller and jester." [12] Mme. du Deffand, whose point
of view is brilliantly representative of the old régime,

---

[12] W. L. Cross, *The History of Henry Fielding,* III, p. 180.

seems to have caught the real Fielding, in spite of the imperfections of the French version. But in her admiration she was, at first, almost alone. It is not surprising that Richardson should have found less favour in the eyes of Mme. du Deffand, who, though she liked his idea of introducing ordinary details of family life into his novels, found that he did not always choose those that were "agreeable." On the whole, *Clarissa* bored her.

The first fifteen years of the eighteenth century were burdened by Louis XIV's unfortunate weakness for swallowing the religious prescriptions of Mme. de Maintenon,[13] of whom it was said that Louis XIV's fear of hell had made her Queen of France. With the death of the formerly less wearisome *roi soleil,* the court revealed that it had not been converted to any of Mme. de Maintenon's principles, and the literature of the Regency showed a kindred spirit. *Gil Blas* had begun to appear, but its directness and narrative excellence were a pleasure to French readers rather than an example followed at once by Lesage's contemporaries, though his influence in England, notably upon Sterne, affected Diderot through the work of the English novelist. The Spanish source of inspiration had declined, and Lesage is the last great French novelist, before the Revolution, to profit notably by the example of Cervantes.

The *conte,* a type of short story which reached its final and, perhaps, most brilliant stage in the dialogues of Crébillon *fils,* gave what Sainte-Beuve calls "the tone of raillery, the exquisite perception of the ridiculous in its most

---

[13] Mme. de Maintenon may have acted on Rivarol's proverb that "impiety is the greatest of indiscretions."

secret hiding-places," [14] the flexibility of a practised wit. It had been boasted that a hundred reputations were not worth an epigram. La Fontaine, in whose *contes* this species of tale had an auspicious origin, wrote in his preface that if he could not deny the licentiousness of some of his stories, neither could he avoid it, for the subject demanded such treatment. He did not wish to be taken too seriously, for he wrote primarily to amuse; he had considered the "taste" of his century, and judged that in order to "please," he must be *galant et plaisant,* a remark which is more frequently made in reference to the following century than to the seventeenth. In regard to his *Psyché,* he could not at first decide whether to write as historian, novelist, or poet. The first seemed too "simple," the second insufficiently developed, as yet, and the last too "ornate." He finally chose the second, though he found it difficult to write prose, and did not hesitate to put in sets of verse, here and there.[15]

The style of La Fontaine's *contes* is simpler than that of Crébillon *fils,* but his stories are as cleverly suggestive, though he has not the wealth of epigram, the quotability of the later writer. *Mettre l'esprit dans la volupté*—this was typical of the early eighteenth century and especially so of Crébillon *fils.* His stories, for origin other than La Fontaine, go back to Perrault, whose dispute with Boileau

---

[14] Sainte-Beuve, *Portraits Contemporains,* II, p. 412.

[15] Chamfort called La Fontaine the model for the writer of the *conte.* Chamfort's *contes* are in verse, like most of La Fontaine's, and he wrote more directly under La Fontaine's influence than did Crébillon *fils,* though the latter had published his first dialogues at an earlier date. Chamfort's are few in number, but of an excellence rare in the late eighteenth century, in that type of fiction.

(1687) was the beginning of the revolt from the restrictions of classicism. Through the *contes* of Perrault, and those of his contemporary, Hamilton, and the *Lettrès Persanes* of Montesquieu, one follows the progress of the *conte* in the oriental setting in which satire of the France of the time was frequently disguised, though as to style, notably in comparison with Hamilton, as with that of La Fontaine, the writings of Crébillon *fils* lack a finished simplicity.

After Crébillon *fils*, the *conte* became philosophical with Voltaire, in whose stories, however, direct narrative plays a more conspicuous part; and Voltaire could arouse pity, in *L'Ingénu*, as Crébillon *fils* never even tried to do.[16] The *Contes Moraux* of Marmontel are not all that their title implies, and they have a lightness and facility that carried on the general tradition of their kind, until, with Restif, the *conte* became serious, and at once lost all its original aim and manner.

The progress of the French novel in the eighteenth century is by no means a steady advance in any one direction. As late as 1782 appeared Laclos' *Liaisons Dangereuses*, which, though it has many of the qualities of form and style of the early part of the century, entirely lacks the sentimentality which had so firmly established itself before this novel was published. The restrained and reserved form of the *sensibilité* novel had its celebrated origin in France, in Mme. de La Fayette's *Princesse de Clèves*, in the seventeenth century. The *sensibilité* of the

---

[16] In *Candide* there are some likenesses to the frank good-nature of Diderot's character of Jacques, with some suggestion of the lightness and graceful scepticism of La Fontaine and of Hamilton.

novels of Marivaux and of Prévost was less austere, less
reserved, but not so painfully super-sensitive as it was to
become in later writers.   There is some of this quality in
Diderot, which, though held in check by other elements,
proved to be too self-assertive for those who chiefly admired the serenity of Mme. de La Fayette's *bon goût,* in
spite of the far greater power and variety of his genius.
With Rousseau and Restif, *sensibilité* became abnormal
and hysterical, to the disgust of Voltaire, who had no use
for even the milder manifestations of this sort.   The later
sensibilité tended always toward the shedding of tears; and
weeping was not fashionable in the strongholds of *bon
goût.*

How was it that Richardson in England, and Rousseau
in France, not to mention other writers, found so wide and
so warm a public, even in the face of much ridicule?   The
novelty of the tears and sentiments in which they indulged,
after the formality and restraint of the preceding century,
made many of their readers ignore the fact that there were
too many tears and too much sentiment.   The reaction
was to be more violent and more rapid in France than in
England.

Mme. du Deffand expressed herself only less positively
on the subject of Rousseau than she would have done in
regard to Restif if he had not been beneath her contempt.
Horace Walpole wrote:[17]   "Mme. du Deffand's understanding was too just not to be disgusted by Rousseau's
paradoxes and affectations.   His eloquence could not cap-
tivate her, for she hated eloquence.   She cared (among

[17] July 24, 1778.

modern writers) for no style but Voltaire's. She had an aversion for all modern philosophers. She was born and she lived in the age of true taste.[18] She held that all but Voltaire had corrupted their taste and language. La Fontaine was her idol, that is, simplicity." She and Diderot did not care for each other. "He had enough," she wrote,[19] "after one visit to me. I am not a collection of related atoms."

The wit of the eighteenth century can be quoted in numerous anecdotes:—"I love my husband so devotedly that I would sacrifice anything to him, except my lover."— A husband to his wife: "My dear, I allow you any indulgence except princes and lackeys, for these extremes might cause scandal."—Mme. X is discovered by her husband; he says: "What an indiscretion! Think of the disaster if any one but your husband had found you thus!" —Duclos, in his youth, swimming in a lake, came to the shore to rescue a lady whose carriage had overturned in the mud. She objected to his nakedness. He apologized for having saved her life without putting on his gloves.— "In this century," said some one, "virtue is ridiculed so remorselessly that hypocrisy has been abolished."

Mme. du Deffand asked the *Président* Hénault, on his death-bed, if he remembered Mme. de Castelmoron. Both she and the lady in question had formerly been his mistresses. The *Président* did not recognize Mme. du Deffand, and at the mention of Mme. de Castelmoron he

---

[18] "The brilliant society of the eighteenth century had become too enlightened to dare to make a mistake, too fastidious to risk imperfect work." —Saintsbury, *Essay on Chamfort and Rivarol.*

[19] Mme. du Deffand, *Lettres à H. Walpole,* II, p. 361.

burst forth in loud praise of her, contrasting her virtues with the vices of Mme. du Deffand. He died without knowing that he had thus insulted one of his life-long friends. On the evening of his death, Mme. du Deffand went to a large and fashionable dinner. When she entered the room, she was asked about the *Président's* health. "Alas, my friends, he died two hours ago—otherwise I should not have been with you this evening."

At the tomb of the Abbé Paris in the graveyard of the church of Saint-Medard, many miracles were said to have been performed until, in 1732, Louis XV put a stop to them. This act inspired the following lines which someone wrote on the tomb:—

> *De par le roi, défense à Dieu*
> *De faire miracle en ce lieu.*

An "ideal" image of passion has been said to have been the aim of Racine and of his contemporaries. A witty satirical image of pretended passion had been the amusement of the Regency. The crudity and violence of passion found their way in the late eighteenth-century novel, which was more inventive as to style and plot, and less concerned with smoothness of surface. "It was the eighteenth century that brought life-likeness into novels, and, for so doing, may it and the Lord be thanked." [20]

The later writers of the eighteenth century were more serious than their predecessors, but they were not only less interested in wit—they were less witty. The tremendous output of epigrams, the *bons mots* which everyone had tried

---

[20] Saintsbury, *The Peace of the Augustans,* p. 176.

to say or to remember—and in both endeavours many succeeded in astonishing degree—these pastimes had begun
to seem more trivial than funny. Neither Rousseau nor
Restif was witty. The sacrifice of personal feeling for the
sake of an epigram was incomprehensible to them, and their
feelings were wounded by sarcasm. Diderot was less
sensitive. He could be brilliant; but the endless interest of
the old régime in repartee seemed to him trivial, and his
love of eloquence excluded him from the most traditional
of the salons, though, in others, his ardent discourse found
favour. Voltaire alone could keep pace with the progress
of thought, and at the same time appeal to the manners
and prejudices and interests of the old order.

The literature of Germany had a certain influence, but
not nearly so great as that of England, on the France of
the middle-eighteenth century, while the admiration of
Germany for French literature operated much more pro-
foundly throughout the century. In 1762 Grimm wrote [21]
of the vogue of certain German authors in Paris, a vogue
which would have been laughed at as an impossibility, a
few years before.

The last phases of the eighteenth-century French novel
show the influence of journalism,[22] especially in Restif's
collections of short stories. He reported the facts of life
which he saw about him without regard to their importance
or, rather, in accordance with his conviction that everything
was worth writing. His work is thus extremely uneven,
and much of it quite worthless. His practice of regarding

---

[21] Grimm, *Correspondance*, V, p. 11.
[22] Restif, *Les Contemporaines* and *Les Nuits de Paris.*

all quarters of Paris as fit subjects for pictures was, at that time, unconventional and highly objectionable, for it had been considered good taste to write chiefly of the Faubourg Saint-Germain. The journalistic influence gave the novel wider scope, broader sympathies; but it broke down certain artistic barriers and tended to cheapen style, to ignore proportion and selection, while it gave opportunity for deeper investigation, for greater sincerity and completeness. New dramatic and pictorial subjects for the novel were to suggest themselves, and this was specially encouraging, since the rigid formalism and the extreme fastidiousness of the seventeenth century had done what they could, had reached their narrow perfection, and could, in continuation, have sunk but more deeply into artificiality.

Richardson's habit of using letters as a form of novel-writing, and the same method in the otherwise totally different work of Laclos, may be observed. From Richardson, Rousseau adopted the epistolary narrative, and Restif told some of his stories in this way, though, in his case, the letters were frequently real. He kept them in great numbers, and they occupy a large place in the part of his fiction which is to some extent a diary.

The most striking feature of some portions of Restif's novels is their distorted *sensibilité,* and, of others, a directness of reported facts and conditions of ordinary life—a directness which foreshadows much of Zola's work, except Zola's powerful mentality and concentration. Assézat [23] gives an excellent account of Restif's position in the progress of the novel. "At the time when Restif began

---

[23] Assézat, introduction to Charpentier edition of *Les Contemporaines.*

to write, the state of the French novel was confused and
compounded of various elements. It had passed through
so many forms, manners, purposes, that it was doubtful
which element would predominate in the future. The
majestic compositions of the sixteenth century—of d'Urfé
and of Scudéry—were strictly out of date. The novels of
Scarron and of Furetière were forgotten. The tales of
Crébillon *fils* were too specialized and polished for reduc-
tion to a popular type, and Rousseau's *Nouvelle Héloïse*
was a masterpiece which one might hesitate to copy,"
though Restif dared to do so, as he partly admitted.
Restif's particular significance consists in his explorations
of the poorest quarters of Paris. He was not the first to
write of the lower classes, but he pictured them with
greater realism and sympathy. His predecessors, Scarron
and Furetière, had aimed at novelty, amusement or adventure. How differently Furetière sketched the bourgeoisie
of the seventeenth century in his *Roman Bourgeois*—"I
sing of their loves," he wrote in his preface. Scarron's
Roman Comique had told of strolling players, of their adventurous lives and amusing scrapes, in the style of
Spanish picaresque fiction. Restif hardly ever tried to be
amusing; he called his purpose philanthropic, and hoped
his books would stimulate reform. He would not let his
pictures speak for themselves; he felt called upon to do his
own preaching, on the texts of his narratives.

Saintsbury [24] comments upon Restif's relation to various
English authors: "Restif has been compared, not unfairly,
to Defoe as well as to Rousseau. In a way he is like

---

[24] Saintsbury, *History of the French Novel,* I, pp. 454–6.

Pepys, and all four share an intense and unaffected reality of a dreamy kind, and with other dream-quality which reminds one of Barrow and even of DeQuincey. Restif's absolute shamelessness is less unconnected with his dream-quality than may at first appear. Could he ever have taken holiday from his day and night devotion to Aphrodite, he might have been a most remarkable novelist, and, as it is, his narrative faculty is such as by no means every novelist possesses. He counts in the advance toward real things in fiction. . . ."

Though the journalistic element has been noted in Restif, he is altogether distinct from his younger contemporary, Pigault-Lebrun,[25] as a novelist. In contrast, also, to Restif's life, which began with some prospects of happiness only to advance rapidly in the opposite direction, Pigault's youth was flippantly scandalous; but eventually he married happily and became a respectable old patriarch, as thoroughly "proper" as his past would allow him to appear to be. His father was a lawyer, and wished his son to study law, but Pigault became a clerk in an English commercial house. "He seduced his master's daughter, ran away with her, and would no doubt have married her—for Pigault was never a really bad fellow—if she had not been drowned." [26] His father, tired of repeated reports of his son's disorderly life, wrote *lettres de cachet,* and Pigault would have spent more time than he consequently did in the Bastille, had not that prison been destroyed. He became a "gentleman trooper" in the king's service; then he joined a company of actors. As a writer of plays he was

[25] 1753–1835.
[26] Saintsbury, *History of the French Novel,* I, p. 457.

successful, but the military fever of 1792 interrupted his writing, and he fought in the battle of Valmy. Late in life he began to write novels. Whenever he could, he attacked the fallen government which had so annoyingly interfered with the dissipations of his youth. In his novels, Pigault appealed to the coarser elements of public amusement, with a sharp eye open to the market value of cheapness of style and presentation. He liked horse-play; he had none of Restif's sincerity and *naïveté;* he has been called the first of a long line of novelists whose work is a trade instead of an art. Though he made some effort to improve his style, he never succeeded, and his general attitude toward fiction remained unchanged.

As novelists, Restif and Diderot have some points in common. Both wrote too much and too rapidly to allow time for careful revision; both hated the cruelty and indifference of the court; both were too emphatic, too much inclined to exaggerate, and both hated the restraints of the conventional novel. But Diderot thought little or nothing of his own fiction, whereas Restif regarded the novels he wrote as of supreme importance, not only to himself but also to the public—an opinion which goes as far wrong in one direction as Diderot's in another.

The spirited lightness of Crébillon *fils,* the analytical clarity of Laclos, the ego-mania of Restif and the humanitarian ardour of Diderot's genius, serve the purpose of setting certain aspects of the early and of the late eighteenth century over against one another. And if preferences be expressed, there are difficulties resembling those of Horace Walpole when he compared the France of the eighteenth century to the England of that time, for there

was no greater difference between the two countries of
Walpole's knowledge, than between the early and the late
eighteenth-century French novel.   In the history of France
and of French fiction, no era is more extraordinary, or
more significant, than the eighteenth century.   Whether or
not the old régime deserved the "deluge," it is easy to see
in the work of the novelists under discussion many of the
features of social life to which the revolutionists so violently objected—the triviality and selfishness and useless-
ness of the characters drawn by Crébillon, the wickedness
of those of Laclos, the misfortunes and sufferings of those
of Diderot and of Restif de la Bretonne.

CHAPTER II

Crébillon

THE dull, conventional tragedies of Crébillon *père* are as different from the clever dialogues of Crébillon *fils* as their authors. The father and son in temperament, appearance, disposition, and aims of authorship, were at opposite poles. Their quarrels, however, were natural and unimportant, and they lived in the same house, happily enough, though their ideas of pleasant living were at variance. In their attitudes toward literature, there is much of the contrast between the seventeenth century and the early part of the eighteenth.

Claude-Prosper-Jolyot de Crébillon was born in Paris, February 14, 1707, two weeks after his father's marriage. He was baptized in the church of Saint-Étienne du Mont on the day after his birth, and it was hoped that the promptness with which the christening was accomplished would help to compensate for the delay in the performance of the wedding ceremony of his parents. When he was four years old, his mother died; but his improvident father's friends eventually sent him to the Jesuit Collège Louis-le-Grand, where Claude did well in his studies, and graduated without the slightest inclination or the vaguest intention of ever becoming a Jesuit.

"My family," he wrote in 1750, "is said to be ancient and honourable in Burgundy, but that does not prove that I am descended from the nobility." He doubted the

Crébillon tradition that Anne of Brittany was one of his ancestors.

Crébillon *père* was devoted to declamatory pomposity and elaborate moral soliloquies.[1] He gained an undeserved fame due to unmerited court favour, and it is not surprising that his plays lost their vogue before the court was overthrown.

Though his peculiar character and habits were thoroughly distasteful to his son, Crébillon could not be expected to alter them, and Claude managed to laugh at what would otherwise have been quite insufferable. He was not ill-natured, and his affection for his eccentric father was real. Crébillon was generous when he could be so, which was not always the case, and it was not so much his personal peculiarity as the disorder of his house which would have driven Claude away in disgust, if he had not inherited some of his father's laziness. The Crébillon residence in the Marais, as an asylum for stray cats and dogs, knew not the word intrusion. As the dignified tragedian walked about Paris, he adopted a cat here, a dog there, until his collection resembled that of the Ark. There must have been at least two of every kind, especially of all cases of feline and canine sicknesses, for ill-health in an animal was the shortest road to the great man's heart.

The Crébillon house [2] was inconveniently arranged, sparingly furnished, and always cold, except in summer. No effort was apparently made to sweep or clean the house

---

[1] Rivarol said of him: "Critics economize their time when they search for faults in Racine, and for beauty in the work of Crébillon."

[2] O. Uzanne, *Notice sur Crébillon fils*—preface to edition of *Contes Dialogués* (*Collection des Petits Conteurs*), Paris, 1879.

J. DE CRÉBILLON fil.

CRÉBILLON FILS

at any time, though twenty-two dogs and ten cats and several ravens had made it their permanent home, and found it convenient to ignore the rudiments of sanitation. One's nose could not have suffered more than one's ears in this auditorium in which a croaking, miauing, barking orchestra performed at all hours.

The names of poodles, pugs, greyhounds and mongrels were donated in accordance with the dispositions of the animals. Those that were "gentle" were given "gentle" names, and for others there were other appellations. The first nine cats were named for the nine Muses, and the tenth was called Boileau—a natural association for a seventeenth-century literary orthodoxy.

In the midst of the beautiful sounds that came from the mouths of Boileau, the Muses and other creatures, the great tragedian wrote his tragedies, recited his verses, and puffed at his pipe, till the air groaned with noise and choked with smoke, and sometimes the plays caught the infection of the atmosphere. Crébillon was stocky of build and deep of chest, and the dignified expression of his face was slightly lessened, in effect, by his surroundings. In this bedlam there was a figure of incongruous elegance. The perfumed, ribboned, graceful Claude indolently petted one of the cats, or hummed a popular tune, while irony played with his lips as he watched his father with amused condescension, and ignored the indignant protest with which he who listened to the "true" tragic Muse expressed, now and then, his resentment at the interruptions of her namesake. The shade of over-elaboration in Claude's manner saved itself in a suggestion of ironical arrogance, and he did not take either himself or a prospective career too seriously,

Mercier [3] wrote: "I was nineteen years old when I went to see the two Crébillons. The barking of many dogs at once greeted me. I entered. Their uproar continued as they escorted me to the room in which Crébillon sat, his legs and arms bare, his pipe in full blast. He got up to drive the dogs away with a whip, so that I might have one of the chairs in which they had at once ensconced themselves. Finally a comparative peace was established, broken only by intermittent growls. Crébillon's mistress,[4] an unattractive woman, very short, bow-legged, and with the most malignantly sparkling eyes I ever saw, entered the room. The dogs permitted her to occupy a chair without waiting for Crébillon's command. Crébillon stopped smoking to recite some of his verses; then he returned his pipe to his mouth and said no more. When I got up to go, the dogs at once arose, barking more furiously than ever, and accompanied me to the door. I heard their master rebuking them too gently, and their clamour continued until I had gone some distance down the street." [5]

Some of Crébillon's experiences are interesting in comparison with those of his son. He was one of the first

[3] Mercier, *Tableau de Paris*, X, chapter on the Crébillons. Mercier reports that he once saw "Crébillon *fils* eat, at one sitting, a hundred dozen (*Cent douzaine!*) oysters." (Perhaps he meant to say one hundred and twelve.) "He drank milk while I drank champagne; we agreed on the subject of digestion. It is true that milk is the best dissolvent of oysters." Ibid., X, p. 87.

[4] Voisenon, *Anecdotes Littéraires*, IX, p. 49. "Crébillon's mistress was unfaithful to him in his youth, and robbed him in his old age."

[5] Crébillon's partiality for animals resembles that of the Russian composer Borodine, whose cats jumped onto the table, ate out of the guests' plates without suffering an adequate punishment. Crébillon once remarked: "I began to love animals when I learned to know men."

habitués of the Café Laurent, the first of the Parisian
cafés littéraires, which became the usual meeting place for
the idle, who smoked and talked by the hour. "No one
was ever so lazy as Crébillon *père,*" said Collé—an obvious
exaggeration, for Crébillon wrote a number of plays.
While he was at work on one of them, the scientist Duvernet offered him the use of his garden. It was very hot,
and Crébillon, thinking that no one could see him, took off
most of his clothes as he often did in warm weather, and
walked up and down, declaiming his verses in a loud voice,
and making violent gestures. The gardener, whom Crébillon had not seen, rushed to tell Duvernet that he had
discovered a lunatic behind the house; and Duvernet was
much amused. When Crébillon was appointed "royal
censor," [6] his obscure and comfortless manner of living became known to Mme. de Pompadour. Through her help,
his plays were favoured at court, and he was given a house
and garden and a small income. But he continued to live
very quietly; he did not care to go where he could not
smoke incessantly, and he was too indolent to take advantage of his opportunities, though at times, in a small,
congenial circle, he could talk "delightfully"—about his
plays.

When he went to thank Mme. de Pompadour for her
kindness, she was touched by the old man's appearance, and
received him graciously. "She thought," wrote Sainte-
Beuve,[7] "that she had discovered a genius." He was bend-
ing over her bed, to kiss her hand, when the king entered.

---

[6] "Mercure de France," July 1762, *Éloge de Crébillon;* see also Marmontel,
Mémoires, I, pp. 287–8.
[7] Sainte-Beuve, *Lundis,* XII, p. 495.

"Ah! Madame," cried Crébillon, "His Majesty has discovered us; we are lost!"   The wit of this octogenarian pleased Louis XV, and seemed sufficient to assure Crébillon's success as a writer of plays for the court.   The royal printing-press was ordered to publish a special edition of his works, and, for a time, Voltaire was coldly received at Versailles and discontinued his visits.   His revenge consisted in writing a cruelly truthful criticism of Crébillon's tragedies after the death of their author.   Voltaire could have included many of his own plays in the condemnation, though Crébillon, as royal censor, had praised them.

As one of the directors of the Académie Française, Crébillon made a speech the frankness of which astonished his friends.   "And why," he asked, "should I be afraid to speak thus of a prince who cannot make his subjects tremble except by the fear of losing him?"—an odd mixture of defiance and deference.

Casanova [8] studied French with Crébillon, and heard anecdotes of Louis XIV.   That monarch had told Crébillon not to write about Cromwell, as he had planned:— "Do not devote your talents to the description of even one incident in the life of a rascal."

After Crébillon *fils* left the Collège Louis-le-Grand, he often went with his father to the Comédie-Française.   He enjoyed the performances, and made friends among the members of the company. [9]   He knew an actress, called La

---

[8] Casanova, *Mémoires*, V, p. 20.

[9] The friends of Crébillon *fils* included the actor Romagnesi who made his debut in a play of Crébillon *père*, and "Lelio" the son of the novelist Mme. Riccoboni.   Crébillon *fils*, Collé and others wrote short pieces or verses for amusement, and sometimes succeeded in having them acted or recited.

Gaussin, who consented to marry him. But when he brought her the marriage license, she said she had found a rich lover whom she preferred to a poor husband.

"He told me," wrote Mercier,[10] "that the manners of the time of the Regency appealed to him more than those of the present. He said that he had not read all his father's plays, but that some day he probably would. He regarded a typical French tragedy as the most perfect farce that the human mind could invent. He laughed till the tears rolled down his cheeks at certain dramas which were seriously admired by the Parisian public. The audience always managed to see in the virtuous, heroic kings of French tragedy, a series of portraits of Louis XV."

The gaiety of Crébillon *fils* made him popular in the Caveau club, of which he was a charter member. It existed chiefly for the enjoyment of wine, wit and song.[11] The regular Sunday meetings were specially provided for, and Gallet, one of the founders, easily added special

---

[10] Mercier, *Tableau de Paris,* X, chapter on the Crébillons.

[11] The first organization (1729) of the "Society of the dinners of the Caveau" was the work of Crébillon *fils,* Collé, Gallet and others. The Caveau existed, under various names and with varying fortunes, for more than two centuries. In 1759 Pelletier, the rich farmer-general, regularly entertained the second Caveau, and among his guests were Marmontel, Suard, Garrick and Sterne. Other members were Duclos, Moncrief, Boucher, Helvétius and Rameau. Women were seldom admitted, but an exception was made in favour of the voice and wit and beauty of Sophie Arnould, whose disposition suited the general atmosphere of the club, if not the taste of some of its later members. "Panard was the singer of the first Caveau, and his glass (holding a full bottle of claret) is religiously preserved by the society which inherits the title, to this day (1890). Panard's character appears to have approached the ideal of this anacreontic and epicurean band." George Saintsbury, *Miscellaneous Essays,* p. 355. See also, P. Laujon, *Œuvres,* IV, p. 225.

gatherings by letting his best friends dine as often as they
liked, free of charge, at his cabaret. They not only ate
and drank, but made jokes at his expense and to his
amusement. Crébillon *fils* could not often persuade his
father to come to the Caveau, for the tragedian disliked
hilarity, as a rule. Now and then he enjoyed such an
evening, but on one occasion he lost his temper. Duclos
asked him which of his works he thought the best, and
Crébillon *père* replied that the question was difficult to
answer. Then he pointed to his son:—"There, at any
rate, is the worst of them." Claude retorted: "Not so
much pride, Sir, if you please. Wait till there be proof
that all your works are your own." He referred to a
rumour that a certain monk had been the author of some
of Crébillon's plays, and the gibe was too much for the
tragedian's dignity, though he had brought it on himself.
He glared at his son for a moment, hurried away, and
never appeared at the Caveau again.[12]   Everyone laughed,
and no one objected to the departure of anyone who could
not "take" any joke. Boring, jealous, vain, pedantic
writers were not admitted, but young authors who knew
how to be amusing and amused were always welcome;
whether successful or not. Their writings were read aloud,
and frankly discussed; they were given good advice instead
of foolish compliments, and frequently their membership
in the Caveau was more practically valuable to them than
if they had belonged to serious literary clubs which were
sometimes as useless as they were tiresome.

Crébillon *fils* was unanimously elected president of the

---

[12] C. Collé, *Journal*, I, p. 5.

Caveau, and held the office for several years. He allowed neither dullness nor uproarious behaviour nor dishonesty, and in the course of time it was found necessary to dismiss the hospitable Gallet for the crime of usury. Crébillon *fils* wrote him the following note: "M. Gallet is invited to dine anywhere except at the Caveau on Sundays." The convivial Panard objected to the severity of this sentence; but the rest of the club supported the president.

The power of the court,[13] even in such intimate and private affairs as the meetings of literary clubs, was demonstrated one night when two gentlemen arrived from Versailles, having heard that the Caveau afforded amusement. When they were asked to sit down, they snobbishly refused, and seemed to say: "Come, now, show us your wit." The Caveau at once became silent, and the annoyed courtiers took their departure. Their revenge consisted in spreading false charges of political meddling, and the Caveau was forced, for the time, to disband. Its members soon formed another association, and persuaded the authorities that they had no interest in politics.

Though Crébillon *père* thought the life of his son a series of disgraceful indulgences, or a far too complacent surrender to laziness, the friends of Crébillon *fils* were in the habit of telling him that his decorous behaviour should be altered to fit the quickness of his wit. "Between Crébillon *fils* and Collé there was a continual rapid-fire of repartee. Anyone else might put in a word where he could, but at great risk, for, in any conversation, Collé or Crébillon would be sure to out-do him. Crébillon had the gift of

---

[13] See E. Dentu, *Historique du Caveau*, for a picture of these scenes.

drawing out Collé's wit,[14] and I contented myself with listening to their epigrams. When I tried to take an active part in their talk, I learned rather severe lessons in modesty." [15]   Marmontel said that the Caveau was in some ways more agreeable than the salon of Mme. Geoffrin, for she acted as a brake on conversation, and kept free speech and frank discussion too closely in check.

An incident in connection with some of the friends of Crébillon is an example of the mild adventure in which they would have been glad for him to join them. After a late dinner with two other men, in the early days of the Caveau, Piron started to go home alone. He announced that the wine had inspired him, and he meant to compose a poem on the way. They told him it would be a dangerous walk at such an hour, and proposed to go with him. "You are wearing a handsome velvet coat, and you will be murdered for it and for the money which you appear to have." "Oh!" cried Piron, "why didn't you say at once that you wished to escort my coat? Here it is. When I am seen in my shirt, I shall not be robbed." He dashed down the street; his friends picked up his coat and followed him. Presently they saw him coming back, guarded by two or three policemen who had apparently arrested him on the ground of his having been robbed. "Are these the thieves?" they asked, when they met Piron's friends.

---

[14] In Collé's comedy, *La Vérité dans le Vin,* a woman says: "I love this child of mine as if it were not my husband's. And in truth it cannot be my husband's, for it is my first."—A husband says to his wife: "Are you happy with me?" "You and I are admirably matched," she replies, "we are as one soul and one body—and it bores me to be alone." Collé said of a man: "His vice is most shocking—it is no longer fashionable."

[15] Marmontel, *Mémoires,* II, pp. 100-111.

"Yes," said he. Collé was ordered to surrender his sword, which he did in a majestic manner, reciting a speech of the hero of a popular drama, in a more serious predicament. Piron walked with the sergeant, at the head of the party, and laughed at his friends. "What are you going to do with them?" he asked. The sergeant solemnly replied: "They will be hanged, if nothing worse happens to them." Piron, rather worried, told the true story, and requested that his friends be released. "Well," said the sergeant, "now that you have your coat, do you want the thieves to escape? You must be in league with them."

The party arrived at a police station. The clerk took notes on the various accounts of what had occurred. "Shall I help you put the story into verse?" laughed Piron. "What are verses?" asked the clerk. Then, turning to Gallet, "What is your occupation?" *"Je fais des chansons,"* he replied, truthfully enough, but the words can also mean "I do nothing," and the clerk assumed this to be his meaning, till Gallet sang a song, which was still more annoying. Collé interrupted him:—"To save these gentlemen the trouble of questioning me, I announce that I am Charles Collé, that I live in the rue du Jour, and that *my* profession *is* to do nothing, much to the anger of my family. When Gallet's couplets are good, I recite them." "And when Collé recites them," broke in Piron, "I sing them." Then, in the manner of an opera singer:—

"J'ai tout dit, tout, seigneur, cela doit vous suffire,
Qu'on me mène à la mort, je n'ai plus rien à dire."

They were hurried off to the commissary of police, who slept soundly, and awoke slowly, in a bad humour. The

actors in the farce had assembled in front of his house.
People stuck their heads out of windows and laughed at
them. "Oh, Sir," cried Piron, when the commissary at
last appeared, "do not destroy us, we are the children of
our parents." "Who are you?" "I am the poet Piron."
"I never heard of you." "Where have you hidden yourself, never to have known my fame? My writings are celebrated, my plays are successful in the theatres." This was
true enough, and the officers of the law consented to laugh,
and the commissary decided to release the prisoners, in-
viting them to lunch the next day. He remembered having
met Piron recently at dinner. As they went away, Piron
said to his friends: "Nothing now is lacking to my glory.
I have made a policeman laugh." [16]

Before attempting to turn the manners of his time into
fiction, Crébillon *fils* made friends at no dizzy height, but
at a sufficient elevation for more or less extensive social
observation. He took notes less solemnly, but no less carefully than Laclos. But this "child of a Crébillon," as
Voltaire called him,[17] was not popular, according to some
of his contemporaries; his wit appears to have been more
evident at the Caveau than elsewhere, and he was accused
of mannerisms and affectations, though, to some people,
his coolness and ironical indifference and the involved construction of his phrases gave the effect of subtlety of
thought. His habit of not laughing at his own jokes was
sometimes adopted by those who heard them, and the fact
that he did not emphasize his *bons mots* caused them occa-

[16] Rigoley de Juvigny, *Vie d'Alexis Piron*, preface, edition 1776.
[17] In a letter, Dec. 1734.

sionally to pass unnoticed. In some parts of the fashionable world he was admired as an epicure, but he was not so
successful among actors and actresses, who thought him too
cold and too fastidious. The great salons were too formal
to please him, and his "tone" was not sufficiently "good" to
give him the entrée if he had wanted it.[18]

His love affairs do not seem to have been numerous.
According to Montifaud,[19] his only liaison of any duration
was with a Mme. de Margy, whom he described in *Les
Égarements* as the friend of Meilcour, Mme. de Lursay.
"She tried to obliterate the memory of her youthful follies
by making her heart appear to be extremely difficult to conquer, and by demanding so many good qualities in a lover
who should be worthy of her affection, that those for whom
she did not care were usually discouraged."

After the publication of his first novel, *L'Écumoire,*
Crébillon *fils* was imprisoned for a short time at Vin-
cennes,[20] for supposed allusions to the Duchesse du Maine,
Cardinal de Rohan and others. But he was released

---

[18] *Souvenirs* attributed to the Marquis de Créquy, written by Courchamps
(or Causen), IV, p. 153: "Crébillon *fils* was pedantic, serious, dry, formal,
offensive, tiresome; he could think of nothing better to do than to bow in an
old-fashioned manner, and nothing better to say than: 'I have the honour to
present you my deep homage.'" Mme. du Deffand wrote to Walpole
(March, 1777) that she considered Crébillon *fils* "an insignificant little person
whose friends were impossible people." She thought his style incomparably
inferior to Hamilton's. Walpole wrote to her that she reminded him of
one of Crébillon *fils'* heroines—he did not say which. Mme. du Deffand
replied: "You might as well compare me to the fairy Urgèle." (According to popular legend, Urgèle was a good fairy; the character appears in
an eighteenth-century comic opera.) See *Lettres de Mme. du Deffand à
Horace Walpole,* Toynbee edition, I, p. 528.

[19] Introduction to *Le Hazard du Coin du Feu,* edition Gilliet, 1880.

[20] P. Bonnefon, *L'Exile de Crébillon; Revue de Paris,* Aug. 15, 1898.

through the intervention of the dowager Duchesse de Conti, who did not wish it to appear that she thought his supposed portrait of her daughter sufficiently lifelike to be recognizable.[21]

A few years later, his novel *Le Sopha* got him into more serious trouble.[22]   In March, 1742, he was exiled to a distance of forty leagues from Paris by the Chancellor d'Aguesseau, not only because of the licentiousness of the book, but also because Crébillon *fils* had neglected to get permission to publish it.   After leaving Paris, he wrote a letter of affected humility to Marville, chief of police:—"Undoubtedly I am guilty, or I should not be punished; but I have also been told that my book is too restrained, as a picture of the kind I had chosen to present."   Later, he wrote that his father's financial difficulties demanded his return and assistance.   He promised to write no more books like *Le Sopha,* and pleaded that he had written that novel at the command of Frederick II.[23]   Why this argument should have been thought acceptable to Louis XV, whose worst enemy was Frederick II, is not explained.

After a few months, Marville managed to persuade d'Aguesseau to shorten the sentence, but Crébillon *fils* did not return to Paris till 1747, after spending some time at Sens, and going south to Dijon and other cities of Burgundy.

Soon after his arrival in Paris, he found himself serving on a committee including Helvétius, the *Président* Hénault

---

[21] When he called to thank the dowager, she asked him what he knew about "absent-minded princesses" to which *L'Écumoire* had referred.

[22] P. Bonnefon, supra.

[23] M. Dutrait, *Étude sur Crébillon père,* p. 72.

[24] L. Vian, *Histoire de Montesquieu,* pp. 231–2.

and Fontenelle, to which Montesquieu had submitted the manuscript of *L'Esprit des Lois,* for competent advice.[24] Crébillon *fils* and Fontenelle thought the book should not be published, for the style could not be called *le bon genre* of French literature. The book was not withheld on account of this verdict.

About this time, Crébillon *fils* met Henrietta Maria Stafford, daughter of a deceased English nobleman, John Stafford, formerly chamberlain to James II. There was a story [25] that she had read *Le Sopha,* had at once fallen in love with the author, had crossed the Channel to find him and offer herself to him. Though she actually met him by chance, she decided to become his mistress, since they were too poor to marry. This affair lasted for four years, and resulted in matrimony, April 23, 1748, a "case of thirst wedded to hunger," it was said; and consequently it appears that the original obstacle to marriage was rather an excuse than a reality. A child, born two years before the wedding, died two years afterward, followed in a few months by his mother. M. and Mme. Crébillon *fils* had lived quietly, and apparently happily. According to Collé, Miss Stafford was awkward, not at all pretty, and squinted badly. Her life was absorbed in her husband's, and his did not consequently become more brilliant. He had married her chiefly because she was in love with him, or possibly because of her family connections.[26] But not enough is known of the life they led to warrant any definite conclusions.[27]

---

[25] A false account in the memoirs falsely attributed to the Marquise de Créquy. See *Notice* by Uzanne, supra.

[26] *L'Artiste,* Dec. 19, 1847.

[27] Collé, *Journal,* I, p. 124.

In 1749, Crébillon *fils* had written again to the chief of
police, to ask for the office of censor which his father had
formerly held, but there was no immediate reply.   In 1755,
Crébillon *fils* was somehow brought to the notice of Mme.
de Pompadour, and four years later she decided to recommend him as *censeur royal pour les belles-lettres*.

The income which he drew as royal censor seemed to
Crébillon *fils* the only really serious aspect of that office.
He very intelligently suppressed only the works of such
authors as he thought vapid and insignificant, but many unknown and deserving writers found him helpful.   Mercier
describes a visit to his *bureau* after Crébillon *fils* had had
several years of experience, during each of which his tedious
task had been to consider forty or fifty thousand verses, not
to mention other productions.   "Crébillon *fils* said to me:
'Stay here till one o'clock and watch the poets come in with
their manuscripts.'   One of them entered in a sprightly
manner, took a chair, and pulled a paper out of his pocket.
'What part of France do you come from?' asked Crébillon
fils.   'From the vicinity of Toulouse,' replied the young
hopeful.   'Good,' said the censor, 'leave your poem here,
and come back in a day or two.'   When he had gone,
Crébillon *fils* said to me: 'That fellow's talk is easy and
spirited.   What will you bet that his verses are good for
nothing?'—'What makes you so sure?' I asked; but as I
glanced at the poem, I saw he was right.   It was altogether nonsensical.   Now a shy, awkward person came in.
'Where do you come from?'—'Rouen'—'Good.   Come
back in three days.'   He stumbled out, nearly upsetting a
table; and tripping on the landing.   'This piece will have
merit,' Crébillon *fils* announced.   He proved that this was

the case, and then explained. 'An experience of several years has shown me that out of twenty authors that come from the south or centre of France, nineteen are worthless; and that out of twenty from the north, ten have talent and are capable of improvement. The worst possible verses come from the region between Bordeaux and Nîmes. This seems to be the latitude of platitude. They have nothing but wind in their heads.'" Mercier adds that this had often been his experience. The people from the Midi seemed generally lacking in logic and originality. He said of the verdicts of most of the eighteenth-century censors that they were more useful as guides to what *not* to read than anything else. He found Crébillon *fils* an exception, and, later on, when one of his own books had got him into trouble, Crébillon *fils'* help saved the situation.[28]

His advice proved valuable for his friend Collé, who says in his diary that, at first, he only wrote couplets which, at best, were mildly amusing. Crébillon *fils* told him he could do better things, and kept at him till he wrote *La Vérité dans le Vin* and other clever comedies.

When Crébillon *père* died in 1762, Mme. de Pompadour transferred to Crébillon *fils* the two-thousand-franc pension of his father. The mistress of Louis XV had managed to forget her original disapproval [29] of *Le Sopha* and other novels of its author.

Between 1762 and 1777, Crébillon's life is obscure. In 1774 he became *censeur de police* in addition to royal censor, and acquired another pension which had belonged to

---

[28] Mercier, *Tableau de Paris*, X, chapter on the Crébillons.
[29] F. Loliée, *Revue Bleue*, Dec. 14, 1901; article on Crébillon *fils*.

M. de Sainte-Foix, in connection with the *Mercure de France*. At the age of sixty, Crébillon *fils* had grown dull. Unkind persons referred to him as "the late M. Crébillon *fils*." In 1765, Horace Walpole wrote [30] that Crébillon's novels had gone entirely out of fashion with the coming of the *philosophe* vogue which Walpole called "unsupportable, superficial, over-bearing and fanatical." A more modern critic [31] asserts the stories of Crébillon *fils* continued to be read "only by young officers in garrisons." Probably they were still popular *en province*, on account of their Parisian reputation.

Walpole's admiration of Crébillon *fils* was at its uncritical height when he wrote in 1752 [32] to Horace Mann: "You know my passion for the writings of the younger Crébillon. You shall hear how much I have been mortified by the discovery of the greatest meanness in him, and you will judge of how much one must be humbled to have one's favourite author convicted of mortal mercenariness." Walpole had determined to have a portrait of Crébillon *fils* by Liotard, and his "favourite" author was persuaded to sit for the picture; but when it was finished he liked it so much that he demanded a copy. This being refused, he insisted on having the original. Liotard had asked sixteen guineas for the portrait, and Walpole adds: "I am satisfied that a man who could beg sixteen guineas will not give them away, so I may still have the picture." But next year he wrote that Liotard had actually kept the original, and he damned Liotard's "foolish dirtiness" when he could no

---

[30] *Letters of Horace Walpole,* Toynbee edition, VI, p. 352.
[31] F. Godefroy, *Histoire de la Littérature Française,* V, p. 266.
[32] *Letters of Horace Walpole,* Toynbee edition, III, pp. 105, 147.

longer accuse him of over-charging. There was, at any rate, some consolation in the fact that, though he himself could not get the picture, neither could Crébillon *fils.*

Sterne once remarked: "Before I wrote, I read Rabelais and Crébillon *fils.*" When he went to Paris he met the latter, in whom he was interested on account of the fact that the Frenchman wrote even more daringly than he. Sterne [33] recorded the result of their meeting:—"Crébillon has made a convention with me, which, if he is not too lazy, will be no bad persiflage. As soon as I reach Toulouse he has agreed to write me an expostulatory letter upon the indecencies of *Tristram Shandy,* which is to be answered by recrimination upon the liberties in his own works. These are to be printed together—'Crébillon against Sterne, Sterne against Crébillon'—the copy to be sold, and the money equally divided. This is good Swiss policy. . . ."

This scheme of self-advertisement was never carried out.

Crébillon *fils* died April 12, 1777, in his lodgings in the rue du Chantre, near the Louvre, where he had lived for nearly twenty years. Most of his friends were dead or had forgotten him, but Collé, whom he had made executor of his will, was with him when he died, and saw him buried in the church of Saint-Germain-l'Auxerrois.

---

[33] Letter to Garrick, April 10, 1762.

CHAPTER III

The Novels and Tales of Crébillon

CRÉBILLON'S first novel [1] was written as a satire on eighteenth-century manners and literature, in the disguise of a Japanese story, which, in an elaborate preface, he pretends to have discovered in the form of a French translation of a Japanese version of a prehistoric tale. This denial of invention is as clearly satirical as the intention with which he wrote. Voltaire read *L'Écumoire* and found it thoroughly entertaining. Crébillon had been shut up in the prison of Vincennes, for a short time, on account of the book, and Voltaire commented [2] on the absurdity of such punishment:—"What a century we live in! It seems that La Fontaine would have been burnt at the stake, if he had lived in our time. It would be sad to be alive, my friend, if there were not some people, like you, who think as one thought in the brave days of Louis XIV."

There were minor quarrels and jealousies at this time,[3] and Crébillon used *L'Écumoire* as a means of ridiculing Marivaux's habit of hair-splitting, of analyzing too minutely a series of insignificant incidents, a process called *marivaudage* by his enemies.[4] The prince Tanzaï scoffs at

---

[1] *L'Écumoire*, or *Tanzaï et Néadarné, histoire japonaise,* 1733–4.

[2] *Correspondance de Voltaire,* April 1734, Letter to Comte d'Argental.

[3] The Abbé Prévost attacked Crébillon in his periodical, *Le Pour et le Contre.* In *Le Paysan Parvenu* Marivaux ridiculed Crébillon's pretensions to literary merit.

[4] At end of second book of *L'Écumoire.*

the princess Néadarné's bad taste. She says to a story-teller whom Crébillon meant for a caricature of Marivaux: "Tell me all you have done, all you have thought, and all that you would have wished to think. Do not omit the least circumstance. You tell a story so well!" The prince marvels at her interest in such pretentious, long-winded repetitions of nothing. "What does it matter," she replies, "if one repeats, so long as one can give an air of newness to what has already been said?" Of an unusual arrangement of words, she thought it well to introduce them to each other. They had never met, and they would enjoy meeting.

The general course of the narrative includes a number of difficulties, practical jokes of devilish malice which the prince and princess found in the way of matrimony, and which were devised by evil spirits for their confusion, but from the toils of which they eventually succeeded in extricating themselves. There are amusing passages, but many are tediously coarse, and the story is by no means Crébillon's best.

Le Sopha, for which Crébillon was exiled, is too long, but some of it is better than any part of *L'Écumoire.* It concerns a silly sultan who insists upon having stories told to him, and who refuses to listen to any but the most improper. No one dares to moralize in his presence, for he has said: "I do not like morality," with a simplicity not of greatness, for "the sultan was ignorant and effeminate. It would be impossible to be less witty than he, or to consider oneself more witty than he felt sure he was. He was always astonished by ordinary people and the common routine of life, and he understood and believed only absurdities and improbabilities—with the exception of immoralities. In the course of a year he could hardly be said to have had an idea; and in the course of a day he rarely stopped talking. He regarded his mental powers as unparalleled, but, in spite of the interest which he took in the lives of his pet animals and in the personnel of his harem, he was flattered at finding himself frequently bored."

An article [5] on Crébillon asserts that Louis XV was wise enough not to see a caricature of himself in this picture of the sultan, and he exiled the author on other grounds. But if Crébillon had attacked the government from a political standpoint, his punishment would probably have been more severe. At any rate, the "shock" caused by the immorality of the story was not of long duration.

Upon Horace Walpole's admiration [6] for *Le Sopha,* Macaulay [7] brought his heaviest condemnation to bear. "Even of Montesquieu Walpole speaks with less enthusiasm than of that abject thing, Crébillon the younger, a scribbler as licentious as Louvet, and as dull as Rapin. This trash, Walpole extols in language sufficiently high for the merits of *Don Quixote.*" Macaulay's exaggerations are always sincere and well-written. He stands at one extreme, and finds fault with Walpole for his position at the other. Macaulay's eloquence did not flourish in proportion to the accuracy of his thought, and Walpole's critical judgment was not equal to the task of evaluating his own personal tastes.

In *Le Sopha,* Crébillon writes of "important persons,

---

[5] *Biographie Didot* (Nouvelle Biographie Générale).
[6] Walpole's *Letters,* Toynbee edition, I, p. 178.
[7] Macaulay, *Essay on Horace Walpole.*

who, having to talk only to women and courtiers, were more concerned with the elegance of their phrases than with the grandeur or truth of the ideas they expressed." Elsewhere he remarks: "Women are constantly tormented by the desire to know certain things which they persistently refuse to admit." He recommends the brevity of one of his novels.[8] "You have finished it before you have time to dislike it"—forgetting the possibility of dislike at first sight. Sometimes his alertness and penetration are worthy of Rivarol or of Chamfort, but all his stories are too long. If he had concentrated the wit of all of them into his two best dialogues, there would have been little loss in destroying the remains.

The *Égarements du Cœur et de l'Esprit*,[9] though not his best story, is longer, according to the original plan, and more ambitious than the others. He complains in his preface of the scarcity of novels that show any effort to give adequate pictures of the realities of life, and of the number of rhapsodies dealing with impossibly glorious heroes and immoderately virtuous heroines. "Any author who holds himself in restraint in the base fear of displeasing his contemporaries, will rarely be interesting to future generations. A novel is supposed to amuse or instruct, and consequently it is usually either too frivolous or too dry." In the *Égarements* he tries to avoid both defects, but in most of his stories he worries very little about the former failing. The novel tells of the difficulties encountered by Mme. de Lursay in ensnaring a youth named Meilcour whose shyness, in her eyes, closely resembles

---

[8] *Atalzaïde.*

[9] Or *Mémoires de M. de Meilcour,* published incomplete and never finished.

stupidity. "She had felt that, in the long run, she would not be able to resist this young man, so why attempt to avoid the inevitable?"

The chief figure in the story is the Comte de Versac, who, with Richardson's Lovelace and Laclos' Valmont, was accepted by the eighteenth century as the personification of wickedness in the form of a lover. "He had the air of having vanquished even those ladies who had resisted him." He was, of course, aristocratic, witty, imperious and cruel, and his "most seductive face and person" were adored by all the broken-hearted women whom he had betrayed and forgotten. Versac informs Meilcour of the obliging nature of Mme. de Lursay, whose hints had not been sufficiently bold to convince the innocent youth of her intentions and desires. Then, having broken Meilcour's illusions, Versac introduces him to a still less admirable person, for Mme. de Lursay was capable of affection, but Mme. de Senanges "gave herself freely to a variety of indulgences all of which fell short of her expectations. It was a consolation to her to know that though she continued to find life less pleasant than she resolutely hoped it might prove to be, she had, at any rate, denied herself nothing that could be expected to afford her any satisfaction. She always appeared, meanwhile, to be astonished at the vices of the century, to complain and even to despair of them. She attempted to atone for her unmistakable lack of charm by denouncing all vices and practising most of them."

Versac tries to teach Meilcour the principles of worldliness, and to make him a successful and heartless lover. "You must say cruel things or you will not be feared."

But Meilcour proves unworthy of Versac's efforts in his behalf. No one fears him, and, worst of all, he has the bad taste to fall in love. Evidently he is hopeless.

Crébillon's sketches of Versac and of Mme. de Senanges are finely drawn, but they are incomparably less vivid and powerful than Laclos' portraits of Valmont and of Mme. de Merteuil. Crébillon plays skilfully with his comedy, but Laclos is a dramatist, shaping the fate of a group of strong characters.

The best of Crébillon's stories are the dialogues, *La Nuit et le Moment* (1755), and *Le Hazard du Coin du Feu* (1763).[10]

The *Nuit* is full of expressions of the philosophy: "if love-making is not always a pleasure, at least it is always a kind of occupation," which might have been suggested by a remark in *Gil Blas*.[11] Crébillon elaborates the theory: "In the world we live in, a liaison is quickly formed when there is mutual attraction, easily broken off whenever the attraction fails, promptly taken up again, as ardently as at first if the attraction returns. Above all other considera- tions, the essential point is to avoid a quarrel. It is true that 'love' plays a small part in all this. But what is that

---

[10] Pierre Nozière dramatized *Le Hazard* and published it with a stage version of Laclos' *Liaisons* in 1907. The *Hazard* was performed at the Théâtre Femina, April 25, 1907.

It is not necessary to mention all the novels attributed to Crébillon. Some of them, like the *Lettres de Mme. de Pompadour,* are of doubtful origin, and many are distinctly worthless.

[11] *Gil Blas,* last page: "For a young man it is a pleasure to get ready to see his mistress. For a man who is beginning to grow old, the prepara- tions amount to an occupation."

exaggerated thing called love? What is it but a sensation which it has sometimes pleased the vanity of man to regard as a virtue?"

Clitandre has come into Cidalise's room clad, as she guesses, only in a dressing-gown, but she asks him if this is so. "Why not?" he replies. "We are still enjoying the lingering warmth of early autumn." She agrees, and then they discuss the bad taste of some of their friends. They make a pretense (of which neither is to the least extent the dupe) of love, virtue, jealousy, hate; they enjoy the cleverness with which they act their successive rôles. There is even a touch of sincerity when Clitandre tells Cidalise of an affair, a rare experience in that it really touched him, for the moment. They are not afraid to pose, they are capable of graceful affectations which reflect realities; capable of certain realities which their manners have only served to enhance. They know each other perfectly, they have often played this game, but it has not lost its zest.

Le Hazard [12] resembles *La Nuit* in more senses than one. The superficial rather than real insincerity of the characters is a part of the truth of the picture. It was a sufficient reason for the playing of their transparent game, that it appealed to them to play it in an elaborate manner; they had learned it as a science and they practised it as an art. Even if they were occasionally bored, they could make their boredom amusing to each other. The people of the eighteenth century could endure *l'ennui* as gracefully as

---

[12] *Dialogue moral*—the moral of which is solely in the title.

they went to the scaffold.[13]   It would have been vulgar and tiresome to complain.

La Nuit concerns a duke and Célie.   In reply to his insistence, she asks: "Do you love me?"   He replies: "If this kind of familiarity were permitted only to love, what would be the use of friendship?"   He continues to evade her question, and she to put him off.   She knows he does not love her and that she does not love him, but it is so amusing to pretend.   However, she gives her consent before he answers her question.   She knows that he intends to visit a certain marquise as soon as he leaves her, and he frankly asserts, though with probable exaggeration: "I love the Marquise passionately, but that does not prevent me from acknowledging your effect on me, an effect so undeniable that it is difficult for me to be sure that there is all the difference between these two emotions that there is said to be."   They are both fully aware of the reality of the difference, and that is a perfectly definite part of their game.   If this game had ever become a serious affair, threatening a war such as the characters in Laclos' novel brought upon themselves, the ending of *La Nuit* would probably have been the same.   Either Clitandre or Cidalise would have laughed, and lost all but the saving grace of another laugh at defeat itself.

In Marmontel's stories, written soon after those of Crébillon, there are many signs of the influence of the

---

[13] Duclos wrote in his *Considerations sur les Moeurs du 18me Siècle,* not without vanity: "the French are the only people for whom it is possible for morals to be depraved without corruption of heart or weakening of courage."

older writer, in description and comment. There is a gentleman whose one ridiculous ambition was to be loved for his own sake;[14] elsewhere,[15] a liaison is referred to as a chance meeting, and it is said to be "cruel enough not to be able to love forever, without condemning oneself never to love at all"; a man is described[16] as thinking himself kindhearted when he makes love to ladies not in their first youth. Of a certain Blamzé, "one dared not say that he was fatuous, for, in his fatuity, there was such an air of aristocracy."[17] The influence is all the more evident in Marmontel's references to Crébillon *fils* in his memoirs.[18]

There were the usual differences between contemporary criticisms of Crébillon's stories. Palissot, who hated Diderot and the *philosophes,* admired Crébillon immoderately. "There is an approach to exact truth in his novels. The characters could not be more finely drawn, nor the situations more skilfully worked out. Crébillon *fils* might have said to many people of his time: 'Is it my fault if these customs are yours?' He was the most faithful historian of the manners of his contemporaries. He was as accurate in regard to the eighteenth century as Petronius appears to have been in describing the time of Nero."[19] Palissot found a piquant gaiety and an originality in

---

[14] *Alcibiade.*

[15] *Le Scruple.*

[16] *L'Heureux Divorce.*

[17] There is practically no influence of Crébillon on writers of the nineteenth century, but there are references to the fact of his occasionally being read, of suggestions in his *contes* for short-story writing. See G. Rudler, *La Jeunesse de B. Constant,* and Sainte-Beuve's *Nouveaux Lundis,* V, p. 11.

[18] Quoted above.

[19] C. Palissot—*Mémoires pour servir à l'histoire de notre littérature,* I, p. 227.

Crébillon which were lacking, he thought, in Hamilton.

Grimm [20] reports that it was said of Crébillon: "Nothing so clearly proves the sterility of this writer as his continued production." Grimm admired his ingenious touch, a subtlety not always inherent in the models from which he chose to draw his sketches; he notes the success of his stories in England,[21] Italy and Germany,[22] and the high opinion in which they were held by Garrick and Sterne. There is a surprising reference to them in Gray's letters:[23] "Now, as the paradisiacal pleasures of Mahometans consist in playing upon the flute and lying with Houris, be mine to read eternal new romances of Marivaux and Crébillon." This eternity could hardly be expected to be "paradisiacal," and it is strange that two such different writers could possibly be so closely associated in anyone's favouritism.

Taine [24] found in Crébillon and Laclos examples of the indestructibility of manner in the eighteenth century. "In the most animated and intense situations, the characters speak in measured and irreproachable terms. For them, indecency may be in things or in deeds, but it must never be in manners or in words." This was true, not only of the highest social ranks, but of some that were conspicuously less lofty. It is clear, in spite of Horace Walpole's attempted parallel, that there is little or nothing of the Cré-

---

[20] Grimm, *Correspondance*, edition Tourneux, XI, p. 479.

[21] Cf. M. de Montifaud, *Notice sur Crébillon fils*, p. iii:—"Crébillon's pictures of life in Paris are as true as the English scenes of Defoe and Richardson."

[22] L. Reynaud, *L'influence allemande en France au 18ᵉ et au 19ᵉ Siècle*, refers to the interest in Crébillon's stories in Germany.

[23] *The Letters of Thomas Gray*, London, 1900, I, p. 97.

[24] Taine, *Les Origines de la France Contemporaine*, I, p. 208.

billon type in many of the great figures of the eighteenth century, though this general distinction is, of course, entirely aside from any question of title or aristocratic privilege.   In the annals of Louis XV there are pages markedly less edifying than in any of the novels of Crébillon.   But there is always the "measured speech," the ease of an accomplished manner, to be found, not only in the great Parisian salons and in the assemblies of the court at Versailles, but in the novel of Laclos and in the stories of Crébillon.   The genius of the eighteenth century, the perfection of its special type of art, is not a question of morals or of practical usefulness.   The old régime had found the medium for adequate expression of itself, and consequently it is not strange that it scorned the talk of "progress." Could the *philosophes* point to a single awkward gesture, find a harsh note in the harmony of tone?   The scorn of the old régime for the new was like the scorn of a cat watching the vulgar enthusiasm and listening to the hoarse barking of a dog.   The "dog" was to have his day, for he had been bullied by the cat quite long enough.

The style of Crébillon *fils* is not so admirable as his wit. There are too many involved phrases, the result of a tendency to mannerism, rather than a necessary method of expressing an elaborate system of thought.   There are times when he fails to acquit himself of the charge of longwindedness which he brought against Marivaux.

His most excellent quality is what Saintsbury [25] calls his "almost elfish" cleverness.   His skill in his special per-

---

[25] Saintsbury, *History of the French Novel*, I, p. 365.

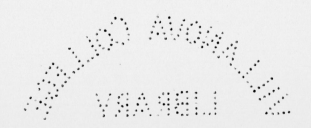

formance is a compensation for his narrowness of outlook; for the fact that he did not attempt a wider or a different field of work. And he could not have failed to see that he must stay in his small enclosure. In that of Diderot he would have been as helpless as Diderot proved himself to be awkward in his effort to copy Crébillon in *Les Bijoux Indiscrets.*

CHAPTER IV

Choderlos de Laclos

THIS soldier, politician, man of the world, made himself famous by writing a novel which, in its portrayal of the calculations of persons who had reduced all their actions to a science, corresponds, in another sphere and century, to the theory of politics of Machiavelli.

Pierre-Ambroise-François Choderlos de Laclos[1] was born at Amiens in October, 1741. His family was of Spanish origin, and of little distinction. One of his ancestors had been valet de chambre to Louis XIV; others had fought for that monarch, or had been inconspicuous writers.

Laclos was given a wider education than the strict requirements of a military career. In 1759, he entered the Corps Royal of Artillery, and became a captain at the age of thirty-six. His older brother had gone as a soldier to the Indies, and Choderlos' ambition had been to follow him, when, in 1762, there seemed a chance that the company to which he belonged would be sent there. But, at the end of the Seven Years' War, he was ordered to Toul, and later to Grenoble. His youth passed in uneventful garrison life, while he longed for active service.

He had been fond of reading, and in 1760 Rousseau's *Nouvelle Héloïse* had seemed to him a "delicious work,"

---

[1] See E. Dard, *Le Général Choderlos de Laclos,* Paris, Perrin et Cie., 1905.

which he continued to admire, though in later life he did
not weep over it as he had done at twenty. He read "with
transport" the novels of Richardson, and shared Rousseau's and Diderot's extravagant feelings in regard to that
author. This is to be wondered at, for Laclos' novel is an
extreme case of the most completely different attitude and
method, except that the Lovelace of Richardson has some
of the character of Laclos' Valmont.

Laclos was tall, thin, and narrow-shouldered. His serious expression, his reserved manner and self-possession,
were favourably impressive, in Grenoble. He could find
satisfaction in the cultivation of an air of proud indifference
which no misfortune should disturb. But he followed the
example of his regiment which had the reputation of enjoying life, and, like most of the fashionable young men of his
time, he wrote verses which the ladies to whom they were
addressed were graciously inclined to call poetry. His
Epistle to Margot was supposed to allude to Mme. du
Barry, and caused a certain sensation in Grenoble; after
this, he turned a novel by Mme. Riccoboni into a libretto,
which failed when somebody set it to music. In Grenoble
he passed for a wit; and he enjoyed the social life which
that city afforded, though observation appealed to him more
than mere amusement, and he took notes on the characters
and manners of prominent persons. His even temper and
his regularity of conduct appealed alike to his friends and
to his military chiefs. His self-indulgence was moderate,
and his interest centred in a study of the inconsistencies
of the provincial point of view, its affectation of contempt
and hatred of Versailles, "the centre of all abuses," which
fascinated those who spoke most bitterly against the habits

which it was their highest ambition to imitate successfully. Laclos' notebook needed to be large.

In several of the regiments there were clubs formed by freemasons who met in halls or barracks where many of the officers and non-commissioned officers assembled. There were literary, philosophical and other discussions, especially criticisms of all established institutions. The idle came to these meetings to be amused, the clever to parade their wit, the ambitious and discontented to make useful acquaintances and to air their views. Laclos attended frequently, and his conversational powers attracted attention, while he gained experience and facility which were of value to him in the days of the Revolution.

In 1779 he was given a commission to aid the Marquis de Montalembert in the construction of a fort at the Île d'Aix, near the mouth of the Charente, on the west coast of France. The journey from Grenoble, near the eastern frontier, was necessarily slow in the eighteenth century, but Laclos was interested in the changing scene. Soon after his arrival he became intimate with Montalembert. They were both ambitious, and dissatisfied with the accepted theories of military science. They saw the chance for more active service than the particular task assigned to them, for it was expected that the English fleet would approach at any time. The English fleet, however, did not appear, and they were especially disappointed, for the fort which they had built was completely satisfactory. All the guns could fire at once without shaking it. Laclos had dreaded the peace which was formally declared in 1783, and he had no intention of remaining inactive and unknown for another quarter of a century, or of passively watching

CHODERLOS DE LACLOS

the intolerable spectacle of soldiers returning gloriously
from the French wars, while he sat in a fort or lived quietly
among the friends he had made in the neighbouring city of
La Rochelle.   It had occurred to him that he might make
a name for himself by putting the notes he had taken at
Grenoble into the form of a startling novel.

In 1781 he was granted a leave of absence of six months
which he spent in La Rochelle and Paris.   He planned a
political pamphlet, and occupied himself more especially in
writing *Les Liaisons Dangereuses*.   There was danger of
the Bastille, or of other results of the wrath of censorship,
but these risks only served to spur him on.   At the end of
the half-year his novel appeared, and caused inevitable discussion and wide notoriety.   The Marquis de Ségur, Marshal of France, greatly shocked and indignant, ordered
Laclos to return at once to his regiment, which was being
assembled at Brest.   Montalembert wrote to Ségur, re-
questing that Laclos be sent back to La Rochelle where he
needed him, and Ségur agreed to this on the understanding
that Laclos was to be replaced as soon as possible.   Nevertheless, Montalembert managed to keep him at La Rochelle
for several years.

The first edition of *Les Liaisons Dangereuses* had furnished Laclos with sixteen hundred francs which were soon
spent.   He wrote an article called *The Education of
Women,* in the worldly sense, and for this purpose his in-
vestigations at Grenoble were of use.   The essay was a
failure in spite of the reputation he had gained by his
novel, and he had neither the material for another article
nor the imagination for another novel.   For a time he
lived quietly at La Rochelle, where his experiences were

similar to those at Grenoble.   It was thought that the notes
for the *Liaisons* had been gathered in the western city, but
this idea, though quite reasonable, happened to be untrue.
The Academy of La Rochelle did not object to Laclos'
notoriety, and elected him a member in 1785.   His general
popularity was not injured by the alteration in his reputation since the days of Grenoble, in spite of the fact that
his military superiors were less satisfied with his conduct.

At La Rochelle there was a Mme. Duprée who prided
herself on her salon, the most attractive feature of which
was her eighteen-year-old daughter.   She had resolved not
to receive Laclos, but he managed to overcome her objections.   It was probably not surprising to the author of the
Liaisons that Mlle. Duprée became his mistress, but he had
no intention of practising all the theories elaborated in that
novel, for eventually he wrote to Ségur for permission to
marry, and received official consent with leave of absence
for a month.

Mlle. Duprée became his wife in 1786, and they went at
once to Paris.   In a few days there appeared, both in La
Rochelle and Paris, an article on the Maréchal de Vauban,
signed by Laclos.   Vauban had been admired by such
sceptical writers as Saint-Simon and Voltaire.   He had
died in 1707, but his military theories were still accepted
as indisputable.   He was said to have taken every city to
which he had laid siege, and all the places he had fortified
were regarded as impregnable.   Laclos' article honoured
Vauban as a man, but gave examples of the wastefulness
which the adherence to his methods had involved.   Military science had greatly advanced since Vauban's day, and
the latest discoveries ought to be made use of.   Laclos

mentioned the improvements in the fort at the Île d'Aix, and explained their efficiency. Montalembert, who had, for years, opposed Vauban's theories in the face of blind opposition, heartily approved of Laclos' article. But the Maréchal de Ségur, to whom Laclos sent a copy of his heresy, was furious. He not only hated the loud comments, pro and con, to which Laclos had given rise, but he particularly resented the fact that Laclos had dared to publish such a criticism without asking permission, especially as that permission would never have been granted.

Laclos was hastily summoned out of the Marais where he was staying with his wife, and ordered to join his company at Metz, where he resolved to leave the army as soon as he could get a discharge. In 1787, having served for twenty-eight years, he was made a member of the Knights of Saint Louis, but he was also released from military duty, to his greater satisfaction.

He settled in Paris, where his novel had been widely read, and where the circle of his acquaintances enlarged as rapidly as at Grenoble and at La Rochelle. He wrote newspaper articles in which he criticized the government as freely as he dared, and managed to keep out of trouble and to live comfortably enough, though it was not until he met the Duc d'Orléans in 1788 that he found adequate support.

The duke never lost a chance to scandalize public opinion, and to irritate the court. One of his whims was to employ an adventurous person, the Comte de la Touche, as his chancellor. He thought it would be original and amusing to have a novelist for a secretary, and Laclos was easily persuaded to take the job. "The ambition, the wit, the bad reputation of Laclos endeared him to the duke, who regarded him as gifted in a variety of ways, and consequently a valuable person to have on hand in case of an emergency." [2] Talleyrand refers to the flexibility of Laclos' opinions. This might have served as a warning to the duke, but he suspected or feared nothing in connection with Laclos. The duke was the richest man in France. He lived a dissolute, but, on the whole, a harmless life, and though his character and mentality were insignificant, his manners were charming. He had become interested in England and English ways, and he had introduced English jockeys, English horse-racing, English cabriolets, English gambling and English drunkenness into France. He told the king that in England he had learned to think (*à penser*). "*A panser des chevaux*" (to groom horses), replied Louis XVI, who was not often witty.

Another of the duke's vagaries had been to make Mme. de Genlis (wife of the duke's friend M. de Sillery, and authoress of many dull books) the tutoress of his three sons. She was alternately violent and sentimental, but she had succeeded in establishing in the Palais-Royal a tyranny which Laclos determined to overthrow, and, by the time of the outbreak of the Revolution, Laclos had supplanted her in the duke's favour. Michelet, in his fondness for oratorical exaggeration, wrote in his history: [3] "Look at the windows of the Palais-Royal! There I see, distinctly, the figures of virtue and vice, the two counsellors of the prince: Mme. de Genlis and Choderlos de Laclos." But Michelet admits her charlatanry, though he does

---

[2] Le Prince de Talleyrand, *Mémoires*, I, pp. 208–209.
[3] Michelet, *Histoire de la Révolution Française*, I, pp. 75–76.

not expressly state that she gives evidence of calculations as selfish as Laclos', in regard to the duke.

Laclos had studied the politics of love. Now he became absorbed in intrigues of state. He met important persons, he discussed with Mirabeau the possibilities of using the duke's money for their profit. Both expressed contempt for Mme. de Genlis. Mirabeau called her a tiresome preacher, who should be put at the head of a girls' school, or made to teach choirboys how to perform church ceremonies. Brissot [4] preferred Mme. du Barry who had the sense to keep out of public affairs.

Laclos urged the duke to go actively into politics, to make himself popular, and to find means of avenging himself for the ill-treatment which he had suffered at the hands of the king. This was a clever suggestion, for the duke hated the king, and, more especially, Marie Antoinette, who had feared him, and had made it so unpleasant for him at Versailles that he had not been there for some time. The duke had no suspicion of Laclos' motives, and complacently allowed the plans of his secretary to shape themselves. Laclos told him that if the king came to Paris, he would manage to have him disposed of. Though there is no proof that the duke himself was guilty of plots against the king, he would probably have had no objection to the success of Laclos' schemes. Conspiracies were bothersome, whether one cared or not, and he left them to his secretary or to other false friends, or to misguided partisans. Rivarol [5] said of the duke: "The hosts of

---

[4] Brissot de Warville, *Mémoires*, I, p. 262; II, p. 321.
[5] Rivarol, *Œuvres*, V, p. 501.

Mirabeau and of Laclos, that is, the power of crime with the uplifting force of all its levers, could not raise this soul from the depths into which it had plunged."

"Laclos," wrote a better friend [6] of the duke, "was the cause of all the crimes which were attributed to the duke of Orléans and to the Orleanists. I am sure that the duke was ignorant of most of the things that were done in his name." But Laclos was simply one of many.

"Laclos was a fluent speaker and a ready writer," says a modern historian,[7] "but his licentious character kept his power from being real." This is not the whole story, for it was political ability as much as nobility of character that Laclos lacked. The life of Mirabeau was no less corrupt than Laclos', but Mirabeau was a political genius. Laclos had determination, self-possession; but his choice of opinions was not always wise, and he lacked the greater gift of conviction. He would gladly have embraced any theory of government, but he misused the opportunity which unscrupulousness had placed in his hands.

Laclos became a member of various clubs—the Patriots', the National, the Valois and others. In the village which was then Montrouge,[8] the Duc de Biron owned a small house where the Duc d'Orléans sometimes went with Laclos to discuss the Revolution with de Biron and his friends. Would it be well for the duke to offer himself

---

[6] Grace Dalrymple Elliot, *Journal de ma Vie pendant la Révolution Française*, p. 265.

[7] H. M. Stephens, *History of The French Revolution*, I, p. 84.

[8] Chateaubriand, *Mémoires d'outre-tombe*, I, p. 301—"The Duc d'Orléans consulted the devil in the race-course of Montrouge, and returned to the garden of Monceau to preside at orgies arranged by Laclos."

as friend to the king, or could he be appointed lieutenant-governor of the kingdom? These and other plans were weighed. There was much to give credit to the idea that in some way or other the duke might be influential. During the terrible winter that preceded the Revolution, the coldest recorded in the eighteenth century, the Seine had been frozen over, from Paris to Le Havre, and famine had been widespread. The duke and duchess had made themselves popular by giving generously to the poor, and a large crowd had assembled at the Palais-Royal in a demonstration of gratitude. The court at Versailles looked upon this incident as a successful effort on the duke's part to curry favour with the people, to be used against their sovereign, and Louis XVI was also suspicious of various reforms which the duke had attempted. Before the elections of the deputies to the States-General the duke had entrusted to Laclos the task of drawing up a set of instructions for the representatives from his extensive estates. Individual liberty, freedom of the press and other advocated innovations had been popular, but the court took particular offence at the twelfth article of the prospectus: "Divorce should be established as the only means of remedying unhappy marriages." This was thought to be directed against the queen, whom the duke was accused of wanting to shut up in a convent. Sieyès was called in to talk over Laclos' paper. He found nothing good in it, "simply because of his contrary nature which invariably took the other side." [9] He wrote his own version, which, as well as Laclos', was scattered throughout France, and

[9] Talleyrand, *Mémoires*, I, p. 210.

was, at first, better known in the provinces than in Paris.

The duke's popularity grew daily, but he could not become a leader because, among other reasons, his friends continued to dominate him.   Laclos, for the moment, was satisfied with the general course of events, and continued his operations, including the writing of *La Galerie des Etats-Généraux*,[10] a series of articles some of which were the work of Mirabeau and Luchet.   Conspicuous persons were discussed under false names, but there were notes that served to lift the masks.   The article on Talleyrand (Amène), then bishop of Autun, is by Laclos: "The first instrument of his success is an excellent intelligence.   He judges men with indulgence and events with coolness.   He has that moderation which is a chief quality of wisdom. He rightly makes conciliations and compromises for the sake of peace, but his principles do not alter.   The characteristics which work against him are his gentleness, his pleasant face, the charm of his amiability.   He knows men too well to be the dupe of their flattery.   He smiles at the illusions of friendship."   This tone is to be found in the other articles.   Of La Fayette: "His misfortune is to have great pretensions, but ordinary ideas."   As for the Duc d'Orléans, Laclos felt called upon to write nothing but praise.

In spite, or because of his conversations with Mirabeau, Laclos did not trust him.   He told his patron that Mirabeau's real purpose was to serve the king with the duke's money, but he did not wish to break with Mirabeau; he wanted to be sure that Mirabeau did not replace him in

---

[10] Published in 2 volumes, 1789.

the duke's confidence. He walked about the streets, listened to conversations, kept himself as much as possible behind the scenes, but was accused of starting or encouraging riots. It is probable that he approved passively, rather than actively, of many of the disturbances, and though his name was connected with the *affaire Réveillon*,[11] and even with the march of the women to Versailles, his connection with these events was probably nothing more definite [12] than the fact of his being in the services of the duke, whose enemies wished to get him, and incidentally Laclos, into trouble.

On the fourth of October,[13] the day before the insurrection of the women, the Duc d'Orléans was seen at Versailles, wearing a conspicuous cockade in his hat, and acknowledging the tributes of a large crowd that shouted: *"Vive le roi d'Orléans."* But if the duke had hoped for great things on the fifth of October, he was soon disillusioned, and, about the middle of the month he fled, with Laclos, to England. There are numerous explanations of this move. La Fayette, jealous of the duke's popularity, is said to have suggested to Louis XVI that the duke be sent on an unimportant mission to London, a mere excuse to get rid of him, for Louis XVI could expect nothing in connection with England, and would have sent someone else if he had planned an alliance. Mirabeau called the duke a coward when he learned of his departure, and re-

---

11 A strike of factory-workers in the Faubourg Saint-Antoine.

12 See Taine's description of the women marching to Versailles: "Imagine that Chamfort and Laclos are bringing their mistresses." (Cited in Dard, *Laclos*, p. 187.)

13 Dard, *Laclos*, p. 187.

solved to have nothing further to do with him. French diplomats hoped that the duke would clumsily manage to make himself unwelcome in England. Commercial treaties were vaguely hinted at. There was talk of the possibility of making the duke King of Flanders,[14] which was known to be the last thing that England would wish, as well as the least probable of all results of the duke's flight.

The duke paid no attention to all this. He continued to live his dissipated life, drank with the Prince of Wales, and, as usual, left intrigue and diplomacy to Laclos, who shut himself up in his den, cudgeled his brains, wrote letters, and accomplished nothing. He met the Comte de Tilly (whose love affairs had been heard of in England as well as in France) in a room where they were waiting for the Prince of Wales to receive them. There was ample time for conversation, for the prince was never punctual, and Tilly felt an interest in Laclos on account of his novel.[15] "His manner of talking was somewhat oratorical on this occasion, but at other times he was cold and methodical. His skill and tact, as a courtier, were not great. He had the impatience of a *philosophe* or of a conspirator rather than the art of a diplomat." [16]

In spite of Laclos' constant efforts, the duke could not see that any progress had been made, and he began to despair of any success. "I am unlucky in having known you," he said. But he continued to keep Laclos in his service, and to trust him with all serious matters.

In June, 1790, the duke is said to have received a mes-

---

[14] *Annales des Sciences Politiques,* 1904, XIX, p. 581.
[15] Comte de Tilly, *Mémoires,* II, p. 320.
[16] Most of the descriptions of Laclos differ from this account.

sage from Laclos the tone of which is too authoritative, too incongruously indiscreet for the author of the *Liaisons Dangereuses:* "Monseigneur, under what unlucky star was I born that I should have fallen in your estimation? Must I bear all the blame for the failure of our projects? In truth, Monseigneur, I swear by all that is most sacred that I could not have been more faithful to my legitimate sovereign than I have been to you. I hope to hear no more of these reproaches, for they must, if continued, alienate me from one who pays for all my trouble with unjust accusations. That which should have put you on the throne, and me at your side, the 5th of October, 1789, has failed indeed. But did I not make every possible preparation? Pikes were forged and distributed, the victims were marked, the proper persons informed. The murder of the queen in her room, the particular manner in which a shot from a group of armed men was to be fired at the king without the possibility of later discovery as to which of those men had fired;—these things were planned. Our tears were to flow, our zealous search for the culprit, our placing of the Dauphin under your care, the mysterious disappearance of your charge;—these things were planned. . . . I have the honor to be, Monseigneur, (Ah! would that I might say 'Your Majesty!'), your most humble and devoted servant, Laclos." [17]

There are other alleged communications, but their authenticity is doubtful. He would probably not have gone into such details in writing, and he could have waited for

---

[17] *Les Liaisons Dangereuses,* edition 1920, introduction by Ad. van Bever, pp. xxiv–xxxiv.

an opportunity to speak to the duke. He would have written a less melodramatic account of the plot, and laid himself open to less criminal charges, though later, in the Jacobin Club, he will be seen to have urged may of the same atrocities which he confesses to have countenanced in the above letter. But he had more reason to be sure of the Jacobins' approval than of the duke's.

Early in July, 1790, the duke returned to Paris, accompanied by Laclos, and declared himself faithful to the king and queen; but when he called on them, they received him very coldly.

Laclos had no idea of letting the duke escape from his clutches as long as the Orleans fortune held out, but he determined to launch himself upon a more involved career. The duke, alone, had not been a strong enough card; but there were others in the pack that might help; and yet, at this time, thorough republican ideas still seemed too Utopian, not only to Laclos, but to other and more important revolutionists, especially the Jacobins to whom Laclos determined now to look for aid. He became a member, and frequently attended the meetings of the *Société des Amis de la Constitution,* which were held in the library of the convent of the Jacobins. On the 21st of November, he joined the *Comité de Correspondance,* and was made the chief editor of the *Journal des Amis de la Constitution,* and the "occult, active and established director of the manœuvres of the Jacobins. Ambitious persons, demagogues, hired revolutionary agents—each member worked for himself, though all appeared to contribute their efforts with the same end in view—the conquest of power by all or any means, for the sake of the group to

which they nominally belonged." [18]   The chief leaders of
the Jacobins, at this time, were Duport, Barnave, and
Lambeth, the triumvirate which maintained its popularity
until the flight of the king to Varennes. "Who was the
grave censor, the pure and irreproachable man upon whom
these men conferred power? Who would believe it?
Upon the author of *Les Liaisons Dangereuses,* upon the
recognized agent of the Duc d'Orléans, upon Choderlos de
Laclos." [19]   Laclos' chief aim, from the first moment of
his association with the Jacobins, was to make Jacobin-
ism the organized cloak for Orleanist propaganda throughout France, advertised as fully as possible in his newspaper.

The power which Taine and Michelet attribute to Laclos
may be exaggerated; nevertheless it is clear that he had, at
least, a recognized influence of some weight, and a considerable activity as speaker and journalist. "Solemn and
dominating, like priests of a new religion, the Jacobins
thought themselves the sole guardians of revolutionary
theory. Laclos worked audaciously along the lines they
laid down. With the *Contrat Social* in hand, like a new
gospel, Laclos wrapped himself proudly in the imposing
mantle of its principles, but sometimes his recommenda-
tions were even more absolute and ruthless than those of
Robespierre himself." [20]

A pamphlet called *La Jacobinière,*[21] reporting on the
sessions of February 23–28, 1791, thus refers to Laclos:

---

[18] Taine, *Les Origines,* V, pp. 73–4.
[19] Michelet, *Histoire de la Révolution Française,* II, p. 113.
[20] Dard, *Laclos,* p. 269.
[21] Aulard, *Histoire des Jacobins,* II, p. 123.

"His speech on the subject of the *émigrés* was full of the most odious wickedness, the most vile baseness, the most extreme hypocrisy, the most cruel barbarity. It is easier to imagine than to express what fury he showed in regard to the court. As I listened to him, I felt an indignation which rose to the point of torture. Laclos said, on February 27: 'No one must leave France, no one must move from place to place even within our borders. A complete paralysis must strike the people. The red flag must float above the meetings of the National Assembly. At a given signal we shall let loose our light troops; they shall kill, massacre, slaughter all those whom we hate, and even those who annoy us, that is to say, more than seven-eighths of the people of France. Nor will any of the royal family be allowed to escape, except my dear pupil; my honoured master, who will be well-treated. We will fill France with little Jacobite citizens whom we will bring up in fear and respect of our new empire.' "

This violence would have astonished the friends of Laclos' youth. He was one among many whom the Revolution led into extravagant cruelty. The restraint of style and the coolness of impartial observation, the contempt for such excess, were forgotten in a mad effort to seek personal gain at all costs. He now put himself on a level with the Comte de Valmont and the Marquise de Merteuil, whose vices he had held up to scorn and brought to punishment. But his methods were vastly inferior to their cold, subtle science.

He continued to express violently anti-monarchical propaganda in his speeches and in his newspapers; and his bitterness against the king exceeded that of any of his fellow-

Jacobins. In the meeting of March 16, 1791, shortly after the king had recovered from an illness, there were cries of *vive le roi* and it was proposed that, as usual in such cases, a mass should be said in his honour. Laclos objected, but his protest met with scanty response, for many of the Jacobins were, outwardly at least, still in favour of adhering to certain customs. A report of the meeting asserts that the Jacobins had not as yet acquired "that republican fervour which would make them hate that *best of kings,* that most tender of fathers, that most honest of Frenchmen." [22] This absurd flattery did not save itself by satirical intention. Laclos is reported to have suggested that the return of the king's health be celebrated by the selection of four girls of the Faubourg Saint-Antoine to be married to four of the conquerors of the Bastille, for the good of posterity. This motion was shouted down, and Laclos replied: "Well, if you insist, let a *Te Deum* be sung, but without expense, for it isn't worth it. We will use the money which would have been lost in religious luxury, for the dowries of the four girls whose weddings we have proposed to arrange."

It cannot be said that Laclos was in any sense a popular leader. He not only made too many enemies, but his personality could not attract a crowd. It was said [23] that "hell, to avenge itself on humanity, threw upon the earth the monster Laclos." He was not working earnestly for the cause in which he pretended to have faith, and he was playing two games at once. He wrote to the duke on

---

[22] Aulard, *La Société des Jacobins,* II, pp. 193–194.
[23] Dard, *Laclos,* p. 296.

April 18, 1791:—"Everything is going well. If I do not make you play again the scenes of October 5-6, 1789, but this time with success, I consent to be called a man without courage or resources." This letter,[24] like the one of June, 1790, may be a forgery, though the fact that Laclos was still plotting for the elevation of the duke is sufficiently clear.

What Laclos hoped for, at this time, was more probably the flight of the king than his death, though Laclos' name continued to be mentioned in connection with schemes of assassination or other insurrections. On the 21st of June, the duke began driving about Paris in an English carriage, trying to get the mob to cheer for him. On the 23rd he went so far as to apply for admission to the Jacobin Club, but he never could be induced to declare openly his pretensions to the throne. When it was learned, on the 21st, that Louis XVI had disappeared, Laclos found out that at Varennes the king had accused the Orleanists of planning to murder him. Laclos wrote in his newspaper: "I wish to see in France a hereditary and absolute monarchy which shall uphold equality, and keep the nation free from civil war." He hoped to see the duke "made regent by the grace of the people and of the Jacobins," including those in the provinces as well as in Paris.

With the help of Brissot, Laclos is said to have written the *Pétition du Champ de Mars*, July 17, 1791, which was the direct result of the flight to Varennes, and provoked the massacre of the Champ de Mars, which, however, was in no way favourable to the duke, though it reflected a growing

---

[24] *Les Liaisons Dangereuses*, edition 1920, introduction, p. xxviii.

hatred of the court. Laclos, in a group of men including
the then inconspicuous Danton, found more difficulties to
encounter than had been foreseen. Laclos, not being able
to use the Jacobins as he had hoped, retired from all
participation in their activities, including the editing of the
newspaper [25] which he had controlled. Later, he made an
effort to rejoin the Jacobins, but without success. He continued to live at the Palais-Royal, but the husband of Mme.
de Genlis had replaced him in the duke's favour, and he
could only wait for some new opportunity to serve his interests. It was clear that the Orleanist cause had failed
completely, and even if there had been a chance for its recovery, Laclos would have had to oppose the influence of
de Sillery, and that of Mme. de Genlis, now Mme. de
Sillery, who had done much to promote the cause of the
Duc d'Orléans' son, the Duc de Chartres, and whose position at the Palais-Royal had been further strengthened
through the dissatisfaction which the Duc d'Orléans now
felt more strongly than ever, in regard to his secretary.

Laclos returned to the army. Politics now seemed to
him as hopeless for any personal advantage as military life
had appeared to be five years ago; and the great fear of
invasion, the frantic preparations for war which suddenly
took the centre of the stage, at once appealed to him.
Danton had become powerful, and Laclos found that he
remembered him. He was made one of Danton's thirty

---

[25] Once, in this paper, Laclos had found occasion to give an argument
in favour of his novel. The publication of the private memoirs of the
Maréchal de Richelieu revealed a history "which far surpassed the pictures
given in *certain* novels which have been accused of exaggeration in connection with the actual manners and morals of *la bonne compagnie.*"

"commissioners of executive power," and he adopted the
"republican fervour" which carried all before it.   Through
Danton's influence, and in accordance with Danton's nomi-
nation of Laclos, the minister of war (Servan) sent him
to Châlons, telling him that he considered that city one of
the most important points of the outer defense of Paris,
and a military base which needed reorganization.   The
general-in-chief at Châlons was Lucknor, an old soldier
who had fought in the Seven Years' War, and whom Louis
XVI had bought from Frederick II.   He had been made
a marshal of France, but he spoke execrable French.   He
was imposing in the eyes of many of his subordinates, but
Laclos, who was to establish a bureau to help Lucknor in
his correspondence, found him a *vieux débris*.   His slight
means of expressing himself were no more faulty than the
ideas which he had to express, and, though he realized his
incapacity, he had neither the courage nor the loyalty to
resign his post to save himself from still greater embarrassment.

Laclos left Paris September 6, 1792.   The military
situation was considered desperate.   Verdun fell without a
struggle and the Prussians advanced on Sainte-Menehoulde.
Laclos was occupied in a variety of ways as soon as he
reached Châlons.   He felt defeat in the air, and wrote to
Servan: "No one at Châlons, nor at the headquarters
of Kellermann's or Dumouriez's armies seems to have any
idea of making plans for the very possible emergency of a
grave check, or a sudden Prussian advance on Paris."   It
seemed to him that Châlons was not a favourable point
on which to make a desperate stand, but, under Lucknor's
direction, the best position would be equally unsafe.

Everyone with whom Laclos came in contact seemed to have lost his head. Lucknor poured himself out in tears and hand-claspings, and expressed his dependence upon his suggestions. Laclos wrote again to the minister of war:— "You have asked me for the truth, and I must tell you frankly. You wish to know how much confidence should be placed in Lucknor. I reply that in the course of a conversation with me he burst into tears. He has only the shadow of authority, but even that shadow may be dangerous for the French army." Laclos' fellow-commissioners at Châlons agreed with him in this matter. "Of the troops assembled at Châlons, the 'patriot Laclos,' as he was then called, was the real chief. His natural perspicacity was enhanced by the *coup d'œil* of the soldier." [26]

In the critical period of the campaign, Laclos was one of the most useful assistants in the organization of the portion of the army centred at Châlons, for the battle of Valmy. He grouped the volunteers, planned for emergencies, attended to the rear-guard, and provided a strong defence for Paris, in case of an enforced retreat. However, the victory of Valmy, in which Laclos played a minor part, and the declaration of the French Republic, were of little profit to Laclos. He had perhaps hoped that Servan would put him in Lucknor's place, and not only had this not occurred, but the almost immediate resignation of Servan as war minister, and the fact that Danton's services were not at his disposal, left him stranded. The fortune of the Duc d'Orléans had almost entirely disappeared, so that he could have given no help

[26] Chuquet, *La Retraite de Brunswick*, p. 37.

to Laclos even if he had not been executed two months
later.   Servan was soon made general of the new "army
of the Pyrénées" which was to guard the southern frontier.
He took Laclos with him as chief of staff, and headquarters were established at Toulouse.   The battle of
Valmy had infected France with war-fever, and there was
talk of war with Spain and of expeditions to India.   Laclos
had always wanted this kind of adventure, and now there
were additional reasons for wishing to get away.   With
the death of the Duc d'Orléans, trouble threatened his
former adherents, and how else could Laclos expect to
escape?   The armies were pulled in all directions at once.
Dumouriez called for more troops on the Belgian frontier,
Servan for the Pyrénées, and Laclos, if he had not been
summoned north, would have led them to the east.

The Orleanists who had sat on the benches of the Convention, and among the Jacobins in their various clubs, and
had been active in all sorts of intrigues, at the duke's expense, had not been a united body.   They had feared and
hated and consequently were, now, all the more ready to
betray each other, if need be.   On March 31, 1793, the
Convention ordered the arrest of the Citizeness de Genlis
(who fled from France), of the Duc de Chartres, and
many other Orleanists.   Laclos was arrested April first,
and sent to the prison called l'Abbaye, not the most comfortable in Paris.   He had been accused not only of
complicity with the Duc d'Orléans but of participation
in Dumouriez's plan, in which the Duc de Chartres was
said to have been involved, of turning his army against
Paris.

Laclos' wife persuaded an influential friend to have

Laclos transferred from l'Abbaye to his home, where he was
to be watched by his own paid guard.   This extraordinary
arrangement did not last long, for the hired detective became nervous.   He noticed the arrival of packages at the
house of his prisoner, the mysterious lockings of closets
and hidings of keys, and he hastily resigned for fear of
being involved in affairs which his suspicions made it his
duty to report, but which he seems to have preferred to
forget.   For the summer months Laclos was permitted to
transfer his imprisonment to Versailles, where he could take
long walks, under another escort, and where his health,
which had not been good, rapidly improved.

At La Rochelle, Laclos had thought of experimenting
with shells which had, heretofore, been used only against
troops, but which seemed to him adaptable for the destruction of forts or ships.   He wrote to the minister of war,
who gave him permission to get such materials and to move
about as his experiments might require.   Very shortly,
however, Laclos was again arrested, and shut up in the
prison of Picpus.   M. de Sillery, just before his execution,
had accused Laclos of being one of the authors of the *Pétition du Champ de Mars*, for which Brissot had already gone
to the block.   Laclos expected to follow him, from day to
day, though for some mysterious reason he was allowed to
go on with his work.   His only facilities were paper and
pencil, and the necessary experiments had to be postponed.
His wife procured certain comforts for him, and her letters
were allowed to reach him although he was not permitted
to write to her.   He is said to have written some speeches
for Robespierre, but the differences between their styles
were such that the work of the former would have been

more marked than it is, in any of the recorded speeches of Robespierre.[27]

After a period of greater severity in the prison régime, Laclos was finally released in December, 1794.

During the latter part of his imprisonment, he wrote letters which have since been published,[28] and among them is a note written by Mme. Laclos: "He could only mention to me the bare fact that he had been condemned to death by the revolutionary tribunal; but the execution of Robespierre and succeeding events saved him from undergoing his sentence. However, he remained in prison for six months after he had written me the brief message which he thought would be his last." [29] In many of his letters, Laclos refers to his constant devotion to the French Republic, ever since it became established, and he professes frequently and at length that the separation from his family is the source of more regret than any of the other deprivations of prison life. He wrote to his wife: "I have ample courage for my personal misfortunes, but I cannot be so brave in facing yours. When I think that I am the direct or indirect cause of all your sufferings, I have need of all my strength to keep from falling into the abyss of despair. I try to imagine that I am at home with you and the children, and sometimes the illusion is strong enough to be, for brief moments, a source of relief."

Mme. Laclos adored her husband. His writings reminded her of Rousseau's. She felt herself unworthy of

---

[27] Dard, *Laclos,* pp. 405 et seq.

[28] *Lettres inédites de Choderlos de Laclos,* published by Chauvigny, Paris, 1904.

[29] Ibid., pp. 29–30.

the rich qualities of Laclos' mind and character, and when
he told her that her self-depreciation was extravagant, she
accepted his correction:—"You are right at last," he wrote,
"in admitting that you have qualities which justify my love
for you. If I listed them here my letter would be too long.
A charming mistress, an excellent wife, a devoted mother—
these qualities have constantly been present in my daily
thought of you. . . . But I will say no more. I would
rather feel than express these sentiments." He hopes that
their son Étienne [30] will profit by his father's letters, but
does not wish Mme. Laclos to insist too strongly that
Étienne read them. A few years later, when Étienne had
gone to Germany, Laclos wrote to him: "The ability to
speak foreign languages is astonishingly lacking among us,
and, in this regard, foreigners are much more accomplished
than ourselves. The present government [Napoleon's] has
observed this defect, and wishes to do all in its power to
promote the study of foreign languages in France." Laclos continues in a Chesterfieldian manner: "You will
find, my friend, that good manners have a use and even a
charm. In social gatherings which at first appear to be
artificial and uninteresting, you will find, when you learn
how to meet them, that there are persons there whom it
will be to your advantage to have pleased. . . . Believe in
your father, Étienne; to this habit you will owe success as
well as the pleasure that life may bring you. You will
perhaps find this letter too serious, you will think it a
father's sermon; but you will be mistaken. It is simply a

---

[30] Étienne, born before Laclos married Mlle. Duprée, was their eldest son.
He was killed in 1814, in Napoleon's army.

word from friend to friend.   Let us learn to reason together; try to persuade yourself that you have no better
friend than your father."   Laclos wrote to his wife that
he would like, above all things, to own a small farm, and
that he would be satisfied to live there the rest of his life,
and make only just enough money to support his family.
But when he regained his liberty, he returned again to military service.   There are many people who think, at some
time or other, that they would like to be farmers—especially when their lives have been spent in other ways.

For the moment, Laclos could only obtain a small government position, but he was given ten thousand francs for his
former military services to the Republic.   He lived quietly
and happily with his family in Paris, worked at his experiments, and wrote articles for the newspapers on politics,
finance and military science.   He spread anti-English
propaganda, and urged France to prepare herself to assume
the dominating position in Europe, which she seemed to
him to deserve to hold, and which she could never gain if
England's power continued to grow.   The violence and
cruelty of his speeches to the Jacobins are absent from these
post-prison articles.   Laclos had become more genial, less
satirical, less bitter.   He praised the genius of Napoleon,
and Napoleon, who knew every soldier in France, made him
a general of artillery, ordering that he should be considered as having held that rank uninterruptedly since the
battle of Valmy.   Napoleon ignored the facts of Laclos'
Orleanist activities and his imprisonment; he regarded him
as a skilled artillery officer who had distinguished himself
in the defeat of the Prussians.

Laclos was sent to the army of the Rhine, under General

Moreau, with whom he got on very well, though he had trouble with various subordinate officers who were jealous of the favours that had been shown him by Napoleon. His chief difficulty was the weight of his sixty years; the weather was cold and rainy, and he suffered from rheumatism. He wrote: "I should like to lay siege to some fortress, to try out my new shells, and then return home, if a lasting peace could be signed."

Partly on account of his health he was ordered south, first to Grenoble, where he was to be one of the generals in a reserve army, then to join the "Army of Italy" under Marmont. He stayed at Turin for some time, always expecting active service, always disappointed. Finally it appeared that peace would soon be established, and Laclos thought of a diplomatic career in which Talleyrand, whom he had known in the early days of the Revolution, might help him. Laclos' services, however, though not required in battle, detained him still in the army, and his experiences were, at least, pleasantly social. General Marmont liked him, Mme. Marmont enjoyed his reminiscences, the manners of the *ancien régime* which he had not lost in the Revolution, and which were the least noticeable characteristics of the majority of the officers in Napoleon's army. Marmont put Laclos in charge of his special reserve, entertained him frequently, and regarded him as a product of a civilization too much of which had disappeared with the monarchy.

Laclos went to Milan with Marmont, and described the journey in a letter to his wife: "Travelling is dangerous, and bandits are numerous. We saw a company of ten, but our number was equal to theirs, and we were undisturbed,

for these gentlemen never fight unless the odds are greatly
in their favour."

At Milan he went to the opera because it was the fashion.
"There is nothing under heaven so mortally boring as an
Italian comic opera, if grand opera be not more so, and we
are threatened with the latter. This is not because one
does not understand Italian, because, for those who do, the
effect of the absurd libretto might reasonably be to destroy
the charm of the music. But the theatres themselves, and
the scenery, are better than ours in Paris." Laclos went
to the theatres, understood nothing that was said, but "one
sees one's friends, and there is plenty of opportunity for
conversation." In the box of the chief of staff at the opera,
Stendhal was introduced to Laclos, whose novel he had
read and much admired.[31] Laclos was interested in Stendhal because he came from Grenoble, and the impression he
made on the young writer was that of a "conversationalist
whose manner still reflects the charm of the social life of
the time of Louis XV," as Stendhal had read of it, and he
found Laclos a delightful contrast to most of the men he
had met in the army. But Stendhal loved the art of Italy,
and Laclos cared nothing for it. When he went to Pavia
he saw only the botanical gardens and the natural history
museum. He imagined that he could sit in his room and
picture to himself more beautiful sights than those of Italy,
and this appealed to him as an economical way of sight-
seeing. He thought the majority of the people of Milan
were "crude and noisy," and they did not interest him any
more than Italian art and landscape.

---

[31] P. Arbelet, *La Jeunesse de Stendhal,* I, p. 185.

While he was at Milan he planned a novel as different as possible from the story of *Les Liaisons,* and which he feared might be lacking in interest because its motive was to be the happiness of family life, "the only true happiness." Judging by his letters to his wife, his fears were not altogether ill-founded.

When he inquired about his *Liaisons* in the bookstores of Milan and Turin, he found that it had never been translated into Italian, but that it was often read in French, and highly praised. At Pavia, Laclos sent a copy to the bishop, who invited him to dinner and told him that his novel was a highly moral work, an admirable book for anyone to read, and to be specially recommended to girls. This would have been a surprisingly broad-minded verdict, even for a layman.

Laclos returned from Italy to Paris in 1801, and there he lived uneventfully until Napoleon sent him to command the new "Army of Naples." This journey proved a great hardship. "The main roads are bad, but the others are almost impassable; the inns are detestable; the towns we pass through are, for the most part, small and unattractive. There is hardly any way of sending letters." [32]

Much of his discontent was due to the fact that the Italians hated the French, naturally enough, on account of Napoleon, and consequently Laclos' troops were not always treated with a hospitality which might have compensated for some of the discomforts of travel. At Taranto, the headquarters of the Army of Naples, Laclos' health broke down. There was an immense amount of reorganization

---

[32] Laclos, *Lettres,* pp. 263, 269.

to be done, and Laclos over-taxed his strength.   He caught
a fever; the doctors at Taranto were none of the best, and
he was too ill to be moved.   He died September 5, 1803.

He had written to Napoleon and to Marmont asserting
that the journey and his illness had cost him most of his
money, and asking that provision be made for his family.
Napoleon gave Mme. Laclos a pension and made her son
an officer in his army.

The peculiar fact of Laclos' life is that although he
devoted by far the greater part of his time to the study or
practice of military science, his only real achievement was a
novel, in spite of the fact that he lived at a time when advantage was being taken of brilliant opportunities in every
department of the army.   "His contradictory gifts place
him among men of indefinable talent, whose characters
arouse our curiosity while they elude our scrutiny." [33]

---

[33] Paul Bourget, *Sensations d'Italie,* p. 294.

CHAPTER V

Les Liaisons Dangereuses

The original title of the story reads: *Les Liaisons Dangereuses, ou Lettres recueillies dans une Société et publiées pour l'instruction de quelques autres.*[1] The author signed himself M. C—— de L——, but he was at no pains to disguise his authorship, for everyone knew he had written the book as soon as it appeared. His preface stated that he had published these letters to show what means may be used by corrupt persons to ruin the lives of the worthy, the innocent and the respected. "Any woman," he solemnly proclaims, "who consents to receive in her house a man whose principles she disapproves, will end by becoming his victim."

The story concerns Cécile Volanges, a girl of fifteen, who has been brought up in a convent school and whose mother has determined to marry her to the Comte de Gercourt, whom Cécile has never met. Without her mother's knowledge, Cécile has fallen in love with the young chevalier

---

[1] The first edition (1782) has been followed by many others of which the latest (1920) was published by Georges Crès et Cie., Paris. Soon after its original publication, the novel was turned into a play by a relative of Mme. de Genlis, much to the regret of the latter. Another dramatization in 1834, and one by Pierre Nozière in 1907, have been performed in Paris. There have been various translations of the *Liaisons,* among them an English version, *Dangerous Connections,* London, printed for T. Hookham, 4 vols., 1784; and recently (1924-5) there has appeared in the *Broadway Translations* a translation by Richard Aldington (Dutton, London and New York).

Danceny, to whom she had been introduced by the Marquise
de Merteuil.   Cécile regards Mme. de Merteuil as her best
friend, and asks her for advice in the perplexing situation
in which her mother's plans have placed her.   The Marquise tells Cécile dreadful things about Gercourt, and
Cécile vows she will never marry him.

The Marquise de Merteuil had formed an alliance (the
principal *liaison dangereuse*) with the Vicomte de Valmont.
This had come about after the breaking up of a liaison
which she had had with Gercourt, who had deserted her for
a woman whom he had induced to sever relations with Valmont.   The Marquise and Valmont, being thus left in the
lurch, a rare experience for either of them, had become
interested in each other through a common hatred of Gercourt, and because of their respective powers of attraction
and infernal cleverness.

Mme. de Merteuil, finding that Gercourt is to marry
Cécile, determines to revenge herself on him by persuading
Valmont to seduce Gercourt's intended bride.   The idea
appeals to Valmont, but he is busily engaged in an effort to
conquer the supposedly unconquerable Mme. la Présidente
de Tourvel, a handsome young woman whose husband is at
a distance.   Valmont's chief pride is that no one can resist
him; heretofore his most difficult conquest had been that of
a woman whom he could not subdue in less than three
months, and he fears that Mme. de Tourvel may prove as
stubborn.   She is the friend of his aunt, Mme. de Rosemonde, and this serves as an entering wedge for Valmont's
plans.

Mme. de Tourvel informs Mme. de Volanges of her
acquaintance with Valmont, of her knowledge of his bad

reputation, and of her hope to reform him. But Mme. de Volanges knows him better, and warns her against him in the strongest terms. This admonition is discovered by Valmont, whose inclination to carry out the scheme of the Marquise is thereby enhanced. The success of this plan would cause Mme. de Volanges more pain than Valmont could find pleasure in direct vengeance.

Mme. de Merteuil grows impatient. She writes Valmont that his affair with Mme. de Tourvel will make him ridiculous; that his friends will think less of him when he fails as he is bound to do; that the women whom he has betrayed will be ashamed of their easy surrender, and that his career will be blighted. She asserts that the Présidente is too pious to be interesting, and warns Valmont that she might be instrumental in ruining his bad reputation. But, secretly, the Marquise has felt a jealousy which she would scorn to admit. It is evident to her keen sense that this is more than an ordinary affair, and that Valmont's devotion to Mme. de Tourvel has its tender side which he, in turn, can be no less willing to own than the Marquise to confess her jealousy. This fearful situation—the discovery of an element of sincerity—is to be the trap into which both the Marquise and Valmont will fall, in spite of their otherwise masterly plan of campaign.

Mme. de Tourvel continues to be invincible for an annoyingly long time. Valmont indulges in hypocritical and ostentatious charity which she mistakes for conscientious kindness. She tells him, however, that their letters to each other must cease, and she conceals the fact of her alarming discovery that her interest in him is turning into affection.

The correspondence between the Marquise and Valmont

takes the form, for several days, of a discussion of their
relative merits in the sphere of intrigue as an art and a
science.   She is convinced of her vast superiority, and tells
Valmont the story of her self-training.   "Having never
been in a convent, having no intimate friend, cared for by a
watchful mother, I had no definite knowledge of life.   But
before I was fifteen, I had the degree of skill in diplomacy
to which most of our politicians owe their reputation, and
yet I felt myself to be an amateur in the science which I
wished to master thoroughly.   I developed much more
rapidly in mind than in body, and my desire for knowledge
suggested a means of instruction.   The only man to whom
I could safely address myself was my confessor.   I over-
came my embarrassment, and told him I had done 'all that
women do.'   I did not know exactly what I meant, but I
knew that I was lying.   The priest called the sin so great
that I knew its pleasure must be extreme; and at once my
desire for knowledge gave place to my wish for experience."

Fortunately her mother had just arranged for her daughter's marriage to the Marquis de Merteuil—and she was
safely and promptly married.   She made her husband think
her simple and frank when she was almost rashly audacious,
and she trained herself especially to read the thoughts that
unsuspecting or unskilled persons always allowed to appear
upon their faces, while she made of her own face an im-
penetrable mask which revealed not even the fact of her
close observation of others.   She could be gay, serious, sad;
could always put herself in the mood that her judgment told
her would suit the occasion; and it was the astonishing
degree of her excellence in penetration and in acting that
lifted her above her competitors.   She learned not to antag-

onize old ladies, "for they made or marred the reputations of those who were younger." She defined love as an art and a science, "like medicine, to aid nature." When her husband died, she retired to the country to study religion and propriety and other accepted ideas, simply to know exactly what to pretend to believe, and how to act. When she returned to Paris, she appeared to keep at a distance all those for whom she cared, and to be gracious to those to whom she was indifferent, thereby establishing her respectability, for she made the former conduct seem as real as the latter. She regarded every person she knew as having a secret which it was her business to find out;—some point in character or taste or ambition by which each individual could be led. "I follow my principles," she said, "for such they are,—the fruit of my profound reflections and observations."

She had recently won a great battle:—she had ruined a young man named Prévan by having him thrown out of her house as if he had insulted her, after she had given herself to him. He was imprisoned and disgraced, and everyone congratulated Mme. de Merteuil. "He has been cruelly sentenced," writes Valmont, "as guilty of a crime of which he is innocent, and your victory is complete. . . . The longer I live, the more I am tempted to believe that you and I are the only persons on earth who amount to something!"

Meanwhile, Mme. de Volanges has discovered the secret correspondence between her daughter and Danceny, and she forbids him her house. She has learned of this through Mme. de Merteuil, who has thereby posed as her friend, and has made her promise not to reveal the tale-teller, by

pointing out that Cécile would not continue to confide in her
if she knew that her words were to be repeated. Thus
the Marquise has induced both Mme. de Volanges and
Cécile to consider her their most intimate friend. But her
deeper purpose, in revealing Cécile's letters to Mme. de
Volanges, thus putting difficulties in the way of Cécile and
Danceny, was to persuade Cécile of the need of assistance in
the form of Valmont, who is to carry letters between them,
thus opening the way for Cécile's confidence in Valmont
which shall bring about her ruin before her suspicions are
aroused. Cécile accepts the help of Valmont, which the
Marquise offers her, and is at once impressed by his cleverness in giving her a letter in a room full of people, without
attracting anyone's notice. When he tells her he must
have the key to her bedroom, she trusts him as implicitly
as if he were the Marquise. When he comes to her room
at night, she realizes that a cry for help would but serve to
put her in the wrong, and she surrenders herself to him.
When he meets her the following day he is interested in
her inability to hide her embarrassment.

Mme. de Merteuil's plans are still more involved than
was necessary for Valmont's success. She has made Danceny her lover, and she wishes Cécile to be her pupil. Having brought Cécile to grief through Valmont, she wishes
to cause her more misery through future revelations of
Danceny's disloyalty, but also to suggest indiscretions with
Danceny which even her still possible marriage with Gercourt would not need to hinder. But the Marquise wearies
of Cécile's ingenuousness; she gives her up, shortly, as unworthy of her efforts to train her in the ways of the world,

and, aside from this consideration, her time has become more and more constantly occupied by Valmont's affair with the Présidente.

Mme. de Tourvel has taken her departure in order to avoid Valmont, but he, by means of priestly intercession, gains permission to see her once more. Their meeting is, for Valmont, a triumph of strategy. He knows that she loves him, he plays upon her sensibility, he threatens suicide, he starts to go, till finally, in an almost hysterical condition, she gives herself up.

Valmont now writes to Mme. de Merteuil, too boastfully to please her pride or calm her jealousy. He proclaims himself worthy to be her lover, but she now determines to be no more easily won than Mme. de Tourvel, and she induces Valmont to strike the woman whom she sees he has grown to love in spite of his erstwhile boast that he cared nothing for her. The Marquise reminds Valmont that he will be laughed at for not deserting Mme. de Tourvel as much as if she had resisted all his efforts; and she bids him write to her thus:—

"Adieu, my angel. You have been charming. I leave you without regret; perhaps I shall see you again, one day or another; this is the way of the world, it is not my fault." Valmont sends a letter to this effect, and Mme. de Tourvel retires, broken-hearted, to a convent. But even this sacrifice, for such it is, does not satiate the anger of Mme. de Merteuil. She continues to prefer Danceny to Valmont, and the latter sees that he has been doubly fooled. He threatens her; but she scornfully returns his letter, with the words: *"Eh bien, la guerre!"* The first battle of the

war is Valmont's.   He persuades Danceny to break an ap-
pointment with the Marquise in order to see Cécile.   The
next morning the Marquise receives a mocking note from
Valmont asking how she enjoyed Danceny's company the
night before.   She replies by telling Danceny of Valmont's
betrayal of Cécile.   He challenges Valmont to a duel in
which Valmont is wounded, but, before he dies, he convinces
Danceny that his worst enemy is Mme. de Merteuil, and
that a young officer named Prévan can bear witness to her
atrocities.   Danceny is to see Prévan's reputation cleared,[2]
while that of the Marquise appears each day in darker
colours, as, piece by piece, the history of her crimes is
brought to light.

Cécile follows Mme. de Tourvel to a convent, but the
Présidente does not long survive the blow of Valmont's
letter.

Mme. de Merteuil is not only ostracized by all her
friends, but made hideous by an attack of small-pox from
which she miserably recovers to find that her face has at
last become what she had all her life striven to prevent it
from being—"the mirror of her soul."

When the *Liaisons* appeared, a former mistress of Laclos, the Marquise de C——,[3] read the novel, and determined to establish her horror thereof by refusing to see
Laclos again.   She said to her servant: "You know the

----

[2] Prévan was reinstated in public opinion. He was neither a scoundrel
nor a model of virtue in this or other affairs.

[3] Tilly, *Mémoires*, I, p. 290, refers to Marquise de Créquy, or Coigny.

tall, thin, pale gentleman who wears black and who often comes here. I fear to be alone with him and I wish never to see him again." Tilly thought that the Marquise took herself for the original of Mme. de Merteuil, whom she resembled, not only before the attack of small-pox, but afterwards as well. Mme. de Genlis was immeasurably shocked by the book,[4] and tried to use its "licentiousness" as an argument to persuade the Duc d'Orléans to have nothing to do with Laclos. Marie-Antoinette possessed a handsomely bound copy [5] of the *Liaisons,* but the title was not printed on its cover. Mme. Riccoboni carried on a correspondence [6] with Laclos on the subject, telling him he had woefully misdirected his talents, and that the book gave a wrong impression of the social life of the time; to which Laclos replied that such characters had been known to exist, whether typical or not.

Grimm was not at all surprised that women had so much to say against the book. To those of them who were above reproach, it was slander; to others it was a breach of faith, inexcusable in proportion to the undeniability of the picture presented, though, admittedly, an extreme case. In 1782 Grimm wrote: [7] "The success of the *Liaisons* is more brilliant than that of any other novel in recent years." But he thought it might lead as many astray as it could safely warn, by the very fact of the vividness with which

---

[4] Mme. de Genlis, *Mémoires,* III, pp. 178–9.

[5] In collection of the queen's books in the Bibliothèque Nationale.

[6] These letters have been presented to the Bibliothèque Nationale, as has also the original MS. of the *Liaisons.*

[7] Grimm, *Correspondance, Tourneux,* XIII, p. 107.

the truth, particular rather than general, was expressed.

The *Liaisons* has been called "one of the most licentious novels ever written," [8] and Laclos "the most cruel of vivisectors of love." [9]   The majority of critics, from the time of its publication to that of the present century have admitted that, aside from moral questions as to the choice of subject, the novel is a masterpiece of analysis.   Its restraint of style, its sober method of presentation, raises it above the appeal to sensationalism which was a part of Laclos' intention.   Saintsbury, whose judgments of French authors are usually more convincing, omitted it from his *History of the French Novel,* and, when he received letters of protest, re-read the *Liaisons* and added a note [10] to his first volume in which he calls the novel "prosaic and suburban, having neither comedy nor tragedy, passion nor humour, nor even wit, except a little horse-play."   It would be less difficult to prove that the mathematical calculations and cold-bloodedness of Mme. de Merteuil are too inhuman to be possible, even though their perfection breaks down eventually, than to find one definite instance of horse-play in any part of the novel.

The subtlety of character-drawing is not only a question of degree of fiendish ingenuity, but of the manner in which both Valmont and the Marquise are brought to their ruin by a triumph over them of the very weaknesses which they most prided themselves on having mastered—the dangers of any indulgence in sincerity of feeling.   And there is the

[8] H. M. Stephens, *History of the French Revolution,* I, p. 84.

[9] P. Bourget, *Sensations d'Italie,* p. 294.

[10] George Saintsbury, *History of the French Novel,* I, p. xiv.

double effectiveness of the inevitability of doom for both
the innocent and the guilty, in this case.

As for examples in real life of such a character as that
of the Marquise de Merteuil, there is a reference in Dard's
careful study of Laclos.[11] At the house of a friend, Stendhal was shown a manuscript of three hundred pages which
has since been lost. It consisted of notes written by Laclos
concerning many well-known names in French society about
the year 1778. These scandalous reports were collected
in various ways, often through Laclos' direct knowledge
of the events described, and sometimes from persons who
told him of their special experiences or observations. The
truth of this statement is supported by a conversation in
which Laclos told the Comte de Tilly [12] of the origin of
his novel. "I resolved to write a book which should be
totally different from the usual work of fiction. It was to
cause talk, to make a name for me, and to survive me.
One of my comrades in arms who is now famous as a
scientist had had a number of adventures of a notorious
kind, which would be eagerly read by the public, I thought,
if adequately presented. He was born for women, and
for the perfidies in which women are past-mistresses. If he
had been a courtier, he would have had the reputation,
throughout France, of a Lovelace. He had taken me into
his confidence, and I laughed at his escapades, at the tricks
he had played; and when he asked me for advice, I did
what I could to help him. At Grenoble, I had met one
of his mistresses, a worthy subject for the portrait of the

---

[11] Dard, *Laclos*, p. 28.
[12] Tilly, *Mémoires*, II, p. 320.

Marquise de Merteuil, but mine is a feeble copy of the original.   She was a Mme. L. T. D. P. M.,[13] a constant source of gossip.   I took full notes on all that I had heard and known of her, and decided to write her story as soon as I could find the time.   I gradually collected other material, and some of my own youthful adventures were striking enough.   I worked as many of my notes as possible into a connected history, but some parts of my book I invented, especially the more unusual character of Mme. de Tourvel.   I took all the pains I could in perfecting my style, and after several months of finishing and retouching, I threw my book in the face of the public.   I have heard very little of what success it has had, but I am told that it is not yet forgotten."[14]

Grimm[15] calls Mme. de Merteuil the *Lovelace des femmes,* and superior to that prototype as well as to Valmont.   Richardson made of Lovelace a less dominating character, without the resources and the skill of Valmont. The death of Lovelace is less dramatically effective.   He dies without affecting the destinies of the other characters further than he has already done, while Valmont's death results in the ruin of one, the justification of another, and contributes directly to a general atmosphere of mingled suffering and relief, the varied significance of which gives

---

[13] In his *Vie de Henry Brulard,* I, pp. 74–5, Stendhal says: "I knew Mme. de Merteuil. She was Mme. de Montmort, who lived on a large estate near Grenoble." But Stendhal was very young at the time, and did not know the details of her history till he read *Les Liaisons.*

[14] Laclos might have said of his novel as Rousseau said of the *Nouvelle Héloïse,* "I have observed the customs of my time, and I published these letters."

[15] Grimm, *Correspondance,* XIII, p. 107.

the story a concentrated force which has been seen to gather strength from page to page.

If Laclos' purpose, aside from his expressed intentions in the preface, was to let the story speak for itself, he did well to choose the epistolary form of telling it; and whether the book be considered moral or immoral in effect, it is probable that no other form of presentation would have offered greater opportunity for the bringing out of the intensity of the drama—an intensity which has been admitted in a variety of ways by readers of the novel. "The moral effect upon my mind," wrote Greville,[16] "was stronger than any which ever resulted from the most didactic work, and if anyone wants to excite remorse in the most vicious mind, I would recommend him to make use of the *Liaisons Dangereuses* for the purpose." Louis Blanc [17] referred to it as the "most profound of impure books"—a remark which does not necessarily indicate a clear perception of the difference between an impure book and an impure subject.

Napoleon [18] is reported to have said: "What made the Revolution? Vanity. What will end it? Again, vanity." Vanity is the predominant element in the characters of Valmont and of Mme. de Merteuil; it drew them into intrigue and it brought them to their ruin. They were not only led on by a pride in the degree of their cleverness, but by the fact that their cleverness consisted in the refinement of torture which they knew how to inflict on

---

[16] Greville, *Memoirs of George IV*, I, p. 34.
[17] See *Bulletin de Bibliophile*, Oct. 1834, for other opinions.
[18] See Dard, *Laclos*, p. 82.

others, and from which they derived a definite pleasure.

The theme of the *Liaisons* resembles the plot of Lady Bellaston to ruin Sophia in *Tom Jones,* except that in Fielding's novel this plan is simply an episode, while in the *Liaisons* it is the basic situation. It is not probable that Laclos had read *Tom Jones* when he wrote his novel, for though it appeared in France, in translation, more than thirty years before the publication of the *Liaisons,* there is no mention of Fielding in Laclos' letters or other writings.

Baudelaire,[19] who saw nothing worthy of note in the stories of Crébillon *fils,* wrote: "Licentious books comment upon and explain the Revolution. . . . The *Liaisons* if it may be said to *burn,* can but burn like ice. . . . In its purpose, it is as high as the highest of moral writings, and equally profound." In 1856 he wrote to a student of the eighteenth century:—"Put aside, for me, everything that you can find on or about Laclos." He called the *Liaisons* a masterpiece among modern novels, and said that he intended to write a critical article on Laclos. As it happened, he never put his comments into the form of an article, such as he planned at that time. In his notes he observes that Valmont is essentially vain, although, "aside from this, he is generous in any case which does not concern women or his own glory." He calls Mme. de Merteuil a female Tartuffe, [20] always superior to Valmont in

---

[19] Ch. Baudelaire, *Œuvres Posthumes et Correspondances inédites,* 1887, pp. 113, 154. See also the notes on *Les Liaisons* by Baudelaire published in Champion's edition, 1903, of Laclos' *L'Éducation des Femmes.*

[20] Baudelaire calls *Tartuffe* a pamphlet, rather than a comedy, in regard to which "an atheist would say that certain grave questions should not be put before the vulgar throng."

In answer to various questions as to the character of Mme. de Merteuil,

method, though each is eventually the victim of the other. Of Danceny, Baudelaire remarks that he becomes interesting as the story advances, though, at first, his "silliness" is tiresome. He sees in Mme. de Rosemonde, an old pastel, "a charming portrait, with her cap and snuff-box."

In comparison with the Don Juan of Molière, Musset [21] thought Valmont a greater genius, making Don Juan seem merely "the shadow of a *roué.*" And as a type, a master of intrigue, Valmont is a more imposing figure than any criminal of the eighteenth century, except Mme. de Merteuil.

In 1807, when Napoleon's empire was at its height, the Comte de Tilly wrote: "In the new order of things, the *Liaisons* has lost some of its interest," as a picture of contemporary life. "But," he adds, "the novel will live as long as the French language."

If Valmont and Mme. de Merteuil had not been brought to their ruin, the book might have been called improbable, or even impossible. And the skill with which the catastrophe is brought about is no mere matter of the imprudence with which they revealed themselves to each other in writing, for their letters were not the cause of their downfall, nor were they victims of remorse. The reason for their failure was more profound than either of these: it was a question of the hazard of emotion. Not even a Mme.

Laclos said that Molière had probably never known the exact original of Tartuffe, but that he had observed various instances of the existence of Tartuffe's characteristics in persons whom he saw from time to time, and had assembled them in one character, just as Laclos had done in the case of his marquise.

[21] See Dard, *Laclos,* p. 51.

de Merteuil nor a Valmont can be sure that their emotions
will always be completely under control.[22]

[22] Rémy de Gourmont, in his essay *La Femme Naturelle* (*Promenades
Littéraires,* 1ière série, pp. 291-2, 301), refers to Laclos as an author "ex-
cessively known" for *Les Liaisons Dangereuses,* a novel "which, after having
been considered very immoral, may, perhaps, in future be regarded as
almost too moral, in spite of certain characteristics of a daring nature. . . .
Laclos was an ardent and almost fanatical disciple of Rousseau. Like him,
he preached a return to nature. In this respect, the *Liaisons* gives the effect
of an unfinished novel, for there is the marked lack of a second part in
which one should see the virtues practised in a state of nature, after the
disorders which were the result of definite social conditions." But Gourmont admits that this second part would not enhance the best effect of the
novel as written, for, in the work of a certain Abbé Gérard, a "long, edifying novel called *Le Comte de Valmont, ou Les Égarements de la Raison,*
published in 1801, a sequel of this kind was actually attempted. To Gourmont, this is an "absurd epilogue" . . . "If Laclos had read it, he might
have remarked that if his novel did not make one thoroughly detest life,
the novel of the Abbé Gérard, at any rate, could but arouse a horror of
virtue." Gourmont admits, further, that Laclos had in him the stuff of only
one novel; he could neither have improved upon *Les Liaisons,* nor written
anything else of equal merit.

CHAPTER VI

Diderot

THE life of Diderot, his Encyclopedia, his relations with many of the leading men of his time, his scientific and philosophical writings—all aspects of his life except his position as a novelist have been treated at length in various books and articles, especially, among English writers, in the work of John Morley. Of Diderot as a novelist there have been various opinions, too many of which are as unjust as his own.

In his novels there is the directness, originality and sympathy which he brought out in his criticisms of painting and sculpture. But the extraordinary diversity and energy [1] of his interests and the rapidity with which he worked were bound to prevent him from perfecting his novels in the finer values of style and construction, though these defects are much more marked in the *Bijoux* and *Jacques* than in *La Religieuse* and the *Neveu de Rameau*. He wrote the two-hundred-and-fifty pages of the *Bijoux* in fifteen days, nor was this time entirely devoted to that one work.

He was always the first to admit his own faults. He said that he wrote down his thoughts as they came to him, and, afterward, made some sort of arrangement of them. "But it is rare for me to rewrite anything. If I find something

---

[1] "I was born to live a hundred years," Diderot once remarked. "Some say I have abused my constitution, but I maintain that I have merely used it. I have lived more in fifty years than most men do in a hundred. I have lived for happiness; the only duty on earth is to be happy."

useful to me in the work of other authors, I use it freely. If they suggest some new idea, I put it in the margin of my manuscript." [2]   He objected to the petty, rigid demands of contemporary critics, and found the French reading-public "indifferent to instruction, and insisting, above all things, on being amused, even in the most serious matters. For my part, I do not fear the disapproval which my actions and ·my writings may arouse. . . . Truth produces goodness; and beauty is their work."

In Diderot's criticisms of the painters of his day, there was always appreciation of sincerity of feeling, of that which was lifelike, rather than that which showed mere technical skill; and some of his contemporaries found him a helpful guide. "Diderot's criticisms have given me, as it were, a sixth sense," wrote Mme. Necker [3] after reading his *Salons,* "and have taught me how to look at a picture." Mme. d'Épinay remarked: "Four lines of Diderot give me more to think and dream of than a volume of one of our supposed *beaux esprits.*" These effects of Diderot's criticisms, according to Sainte-Beuve,[4] are due to the manner in which he brought to the people of his time, a sense of colour through the medium of ideas.

Diderot's criticisms were always vigorous and interesting. "I care more for country manners than for affected delicacy, and I would give ten pictures by Watteau for one by Teniers. I prefer Virgil to Fontenelle, and Theocritus to both, for, if he has not the elegance of the former, he has a greater fidelity to truth, and he is far from having the

---

[2] Tourneux, *Diderot et Catherine,* II, p. 448.
[3] Mme. Necker, *Mélanges,* I, p. 342.
[4] Cf. Sainte-Beuve, *Lundis,* III, p. 233.

DIDEROT

From a copy of an engraving by Delannoy

affectation of the latter." [5] It is perfectly clear that Diderot, also, was greater than Fontenelle; and Sainte-Beuve [6] places them in contrast to each other, as devoted to different literary theories. Fontenelle admired the literary ideas of the seventeenth century, and wrote with them in mind, whereas Diderot "seemed always to address future generations, with Mirabeau and Danton at their head."

Diderot was at his best in conversation, or in the soliloquies [7] with which he often held the floor. One day [8] Grimm and Diderot were in the midst of an animated discussion of the eighteenth century which Diderot excitedly called "the century of philosophy, which would enlighten and regenerate the world." Grimm had expressed the opinion that a great catastrophe threatened France, but Diderot gave him little chance to reason on the subject. While Diderot's eloquence drowned Grimm's voice, a valet entered the room, and said: "The king has been assassinated." Grimm and Diderot looked at each other, and, this time, Diderot was silent. They found out, later,

---

[5] *Pensées Détachées, Œuvres de Diderot*, XII, p. 75. All references are to the Assézat edition, 1875-7.

[6] Sainte-Beuve, *Lundis*, III, p. 260.

[7] *Correspondance Secrète*, VI, pp. 292, 425. When Diderot called on Voltaire, he talked so much that Voltaire could hardly get in a word, and, when Diderot had gone, Voltaire remarked: "That man is not lacking in ideas, but nature has refused him one conversational talent—that of dialogue." Diderot compared Shakespeare to a great statue between the legs of which the tallest man could walk. This did not please Voltaire, for he did not admire Shakespeare. Diderot said of Voltaire: "He resembles a magic castle which is falling into ruin. But one sees clearly that it is still inhabited by a sorcerer." The Chevalier de Chastellux said that Diderot's ideas were habitually drunk, and chased each other madly.

[8] Grimm, *Correspondance*, Jan. 5, 1757.

that the knife of Damiens had only scratched Louis XV.

Concerning Diderot's extravagant manner, there are stories of his visit to St. Petersburg. When Catherine the Great conversed with him, she found it necessary to set a table between them to escape the rapping of his fingers; and the Princess Daschkoff relates [9] that she could pardon him and be amused, in her turn, when, in the course of a discussion of Russia, Diderot jumped from his chair, walked up and down the room in a great agitation, then suddenly stopped and spat violently on the floor. "What a woman you are!" he cried. "In a moment you have overthrown all the ideas that I have entertained on this subject for twenty years!" This lack of self-control was not always so complacently received in France, but those of his friends for whom he cared most, were indulgent.[10] Indulgence was by no means the usual necessity, for Diderot's brilliant eloquence could arouse the most unqualified admiration, and his personality could make friendship deep.[11] The famous

---

[9] Princess Daschkoff, *Mémoires,* I, p. 220, et seq.

[10] Marmontel, Mme. d'Holbach, Mme. d'Épinay were among those who best appreciated Diderot; and it was a matter of no consequence that the snobbishness of the Marquis de Castries should thus express itself: "Wherever I go I hear nothing but talk of Diderot and of Rousseau. What is the meaning of this? They are men of no condition, they have not even houses of their own. They are lodged somewhere in an attic."—Génin, *Vie de Diderot,* p. lxii.

For the salons of Mme. Geoffrin and of Mme. du Deffand, Diderot cared as little for their formality as he did for the conventional French drama, literature and thought.

[11] Sainte-Beuve, fifty years after Diderot's death, and with his great knowledge of the history of the eighteenth century, thought that Diderot was the only man of that time with whom he would have cared to live.

quarrel with Rousseau [12] has been the subject of no end of discussion, but though it has not resulted in unanimous favour of Diderot, more has been established for him than against him. Both Rousseau and Diderot were given to emotional expressions of friendship in contrast to the reserve of Grimm, who was regarded for some years as the friend of both, though much more truly so of the latter. Diderot wrote of a meeting with him: [13] "We were at dinner when Grimm was announced. I cried out, ran to meet him, threw my arms about his neck. He came in, and sat down next to me. I could neither eat nor speak. I held his hand and gazed at him." [14] These expressions are like many of Rousseau's, but in Diderot's writings, as in his relations with his friends, there is a fundamental logic and sanity which were lacking in Rousseau, while there is a poetry and a dream-quality in Jean-Jacques which Diderot could not approach.

[12] "When Diderot looked at Rousseau he thought he saw a madman. But what he really saw was a ghost of the future. Diderot-Danton beheld the face of Rousseau-Robespierre."—Michelet, *Histoire de France,* XVII, p. 50. This offers an interesting contrast to the theory of Lytton Strachey (*Books and Characters,* p. 214), who regards Rousseau as "modern" in comparison with Diderot. But Rousseau and Diderot were both "modern" in reference to the time in which they lived; Diderot was practical and logical, whereas Rousseau was a dreamer. The *sensibilité* of Diderot was more sensible than that of Rousseau. The reasonable, clear thought of Diderot, however, is quite distinct from the reasonable, clear thought of the typical eighteenth-century man-of-letters.

[13] Letter of Oct. 9, 1759.

[14] Carlyle wrote in his essay on Diderot: "He recoiled in horror from an earnest Jean-Jacques." It is true that Rousseau's face seemed, after their long misunderstandings, a distressing sight to Diderot. But he did not give up hope of helping him till he had tried everything he could think of. Diderot was as "earnest" as Rousseau.

In Diderot's plays, there are many of the qualities which are to be found in his novels, though less effectively brought out. Diderot wrote, however, much more fully on the art of the theatre than on that of the novel. He attacked the conventions and formalities which had, to some extent, hindered the full development of Racine's and of Molière's genius, and which had led to artificiality and tediousness in the tragedies of Voltaire and of Crébillon *père*. Diderot wished to give unaffected and simple pictures of ordinary home-life, and the theatre appealed to him for this purpose, partly because of his excellence in dialogue—a form which he also used almost exclusively in one of his novels, *Le Neveu de Rameau*, and in several of his short stories.[15] Diderot's first play was tearful and sentimental, as in the following scene,[16] when Clairville, "driven almost distracted by sorrow and anger, walks back and forth. He stops and sighs," and says to Dorval: "This is the result of all my tenderness. Leave me! I detest you— Ah!" Diderot's stage directions are numerous: "Clairville's accent is that of despair; he walks again, in an agitated manner, and repeats, with a variety of declamatory violence: 'Leave me! I detest you!' He throws himself into a chair, and says, in a low and muffled tone: 'She hates me. And what have I done that she should hate me? I have loved her too much.'" Diderot's *Le Père de Famille* is no more interesting than the *Fils Naturel*, and it cannot be said that he improved upon the classical manner until he wrote *Est-il bon? Est-il méchant?*, which is much better

---

[15] It may be noted that Voltaire's complaint that Diderot's conversations tended to become monologues does not apply in these cases.
[16] *Le Fils Naturel,* Act III, Scene 5.

than its title—a light comedy, decidely amusing, a comedy
of errors in which the principal character,[17] in his effort to
please everyone, finds he has annoyed all his friends, and
his task is then to appease them before the final curtain.

Est-il bon? has, unfortunately, not escaped the oblivion
into which Diderot's other plays have not regrettably fallen.
They are interesting examples of what Diderot much more
successfully accomplished in fiction, and of what he would
have done still more admirably if he had taken the time to
revise and to polish. There are the marks of these defects
in many of his short stories. An amusing *conte* could have
been made of the merest sketch that Diderot set down in
his correspondence with Mlle. Volland, referring to a conversation at Mme. d'Holbach's. The discussion was of a
man who had three children, one of whom lived righteously,
another became a criminal, and the third died in infancy.
What would be their respective fates at the day of judgment? Supposing that the first should be rewarded with
the joys of Paradise, and the second sent to Hell, would
not the third receive neither recompense nor punishment?
But if the third child should say: "Oh God, if you had
let me live longer, I might have made my life worthy of
my eldest brother's," would not God reply: "Ah, but I
foresaw that, if you had lived, you would have resembled
the other brother?" Then, in turn, the criminal would
ask: "In that case, why did you let me live so long?"

----

[17] According to Meister, *Œuvres de Diderot,* I, p. xviii, the central character was Diderot himself. The play was finished only a few years before
Diderot's death. It was, later, admired by Baudelaire, *Œuvres de Diderot,*
VIII, p. 140, but seems not to have been successfully performed, though Baudelaire made efforts in that direction. In Feb. 1904, at the Odéon, the play
was produced several times.

And the Lord might reply: "I gave you longer life that you might prove worthy; you neglected the opportunity, and now you reproach me for the favour." Then the third child would complain again: "But I was not granted that favour." It was concluded (at Mme. d'Holbach's) that these, indeed, were troublesome children, and could but be a source of deep regret to their earthly parents, as well as to their Heavenly Father.[18]

Diderot neglected not only this slight material, but much that was important, for he preferred history to fiction,[19] and his idea of a novel did not include the necessary selection and composition, for he called it a mirror in which the passing scene is reflected. There is also, in most of his stories, a predominant purpose of which no mirror can be accused. "There is every probability," writes Saintsbury,[20] "that Diderot might have been a very great novelist if he had lived a hundred years later." Would Diderot, at any time, have been less distracted by a number of pursuits any one of which must have been more or less of a hindrance to his proficiency in the others? "As a novelist," writes Strachey,[21] "Diderot has some of Rabelais' stupendous

---

[18] *Œuvres de Diderot*, XVIII, pp. 423-4. In vol. V, pp. 501-2, Diderot tells the "true" story of a Russian dancer, La Nodin, who was a Catholic, but habitually neglected to go to mass. On several occasions she consented to go, as her friends advised, but, each time, when she returned to her home, something had happened, till, at last, she came back to find her house burned to the ground. She knelt in the street, and cried: "Oh, Lord, forgive me for going to mass. I did not wish to go. I swear never to go again. May I be damned if I break my vow!" Diderot asserts that she kept her word.

[19] *Œuvres*, XII, p. 81.

[20] Saintsbury, *History of the French Novel*, I, p. 400.

[21] Lytton Strachey, *Landmarks in French Literature*, p. 165. See also Taine, *Les Origines*, I, p. 104.

breadth, and more of Rabelais' enormous optimism." He
has not, however, Rabelais' imagination and originality.
The special point to be made, is that few novelists of power
as great as Diderot's have cared so little, not only for the
novel in itself, but for the variety of ways in which the
effect of a novel may be produced and enhanced. He was
interested, not so much in the technique, but in the sentiments, the ideas and choice of subject and display of
emotion, in novels that he read. The technical mastery
of certain nineteenth-century novelists was not dreamed of
in the eighteenth century, and "technique" was too much
regarded, by many eighteenth-century writers, as something
to be associated with the seventeenth-century formalities
and rather to be gotten away from, than to be more widely
developed. In his *Éloge de Richardson*,[22] Diderot expressed an admiration which amounted to worship. "Until the present time, the novel has been given over to
frivolous fancies, to a kind of writing which was equally
deplorable in its effect upon good morals and good taste.
I should like to find a name other than that of 'novel' for
the work of Richardson, which elevates the spirit, and
breathes a love of what is good . . . O Richardson!
after reading one of your novels, I feel as a man feels at
the end of a day which he has spent in doing good. . . . I
will go so far as to say, O Richardson! that the most
truthful of histories is full of error in comparison with
your novels. From this day I shall prostrate myself at the
foot of your statue. I adore you, I search the depths of
my soul for adequate expression of my admiration, but I

---

[22] Written in 1761. See *Œuvres*, V, pp. 212–27.

cannot find it.   These lines have been written without plan, without order, in the tumult of my heart.   The ghosts of the characters in your novels wander in my mind.   I hear the cry of Clementine; the vision of Clarissa comes to me; I behold the figure of Grandisson; my pen falls from my hand." [23]

A friend of Diderot asked him if he had been ill when he wrote the *Éloge de Richardson.*[24]   The question seems a natural one, and it is surprising that Diderot should have cared more for the novels of Richardson than for those of Fielding, the frankness and humour of which would seem to have been better suited to his taste.   As writers, there is more resemblance between Richardson and Rousseau than between Richardson and Diderot.   But Diderot seems to have known Fielding's works very slightly, and there is almost no mention [25] of them in his letters and essays.   It is strange that Diderot, who thought Richardson's novels none too long, should have criticized Rousseau's [26] on that ground, for it is difficult to understand why *La Nouvelle Héloïse* should seem long-winded if *Clarissa Harlowe* does not.   The *sensibilité* of both (in spite of many points of difference between the authors, for Richardson, with all his elaborate sensitiveness, seems to have had a more normal point of view than Rousseau) gives the effect of a painful endlessness.   One would ex-

---

[23] In his summary of Holbach's *Système de la Nature,* Diderot apostrophizes nature in the same way: "O Nature!   Sovereign of all beings!   And you, the adorable children of nature:—Virtue, Reason and Truth!   May you be always our only divinities!"

[24] E. Scherer, *Diderot,* p. 40.

[25] *Œuvres,* XVIII, p. 514: *Tom Jones* recommended to a friend.

[26] Comte d'Escherny, *Mélanges,* III, p. 168.

pect Diderot to find many of the same faults in Richardson
that Fielding found, and which he found in Rousseau. It
seems that the laws of taste are often the laws of the unexpected, and Diderot's admiration for Richardson was,
perhaps, more deeply set in the taste of the later eighteenth
century than he realized. Possibly he understood Rousseau
better than he did Richardson.[27]

[27] Of Diderot's short stories and sketches, the *Regrets sur ma Vieille Robe
de Chambre* is one of the most charming. In the midst of the new furnishings which had been provided for him by a friend, he sighs, not un-
gratefully, when he thinks of his equal content and comfort before the arrival of more luxurious trimmings, for himself and for his room. Diderot
concludes with a typical word of caution against the lure of riches.

The *Entretien d'un Père avec ses Enfants* gives one of Diderot's favourite
household scenes, too long, too sentimental.

The story of the much too maternal Mme. de la Carlière, and of the man
whose every action seemed doomed to unjust interpretation, is too long even
as to title: *Sur l'Inconséquence du Jugement Public de Nos Actions
Particulières,* but one feels the sympathy which Diderot intended to arouse
for the object of the "public judgment."

In *Ceci n'est pas un Conte,* the contrast between the coldly cruel Mme.
Reymer and the gentle, kindly Mlle. de la Chaux is effectively brought
out in their relations with a man who is subjected to their successive in-
fluences.

The *Deux Amis de Bourbonne* (possibly suggested by a story of Saint-
Lambert's taken from a play by Beaumarchais) were so devoted to each
other that no sacrifice was too great for either one to make. One of them
lost his life in saving that of the other.

L'Oiseau blanc—conte bleu is an imitation (like the longer *Bijoux*) of
Crébillon *fils,* and equally inferior to the original, but not lacking a certain
dexterity and vigour.

All these stories show traces of a dramatic and narrative power always
in need of more rigorous discipline and practice.

CHAPTER VII

Diderot's Novels

Les Bijoux Indiscrets, the first of Diderot's stories long enough to be called a novel, was the only one to be published before his death, and the least worthy of publication of all his novels.[1] He wrote it [2] during the period of his liaison with Mme. de Puisieux, whose constant demands for money led him to try a "popular" novel. At that time the stories of Crébillon were in vogue, and Diderot remarked to Mme. de Puisieux how easy it was to dash off such tales—it was simply a matter of inventing an amusing situation, to be developed freely, without regard for good taste. Mme. de Puisieux challenged him to prove his statement, and, in fifteen days, he had written *Les Bijoux* and given her the proceeds—fifty louis. In later years he realized that he had not rivalled Crébillon, and he was sorry that he had written *Les Bijoux.* He had satirized the person of Louis XV in the familiar guise of a sultan (Mangogul), and Mme. de Pompadour in that of the sultan's favourite (Mirzoza). The Sultan feebly re-

---

[1] Diderot's criticism of Voltaire's *Lettres d'Amabed* applies more justly to *Les Bijoux:* ". . . without taste, without finesse, without inventiveness, a collection of blackguardisms," *Œuvres,* VI, p. 367. In Grimm's *Correspondance,* I, p. 139, *Les Bijoux* is referred to as an unsuccessful imitation of Crébillon; and in Saintsbury's *History of the French Novel,* I, p. 403, it is called "vulgar, which Crébillon never is." Naigeon (the "foolish Naigeon," as Carlyle rightly called him) admired *Les Bijoux.*

[2] In 1748. See *Œuvres,* I, p. xlii.

calls the foolish monarch in Crébillon's *Le Sopha*, but *Les Bijoux* is heavy and clumsy, and resembles *Le Sopha* chiefly in being too long. Diderot brings in Louis XIV as Erguebzed, "a sensible man who did not want the education of Mangogul to be neglected as his own had been. He assembled the learned men of the realm to teach the youth, who, at the age of twenty, was able, thanks to their instruction, to drink, eat and sleep as well as any other aristocrat of his age." Erguebzed eventually "retired to do penance for the crimes of the most just reign of which the history of his country could boast."

The central idea of *Les Bijoux* is tiresomely coarse, but the book was not censored. Diderot's imprisonment, in the year after its publication, was for a philosophical essay supposed to contain far worse political heresies than the novel. There are only two passages in *Les Bijoux* that are of any value—the "dream of Mangogul," [3] and a literary discussion.[4] . . . "I saw, in the distance, a child coming toward us, slowly and steadily. His head and body were small, his arms feeble, his legs short. He grew larger and stronger, and his features [5] changed as he approached. Gradually he became a colossus. His head touched the skies, his feet were lost in the abyss of space, and his arms reached from pole to pole. In his right hand he held a torch which illuminated the depths of the oceans, and the innermost parts of the earth. He arrived at the door of the temple of Hypotheses, the columns of which

---

[3] Chapter XXXII.
[4] Chapters XXXVII and XXXVIII.
[5] According to a note, the respective features were those of Galileo, Pascal and Newton.

seemed to rest on no foundation, to be but six inches in thickness, and to rise to infinite heights.   At the approach of the colossus [6] the temple trembled, and cracked from side to side.   One blow—and it fell with a sound like thunder."

This alarming vision, like a prophecy of the Revolution, gave Mangogul a headache;—it signified nothing more to him.[7]

Of *Jacques le Fataliste*,[8] Carlyle says in his essay on Diderot :—"a grim, taciturn, dare-devil, almost Hogarthian humour rises in the background.   Like this, there is noth-

---

[6] Experience.

[7] In Chapters XXXVII–XXXVIII, Diderot ridicules the opinion in Europe, in the eighteenth century, that French tragedies of the traditional type were altogether great and admirable.   In this attitude, Diderot unintentionally imitated Crébillon *fils* more skilfully than in the novel itself, an intentional copy.

In Chapter XXII, Diderot gives the following remedy for insomnia: "four pages of Marivaux's *La Vie de Marianne;* one page of any story of Crébillon *fils*" . . . etc.

Diderot "takes off" Crébillon *fils'* style in Chapter XXXIX.   Several years later, in a letter to Mlle. Volland (Sept. 20, 1765), he asks her if she does not think he has caricatured Marivaux as well as Crébillon did in *L'Écumoire.*

[8] *Jacques le Fataliste et son maître,* written in 1773, published in 1796. It was known in Germany before France, for, in 1785, Schiller translated the story of Mme. de la Pommeraye, and called it *The Vengeance of a Woman.*   Diderot's alleged plagiarisms from *Tristram Shandy* were, according to Assézat (*Œuvres de Diderot,* VI, introduction to *Jacques*), intended as a caricature of Sterne's method.   Saintsbury (*Short History of the French Novel,* p. 442) says the book was partly suggested by Sterne, but has a legitimate ancestry in the *Fatraisie* of the sixteenth century, and resembles the *Moyen de Parvenir.*   It may be noted that there is no such excellent story in *Tristram* as that of Mme. de la Pommeraye, but *Tristram* and *Jacques* are alike in lack of central plot, and in a constant flow of broad humour.

ing that we know of in the whole range of French literature; La Fontaine is shallow, in comparison. It resembles
Don Quixote, rather." But though he gives this high
praise, Carlyle does not mention the story of Mme. de la
Pommeraye, or that of Père Hudson, which are, easily,
the best parts of the rambling narrative of the adventures
of Jacques and his "master," a pair of gay, lazy vagabonds,
devoted to wine, conversation and travel. "How did they
meet? By chance. Where did they come from? The
nearest place. Where will they go? Who knows where
he is going? What did they say? The master said nothing, Jacques said that his captain had said that everything
that happens is doomed to happen. Can you tell me how
to avoid my fate? Can I be other than myself?" [9] There
is a great contrast between the companionship of Jacques
and his master, and that of Anatole France's Jerôme Coig-
nard and Jacques Tournebroche, the difference between
what may be called Diderot's optimistic fatalism and
Anatole France's pitying, ironical scepticism, his subtlety of
wit and argument. But both pairs of travellers are fond
of wine and good company, and conversation occupies more
of their time than more active amusements; their philoso-
phies of life are essentially similar, and their good humour
and conviviality are deeply rooted in the history of French
characteristics.

The proprietress of one of the inns in which Jacques and
his master happened to stay, told them the story of Mme.
de la Pommeraye, under great difficulties, for the servants
were constantly calling their mistress, and asking absurd

[9] *Œuvres,* VI, pp. 9, 15.

questions. These interruptions, and some unnecessary remarks of Jacques, are all set down in Diderot's account, a
masterly narrative, in spite of these intrusions. "The
Marquis des Arcis was a man of pleasure, having an attractive personality and very little belief in the virtue of
women. . . . Mme. de la Pommeraye was a woman of
birth, breeding, fortune, and a certain pride." She had
finally consented to live with him, and they had sworn that
their devotion to each other would be lasting. But she
saw, before long, that he grew weary of her, and, to make
him confess, she tells him that she no longer loves him.
He says that he has found, to his sorrow, that time has
changed him, too, and he adds: "We must congratulate
each other that our mutual devotion has ended at the same
time. How sad it would have been if only one of us had
ceased to love!" Their parting is calm, and they express
forgiveness. However, as soon as he is gone, Mme. de la
Pommeraye vows that she will be revenged. She remembers a Mme. d'Aisnon and her daughter who had formerly
lived near her, but had lost their money and had become
prostitutes. She finds them, persuades them to return to
her neighbourhood, to live at her expense, but in the
strictest seclusion, with an appearance of saintliness, to
dress as sisters of charity, to take active part in church
work, never to entertain, never to go out of their house
except together. All this is accomplished and Madame's
trap is set. She sees the Marquis occasionally, greets him
always in the friendliest manner, and one day, having
given Mme. d'Aisnon and her daughter instructions to be
at a certain place at a certain time, she meets them, as if
by chance, in the course of a walk in which she is escorted

by the Marquis, who is attracted by the daughter, but
cannot induce Madame to tell him her address, much less
to introduce him to her. The Marquis now calls frequently on Mme. de la Pommeraye; he tells her he is
desperately in love with the girl; that he must see her.
Madame is without remorse until he promises to marry
Mlle. d'Aisnon, which he finally consents to do, though
Mme. de la Pommeraye warns him that he may be acting
rashly and that he may regret his haste. He feels that
nothing could be more painful than his present unhappiness,
and Mlle. d'Aisnon becomes the Marquise d'Arcis. Soon
after the wedding he receives a summons from Mme. de
la Pommeraye. There is every sign of suppressed anger
on her face when he enters her house. She addresses him
disdainfully: "Marquis, learn to know me. If other
women esteemed themselves sufficiently to experience my
resentment, there would be few men of your character.
You won the affection of a woman whom you could not
appreciate. That woman is I. She has revenged herself
in making you marry a woman who is worthy of you.
Leave my house, and go to the address which I now give
you, where you will discover the kind of life which your
wife and her mother have lived during the last ten years."
But the Marquis entirely recovered from this shock, and
was able to inform his wife that Mme. de la Pommeraye
had rendered him a great service instead of having punished him as she had hoped.[10]

There is a living quality and a distinction in Diderot's

---

[10] A stage version of this story was performed in Paris at the Odéon in
1901, but whether the play or its performance was at fault, the production
was a failure. (*Le Temps*, June 24, 1901.)

portrait of Mme. de la Pommeraye, and it is strange, as in so many of Diderot's short stories, that he did not make a long novel, or at least a more completely developed story of such material. Laclos could have made of it a companion-piece to his *Liaisons,* for the character of Mme. de la Pommeraye offers a wide field for the power of analysis which he brought to bear upon persons involved in other intrigues.[11]

The other important story, in *Jacques,* is that of Père Hudson—a brilliant scholar, an able administrator, with a devilish capacity for getting himself out of the difficulties into which his passions have constantly led him. He arranged and kept secret a series of orgies which took place in the house of an abbé who lived near him; he seduced the women who came to him to confess their sins. When righteous indignation set itself against him in the form of an alliance of his enemies, he managed to catch them in the traps which they had set for him. The greatness of his ability equalled the depravity of his character. He had been put at the head of a monastery where discipline had been lax, the standard of scholarship had been lowered, religious observance had been neglected, and rules of conduct ignored. Père Hudson changed all this. He established strict order, insisted upon all traditions and principles of the organization, and the monastery became an example for others to strive to imitate. While he per-

---

[11] "If Browning did not consciously steal and unconsciously if not unconscionably spoil in the stealing the episode of Jules the sculptor's marriage in *Pippa Passes* from the *Histoire de Mme. de la Pommeraye,* then all incredible coincidences must henceforth be held credible."—Swinburne's Letters I, p. 306.

formed this great service to the community, Hudson continued his immoral practices. His subordinates gradually became aware of his duplicity, but could not escape the severity of his authority. They resolved to ruin his reputation, they watched and followed him with the perseverence of the bitterest hatred, but when they found him in bad company, he reported that they, in being there themselves, had broken the rules of the monastery, and his testimony was believed instead of theirs. At last a former member of the brotherhood, who had no further connection with any religious order, discovered Hudson, by chance, with a woman whose disreputable character he knew. He cross-questioned Hudson, till the latter said:—"My friend, you are mocking me, and you have a right to do so." Then Hudson again escaped. The man who seemed to have him in his power, feared him. He knew him to be a dangerous enemy; or perhaps he was satisfied with having made him confess.

The fate of Père Hudson is left in this inconclusive stage, and Jacques and his master are soon interested in other affairs. There is a description of a woman whose history is not told even to the extent of that of Mme. de la Pommeraye, or of Père Hudson. "Reason had made her wise, but her temperament was that of a libertine. She regretted in the morning her conduct of the night before. She passed her life in alternate periods of pleasure and remorse, nor did the habitual indulgence in opposite emotions tend to a choice of either, to the exclusion of the other. Her husband pardoned her for her unfaithfulness because of the good taste with which she chose her lovers. 'I have made but one false oath in my life, and that was

my first,' she complacently said.   She remarked of religion
and of law that they were a pair of crutches necessary for
those whose legs were feeble.   She almost never went to
church, but she was always ready to give to the poor.
Women who feared her influence on their husbands were
perfectly willing for her to be the friend of their children."[12]   Contrary to her own expectations, this extraordinary person eventually died of a remorse which had under-
mined her health.

The story of Jacques and his master wanders a little
further, to a cheerful conclusion.

In spite of many digressions and unevenness, *Jacques le
Fataliste* is a far better piece of work than its predecessor,
Les Bijoux.   It was written after *Le Neveu de Rameau*
and *La Religieuse,* and it is much less important than either
of them.   Diderot meant it simply to be amusing in the
manner of Sterne, and to this extent he succeeded.   The
chief value of the novel is the short story of Mme. de la
Pommeraye.

Le Neveu de Rameau [13] has generally been accepted as

---

[12] *Œuvres*, VI, pp. 255–6.

[13] Written in 1762, revised a few years later, but not published in France
until forty years after Diderot's death.   It was published in Germany in
1805 in a translation by Goethe.   At the close of the year 1804, Goethe
wrote that Schiller had discovered an unknown MS. of Diderot called the
Neveu de Rameau (Goethe, *Œuvres,* Paris, 1873, V, p. 135).   Schiller, who
died in 1805, wrote his last letter to Goethe on the subject of notes for
Goethe's translation.   In 1891 it was published in French (Plon-Nourrit
et Cie.) from the original MS.   But the differences are slight between this
and the Assézat version.   Between 1804 and 1805, several letters between
Goethe and Schiller are full of praise of *Le Neveu* and of Diderot's style.

After Diderot's death, many of his MSS. were sent to Catherine the Great,
who had bought his library.   Grimm took others to Germany, for safe-

the one masterpiece among Diderot's novels and stories. Scherer [14] called it even more important, as history, than the *Mariage de Figaro,* and a prophecy of the Revolution, disguised as a satire. In the *Neveu* there are many of the features of the eighteenth century that were to result in disaster:—the philosophy of indifference to all but the pleasure of the moment, the utter lack of conviction that anything should be done, if one could manage to get along by doing nothing, the system of flattery and indulgence and parasitism. The nephew of Rameau was a harmless, not altogether sane person who could be amusing. He was too exceptional to be typical except as a caricature, but many of his ideas, in better brains, had set the stage for the drama.[15]

Diderot wrote *Le Neveu* about the time when Palissot attacked him in his comedy *Les Philosophes,* and it was in *Le Neveu de Rameau,* as well as in informal and oral dialogues, that Diderot returned the blow, according to Schiller [16] and Michelet.[17] Palissot has caricatured Did-

---

keeping, during the Revolution. Diderot's brother, Pierre, a priest, tried to persuade Diderot's daughter, Mme. de Vandeul, to give him Diderot's MSS. He wished to destroy them, for he thought that Diderot's irreligious ideas were a disgrace to the family. When he found that Diderot's MSS. were, for the most part, in Germany and Russia, he was relieved, but feared they might be sent back. (See C. Marcel, *Le Frère de Diderot.*)

[14] Scherer, *Diderot,* p. 227. (See also Faguet's *Le dix-huitième Siècle.*)

[15] "The *Neveu de Rameau,*" wrote Morley, in his book on Diderot, "is so much more valuable as a guide to the moral sentiment of the time than merely licentious compositions like those of Louvet or Laclos" (p. 236). Louvet has none of Laclos' dramatic power and distinction of style, but neither one is *"merely"* licentious, as a writer, nor lacking in historical significance.

[16] Schiller, letter of April 25, 1805.

[17] Michelet, *Histoire de France,* XVII, p. 66.

erot in one of the characters of his play, and, on the other hand, it is rather in special references [18] to Palissot, than in any personification, that Diderot expressed himself.

Mercier [19] knew both the composer Rameau and his nephew,[20] whom he describes as "half abbé, half layman, spending most of his time in cafés. He thought he could reduce every prodigy of valour and all the operations of genius to examples of the mere struggle for existence. He said to me, one day: 'My musician-uncle is a great man, but my father, who was first a soldier, then a violinist, then a merchant, is still greater. He, indeed, knew how to provide food for himself! I lived lazily at my father's house till I was twenty-two. At last he lost all patience: "How long do you expect to continue to do nothing? Do you know that at your age I had a profession, and that I was hanged?" "What? You were hanged?" I asked, much amused. My father told me he had been strung up for robbery, but the rope had not been properly adjusted and his feet just touched the ground. A passer-by cut the rope. My father made marionettes with his torn shirt, managed to get a violin, and to set up a tiny theatre in which he acted as stage manager and musician. "Now," he said, "you see what I did. Here are twelve francs. You have a better shirt than I had. Leave my house."' He went away, but he had none of his father's resourcefulness. He was always a tramp. He wrote to the Minister of State for money, on the ground of being the son of a great man, and the nephew of another. But he

---

[18] The "nephew" calls Palissot an "arrant rascal" (*Œuvres,* V, p. 104).
[19] Mercier, Tableau de Paris, XII, p. 110.
[20] Born in 1716.

was shut up in an institute, and I have not heard of him since. On one occasion he called on a lady who owned a dog which he suddenly threw out of the window. The lady protested. 'I could not stand his bark,' said the nephew of Rameau, 'the note was false.' "

Cazotte [21] described him as "the most agreeable man I ever knew. He was my comrade at college, and our friendship was lasting. He had an extraordinary and many-sided talent which his lack of determination never permitted him to cultivate. His humour was comparable to that of Sterne's *Sentimental Journey*. There was in his wit an instinctive knowledge of human nature, rather than a mere capacity for making *bons mots*. His love of music was perhaps greater than that of his uncle, but he could not compose. In conversation he was rarely inspired, but at times he could draw tears of laughter from his friends. He loved glory passionately. He could never make money, but his poverty aroused my respect. He could have gotten money from his relatives, but he refused to ask for it, knowing that they needed what little they had."

Diderot's picture of the nephew resembles Mercier's rather than Cazotte's, and the novel is simply the nephew's conversation with a *philosophe,* not altogether like Diderot, for the nephew has the lion's share of the talk. "If ever I become rich," he says, "I shall live in an extravagant manner, and, like all those who have been poor, I shall

---

[21] Cazotte, preface to his *La Nouvelle Raméide*. The nephew had written a poem about himself called *La Raméide,* which had a mild success. Cazotte's *La Nouvelle Raméide* ridiculed the nephew, but the nephew did not object, for he knew that he was ridiculous.

become the most insolent of rascals. All is vanity, except comfort and pleasure."

He tells the philosopher that he lost his job in a rich household by losing his self-control, and his friend advises him to go back and apologize, but the nephew is obstinate. "You have no idea of the miseries I had to submit to. Imagine a depressed and sullen master, wrapped twice around in a dressing gown, out of sorts with himself and everyone else. He is almost impossible to amuse, though one twist oneself into a hundred mental and physical knots. If he speaks, it is but to show you that your wit has been entirely unappreciated. And you must tell him that he is the cleverest man you have ever known; you must scrape the ground before him, and you must run on a thousand silly errands and return like lightning, with a smile on your face."

"Virtue must be respected," he continues, "and respect is a troublesome tribute; it must be admired, and admiration is a bore. No, I must be what I am, a poor brigand among rich brigands, not a swaggering model of virtue, or even a simple honest soul, munching a crust of bread among other beggars. I cannot adapt myself to the visionary happiness which you profess to enjoy."

His scepticism has carried him so far that he is not even sure of the self-depreciating honesty that seems to be his best quality. When the philosopher says: "In spite of the miserable, abject, vile, abominable part you play, I think you have a certain fundamental refinement of spirit," the nephew replies: "Not at all. May the devil take me if I know what I really am. When I am truthful, it is because I have nothing to gain by lying, and vice versa. I

say whatever comes into my head; if it is sensible, so much
the better; if it is impertinent, no one takes it seriously.
I have never in my life taken the time to think before,
while, or after speaking. In this way I offend nobody,
except in unlucky moments."

In spite of this apparent thoughtlessness, a complete lack
of policy would be too consistent for the "nephew." When
the philosopher tells him that he reads to gain "a knowledge of duty, a love of virtue and a hatred of vice," he
replies: "I search for rules of propriety of conduct and
of speech. When I read *L'Avare,* I say to myself: 'Be
miserly, if you wish, but do not talk like a miser.' When
I read *Le Tartuffe,* I say: 'Be a hypocrite if you wish,
but do not talk like a hypocrite.[22] Indulge in useful vices,
but be careful not to practise, nor even to appear to practise those that will make you ridiculous.' I continue to be
myself, but I act and talk as I am expected to do." He
does not claim to have discovered these principles, although he makes use of them as a science, whereas most
people follow them either by instinct or not at all. He
has warned the philosopher against ridicule, and he adds:
"There are times when absurdity is the best policy, and,
in regard to anything as changeable as customs, there is
nothing absolutely and always true or false. One must always be ready to shift one's ground."

The philosopher looks down upon the vagabond from
every point of view except that of amusement. Thus,
while he protests against the nephew's half-serious perversities, he is unconsciously paying him the only homage

---

[22] Meaning "be sure your hypocrisy is not transparent."

for which he cares, and putting himself in the position of pleasurable toleration which he objects to in those from whom his friend gains his livelihood. "Why have you shown me all the worst elements of your nature, and of your conduct?"—"Because, in the first place, you knew most of them, and I had more to gain than to lose in telling you the others."—"Why?"—"Because, if one is to have an evil character, it is well to have it sublimely evil. One scorns petty wrong-doers, but one cannot deny a certain consideration to a great criminal, whose courage is astonishing, and whose atrocities excite horror, and whose character has a strength and unity."—"But you have not that unity. Even in conversation your principles are not consistently carried out."—"That is true, but I have done my best. Have I not duly recognized my inferiority to Bouret? [23]   He is, to me, the greatest of living men." Rameau's nephew would have admired the Marquis de Merteuil and the Comte de Valmont.[24]

He tells the philosopher of his devotion to his son, and that he will do everything to help him unless he take it into his head to become a musician. "Music leads to nothing, unless one has genius; and who can tell whether a child will have it or not? Do you realize that it is probably easier to pick out a child who will be able to rule a kingdom than one who will be a great violinist?

---

[23] Bouret made himself a multi-millionaire by dishonest means. He is said to have given a fête, attended by Louis XV, which cost 3,000,000 francs. He also entertained numerous parasites like Rameau's nephew, and he died a bankrupt.

[24] *Les Liaisons Dangereuses* was not written till twenty years after *Le Neveu de Rameau.*

No, my son must be rich. Money is everything. If he is rich, he will lack nothing, not even your esteem and your respect, the loss of which, however, he could, with wealth, survive."

And, finally: "Adieu, *monsieur le philosophe,* I am always the same, *n'est-ce-pas?*"—"I cannot deny it."—"May I continue to be what I am for another forty years; he laughs best who laughs last." And in less than forty years came the Revolution—five years after Diderot's death.

The character of the nephew of Rameau is more significant than it appears to be, at a hasty glance. In him are some of the vices of the old world, and some of those of the new. He admits that he would become as insolent as any aristocrat, if he became rich; he confesses that he loves comfort and idleness more than other things. He prophesies the Revolution, and he longs for it to come, although he knows that it is not justice alone that he craves;—his greater thirst is for revenge. He knows he is worthless, and that many worthless persons will profit by the Revolution. Many of these thoughts are vague impressions and feelings rather than definite conceptions. There is in him an inarticulate, steadily growing protest deeper than his many spoken words. The consciousness of helplessness is to keep it down only for a short time.

Diderot brings his dialogue to a climax—*"rira bien qui rira le dernier."* The philosophy of the nephew of Rameau, not of the philosopher, has led inevitably to that warning. The serious drama underlies the caricature and the appearance of a jest. The method is admirable:—the restraint of feeling, the oppressive imminence of a great storm, and the growing weakness of an old established strength—these effects are strikingly though indirectly produced. There is an economy of effort, a selection and concentration which Diderot did not elsewhere achieve. The aim and character of the one novel, strictly speaking, that Diderot wrote—*La Religieuse*—is totally different, and there he reached emotional heights which no other writer of the eighteenth century could surpass.

La Religieuse [25] is one of many protests written in the eighteenth century against the conditions of life in convents. Restif's [26] short story *La Religieuse par force*, has none of the power of Diderot's novel which, however, Restif criticized absurdly as lacking "reality." He thought he recognized the heroine of *La Religieuse*, a girl from Auxerre, whose story Diderot had altered to suit his purpose. Restif, as a critic, can be depended upon to be in the wrong. La Harpe's play *Mélanie*, or *La Religieuse*, which was performed for the first time in Paris in 1770, showed that writers as totally different as the conventional critic and the revolutionary philosopher could be moved to express their indignation on the same subject, though La Harpe confined himself to the forced taking of vows,

---

[25] Written in 1760, but not published till 1796. Some of Diderot's friends knew of the book. He had discussed it with the de Holbachs and Mme. d'Épinay, and had written part of it while visiting the latter. In 1770 Grimm referred in his correspondence to an unfinished sketch of Diderot's—*La Religieuse*—which he thought had been lost. The suppression of the religious orders in 1790, by the National Assembly, was said to have been partly due to the influence of Diderot's novel, but this is improbable.

[26] In *Les Contemporaines*, 1780-2.

and omitted the vices and cruelties which Diderot described. The traditional eighteenth-century drama, in far abler hands than La Harpe's, could not have had the effect of Diderot's naturalness and directness of method.[27]

Criticisms [28] of *La Religieuse*, contemporary and of later date, are of a diversity that is not surprising. If the novel had appeared before the Revolution, there would probably have been more official objection to the description of a convent in which sexual perversion existed, for the power of the church and state were less questionable at that time. But there was no lack of disapproval after 1796. The subject of the novel may partly account for the general acceptance of *Le Neveu de Rameau* as a more admirable work than *La Religieuse*, though not a few critics have held the other view. Saintsbury [29] calls *La*

---

[27] It is probable that La Harpe had not seen Diderot's MS. of *La Religieuse* when he wrote his play, for he was not one of Diderot's friends.

[28] Naigeon, having praised *Les Bijoux* too highly, continued his critical errors by saying that *La Religieuse* should be expurgated. The *Journal Littéraire*, Paris, 1796, II, p. 293, called *La Religieuse* an "obscene rhapsody." —F. Godefroy, *Histoire de la Littérature Française*, V, p. 274, objects to the book "because so much of convent life is beautiful"—but this is exactly what Diderot carefully brings out. His fairness to both sides of the question is a most admirable feature of the book, and emphasizes the tragedy described. Godefroy seems to assume that where there is beauty, there must be thought to be nothing else.—A contemporary of Diderot, A. V. Arnault, in his *Critique*, III, pp. 354–363, notes the "simplicity and truth of the book, the magic of the style," and compares the mother-superior of Sainte-Eutrope to Phèdre, as a tragic figure arousing awe and pity. J. Morley, in *Diderot and the Encyclopedists*, London, 1884, p. 263, wonders how Diderot could have thought it worth while to write on such a painful subject. He admires the power and the Richardsonian detail of the story, but finds it "fatally wanting in tenderness, beauty and sympathy." It may have been Richardsonian sentiment which Morley would have preferred to Diderot's realism.

[29] G. Saintsbury, *History of the French Novel*, I, p. 408.

Religieuse "the latest known and by far the best of
Diderot's novels. . . . It is almost a great, and might
conceivably have been a very great book." It was written
under the direct influence of Richardson, which may account for certain elements of pathos, but not for the
dramatic intensity of the presentation.

"The idea of Naigeon," according to Assézat,[30] "and
of other critics, that *La Religieuse* is a historical document, is absurd. It is a work of art, which enhances the
effect produced." There were the basic facts of deplorable conditions, and the direct incentive of a story in connection with a friend of Diderot's. At the end of the
text of *La Religieuse,* Assézat publishes a correspondence
supposed to have been written by a nun (whose letters
were actually the work of Diderot) and by the Marquis
de Croismare, a friend of Diderot, of Mme. d'Épinay [31]
and of Grimm.[32] At the beginning of 1759, the Marquis
went to live near Caen, and his friends determined to
devise some means of inducing him to return. Before his
departure from Paris, there had been brought to his notice
the case of a nun (Suzanne Saulier [33] of the convent of
Longchamp) whose parents had forced her to take vows,
and who wished to be released. The Marquis knew
neither her name nor all the details of her story, but he
had tried to persuade certain members of the Parliament
of Paris to act in her favour. His appeal had been un-

---

[30] Diderot, *Œuvres,* V, pp. 205–6.
[31] Mme. d'Épinay, *Mémoires,* II, p. 329.
[32] Diderot, *Œuvres,* V, p. 8.
[33] Suzanne Saulier was the Suzanne Simonin of *La Religieuse,* and many
of her experiences are there recorded.

availing, and it was decided that Suzanne was legally bound to continue to live in religious seclusion. It occurred to Diderot and Grimm to write a letter, signed Suzanne Simonin, to the Marquis, with a mention of his former kindness to her, and informing him that she had escaped, and was in need of his further help. The Marquis, with no suspicion of the forgery, graciously replied, and his letter was received by Diderot at a given address. When it seemed that the correspondence had gone far enough, Diderot wrote a letter signed by a supposed friend of Suzanne, informing the Marquis that Suzanne had died. When M. de Croismare finally returned to Paris, Diderot and Grimm told him what they had done. The Marquis gave no sign of offence except that he never discussed [34] the incident with Diderot, on whom the story had made a deep impression, and who now determined to turn it into a novel. One day, while he was absorbed in this work, a friend called on him, and found him weeping bitterly. "What is the matter?" he asked. "I am deeply affected by a story I am writing," replied Diderot.

Although the facts of a special case formed the basis of Diderot's incentive, he wrote *La Religieuse* with a wider purpose than simply to arouse sympathy for a tortured individual. He wished, according to Assézat,[35] to see a change in the French laws that governed convents, and if he approved of the total abolition of monasticism, it was not because there was nothing to be said in favour of

---

[34] The daughter of the Marquis had been for several years, since the death of her mother, a student in a convent school. As a result of Suzanne's story, Mlle. de Croismare continued her studies elsewhere.

[35] Diderot, *Œuvres*, V, pp. 205–6.

such a life, but because of inevitable risks and abuses.

The first words of *La Religieuse* refer to the origin of the story. Suzanne has just written to Diderot's friend, and she begins her memoirs:—"The reply of the Marquis de Croismare, if he answers my letter, will furnish me with the first lines of my account. I have judged, by the deep interest which he took in my case, and by all that I have heard of him, that I do not compromise myself in seeking his aid." She writes her story for him, for she is sure that he will wish to know the details of her troubles, and that he will provide her with a means of earning her living in some quiet place where she will not be found out or disturbed. She is ready to face new hardships, but not those which she has suffered for so many years.

She tells of her youth, of her parents' partiality for her sisters, and of the excuse they found for sending her to a convent—the fact that a man whom they had expected to marry one of her sisters had proposed to her. At first she was no more unhappy in the convent than she had been at home, and when she heard, after several months, that her parents had succeeded in finding husbands for her sisters, she expected that they would dispose of her in the same way, and without long delay. On the contrary, they told her that she must become a nun, and it seemed to her that they hated her, and had deliberately chosen this method of burying her alive. The mother-superior, after promising Suzanne to intercede for her, advised her to become a novice, a step which would not oblige her to take her final vows, but would afford the time and experience necessary in order that a wise decision might be made. Suzanne found that the life of a novice involved no particular discomforts, and that everything was done that could serve to persuade her that her life would continue to be beautiful and happy. She was not convinced, but thought that she could do no better than to wait patiently for a sign of parental kindness.

A letter from her mother informed her of many family troubles, the unhappiness of her married sisters, the fact that her parents could not give her money enough to marry her suitably; and though Suzanne had told her mother that she would gladly live anywhere, no matter how simply, if only she might have her freedom, and that she would never ask or expect anything from her relatives, her mother answered, always, that she must become a nun.

Suzanne had seen a girl who had gone insane in the convent, and she resolved never to take vows to which she felt herself utterly disinclined. Her refusal was of no avail. She could not escape from the convent walls, and when, at the altar, in the presence of her family and her friends, she declined to take the vows, she was merely regarded as disobedient, and worthy of punishment. She had been deceived, and she resolved to deceive, if the opportunity presented itself.

The main cause of her mother's treatment of her she was yet to learn. Mme. Simonin came to see her, and told her of a man whom she did not name, who had loved and deserted her. This man was Suzanne's father. Mme. Simonin, to avoid embarrassment, had resolved to put Suzanne safely out of her way. "Everyone expects you to become a nun," she said, "and you have gone too far in that direction to turn back now. When I die, your sisters will be at my bedside, and you would surely be with them

if you were not here. What would be the effect of your
presence at that time? Could I bear to see you? Do
not afflict your mother in her last hour. Let her pass
away in peace. Let her be free to say to her conscience :—
'I have done all I could to expiate my fault; Suzanne will
never return to trouble my quiet household after I am
gone.' Suzanne, let your good deeds be the penance
which shall take the burden of your mother's sins from her
shoulders." Instead of bursting into just and angry protest against this heartless selfishness, Suzanne was moved
to pity and to doubt. Could she be sure that this was not
God's will? And had not Mme. Simonin promised to
help her? She had said that she would deny herself the
pleasures of society, of theatres, of gambling, to be able
to save what money she could for her Suzanne. It would
be hard to do; she would have to put the money secretly
aside, for M. Simonin would not approve. The family
expenses were great, and much would have to go to the
married daughters who were constantly asking for help.

At the time of Suzanne's greatest need to fortify her
resistance, she was weak and uncertain. At the convent
of Longchamp, to which she was transferred, the true
saintliness of the mother-superior was a revelation to
Suzanne, and she found a comfort in her kindness which
she had never known, and which all her companions ex-
perienced. She could appreciate the beauty of such a life,
and of its appeal to others. There was a new meaning in
the church services, in the various duties and observances,
the self-sacrifice and devotion. If her doubts had been
general, they now became confined chiefly to her own case,
for she felt that this peaceful happiness could never be

hers, and she sought the help of the mother-superior. Mme. de Moni prayed for her all night long, and in the morning knew not what to say to Suzanne, whose doubts seemed to have taken possession of them both. She prayed again, and still there was no answer. Suzanne felt herself doomed to misery, whatever she decided or did not decide, and when the time came for her to take the final step, she was powerless to resist. "No doubt I was questioned, no doubt I replied, no doubt I took the vows. But I have no recollection of them. I found that I had become a nun as innocently as I had been made a Christian by baptism. I could remember nothing of the ceremony, none of the faces that were there, nor the priest who had delivered the sermon. Can such vows be binding?"

Not long after this strange experience, Suzanne lost her father and mother. If they had died the year before, she would have been released. Although she had, in the prison which the convent was to her, a good friend of whom her need was great, and whose help had been the one comfort she had known, there was the irony of which Suzanne grasped the full meaning—the irony of the responsibility of the kindness and affection of Mme. de Moni for Suzanne's failure to assert herself at the critical time. By her beautiful example, she had given the convent life a charm in Suzanne's eyes, and though this charm had not the power to make Suzanne choose definitely, it did, none the less, prevent her from renouncing finally. And then Mme. de Moni died. Suzanne had a greater need for her help, after she had allowed herself to take the vows, than before, for now she must resign herself to the results of her weakness, into which both the selfishness of Mme.

Simonin and the unselfishness of Mme. de Moni had drawn her.

The new mother-superior was, in every way, a contrast to her predecessor. "Her character was petty, her narrow mind was full of superstition. She upset the established customs, and, immediately after her arrival, the house was filled with hatred, calumny and persecution. Corporal punishments, of which Mme. de Moni had disapproved, were instituted; and she took a dislike to everyone in the convent who had formerly been held in highest regard. Suzanne endured these innovations as patiently as she could, observing all traditional regulations, and taking no interest in rules that seemed to her unnecessary, and which she had not sworn to obey. She had been the object of Mme. de Moni's special esteem, and now she fell more and more deeply into a disfavour which grew into hatred. Her companions were encouraged in tormenting her, and the place in which she had known the only happiness of her life became an inquisition. "At the back of the garden there was a deep well. How often did I lean over the edge and look down; how often did I resolve to end my miseries! But I knew that the dearest wish of my enemies was that I should end my life, and I could not bring myself to please them thus."

There was only one of her companions—Ursule—who showed her kindness and sympathy and helped her to gain permission from Rome to have her case tried, through the influence of her friends. When the mother-superior discovered this, she decided that Suzanne was possessed, and that consequently she deserved the most severe punishment.

Suzanne had been locked in a dark cell for other offences, and her spirit had not been broken.

"Now I was made to lie down in a coffin, candles were placed at my side, and I was covered with a winding-sheet; the service for the dead was performed, and each of the nuns threw holy water into the coffin. When the winding-sheet was removed, I was left drenched, with no change of clothing. Everyone was forbidden to speak to me, to help me, to approach me or to handle anything belonging to me. If, by chance, anyone touched me, she confessed it as a sin. I remembered the words of Mme. de Moni: 'Among all these nuns whom you see here, there is scarcely one whom I could not turn into a wild beast.' When I asked for something to eat, I was told that I was not fit to live. This was the life I led while my case was being tried. When I talked to my lawyer or to one of my judges, I was accompanied by one of the nuns, who repeated to the mother-superior all that I had said, with alterations unfavourable to me. I was locked in my room, to prevent my going to mass. When I escaped, the door of the chapel was fastened. I prostrated myself on the steps, and when the door was opened, the mother-superior said to the nuns:—'Walk over her! She is nothing but a corpse.' " There was a succession of cruelties and annoyances. The nuns went into her room, broke the furniture and windows, stole her blankets and her clothes. They thought that they were serving God by persecuting an abandoned creature in the power of an evil spirit, and the degree of their cruelty was the measure of the mother-superior's approval.

Suzanne's case was lost in the courts, and now she was regarded with a deeper contempt by everyone in the convent. She was denied admission to the chapel. "Ah, what a destiny!" cried Suzanne, "to be doomed to live a life for which one knows oneself to be ill-suited, and to pass the days in knocking at the bars of a prison!"

There seemed to be no possible experience of goodness or kindness without a new sorrow. Ursule remained her only friend, whose care for her when she was ill ended in Ursule's sickness and death. Her letters resulted in Suzanne's transference from Longchamp to Sainte-Eutrope, but if she expected to find relief in another prison, her illusion was short-lived, for the new mother-superior was not the good Mme. de Moni, though less cruel than her successor. "Her face had a certain attractiveness, her eyes were lustrous, but in them one noticed a strange, abstracted expression. She opened her mouth before she decided what to say, and there was an impediment in her speech. She was given to a number of nervous habits; she lacked dignity and dependability; one could not tell when she would be gentle or severe. Her face gave every sign of an unsettled mind and character, and, under her direction, there could be no smoothness in the routine of convent life. She would take offence at one of the nuns, and order her to be whipped; but hardly had the first blow been struck, when she would interfere, embrace the victim, caress her, kiss her eyes, her mouth, her shoulders, and praise her charms."

Suzanne's beauty at once impressed the mother-superior. "Her attentions caused me some embarrassment, I knew not why, for I did not understand. I spoke of this to my director, and he regarded the familiarity in which I saw

no harm, as a serious matter, and ordered me to avoid it."
Mme. X persisted in helping Suzanne to dress and undress,
and in bringing her food and drink. "There was a nun
named Thérèse for whom the mother-superior had formerly
shown the same affection. When she heard the words and
saw the signs of Mme. X's affection for me, she walked
about the room in a distraught manner, tried to attract her
attention, and failed." Suzanne left the room, but the
mother-superior continued to ignore Thérèse. Suzanne
could not understand Thérèse's jealousy, but she reasoned
that all she had seen, and more that she might see, must
be the effects of unnatural conditions of life. "Human
beings are born for natural companionship. Isolate them,
and their characters will be changed; a thousand absurd
fancies or perversities will possess them. One must have
even more strength to endure loneliness than other miseries.
Solitude breeds depravity."

It is strange that she could reason in this way, and still
be blind to the fact of the mother-superior's character.

"Why do you dislike the life of the convent?" asked
Mme. X.

"I hate the restraint, the duties we perform. I am
oppressed by ennui, in spite of your kindness."

"Have you never wished to marry?"

"I would rather be married than live this life."

"Do your senses speak to you?"

"I do not know the language of the senses."

"Do you wish to learn?"

"I would rather not."

Mme. X's efforts to teach her, or, as she said, to awaken
her, to make her trust and obey her in every suggestion,

were always in vain, always subject to interruption or
resistance.   The director who visited the convent at stated
intervals talked to Suzanne, warned her repeatedly:
"You must never allow her to caress you or even to enter
your cell.   You must consider her an evil spirit, and not a
religious advisor.   Your very innocence has so far saved
you, for she has somehow been in awe of its purity."

Suzanne's resolution gravely affected the mother-
superior, who grew more and more restless, spent night
after night walking up and down the corridor, passing
and re-passing the door of Suzanne's room.   Day after
day, whenever she saw Suzanne, she stared strangely, or
threw herself at her feet.   "Cruel sister, ask for my life
and I will sacrifice it for your sake, but do not avoid me,
for I cannot live without your love."   Distraction and
melancholy turned to delirium.   She locked herself in her
room, refusing to see anyone; then she would call one of
the nuns and beg her to pray for her.   Finally she resolved
to confess to the director, and Suzanne could not resist
the temptation to listen at the door.   "After a period of
silence, I heard these words, and trembled: 'My father,
I am damned' . . ." [36]   She was comparatively calm, after
she had confessed, and she could look at Suzanne without
distress, but gradually she sank into a state of lethargy,
from which she was aroused by fits of delirium and fever.
She would laugh wildly, then burst into tears.   One night
she found her way to the chapel, and prayed in a loud

---

[36] These words were suggested to Diderot by Mme. d'Holbach, whom he
had consulted as to how he should begin the confession of the mother-
superior. Mme. d'Holbach told him there was no choice—that this was
what would have been said. "Only a woman," said Diderot, "would know."

voice. She saw a vision of angels moving toward her through the open gates of heaven. There was anger in the faces of the angels, and there was God's countenance, more in anger than in sorrow. Mme. X was carried to her room in an agony of fear. Next day she had no recollection of the vision. She tore off her clothes, ran naked from one end of the house to the other, and when she was brought back to her bed, she said: "Yes, you are right— alas! I know I am insane." For several months she lived in the firm belief that she was doomed to eternal torture, and in her last hours she was haunted constantly by visions of devils coming to carry her to hell.

Mme. X was replaced by an ill-natured, old and superstitious woman who believed that Suzanne had bewitched her predecessor. "The new director of the convent could not help me, for he was dominated by his superiors as I continued to be by mine; he advised me to escape, and my flight was planned. Ropes were thrown to me over the garden wall. Instead of a post-chaise, I found an ordinary public vehicle, and instead of a proper companion, I was accompanied by a young monk of bad character. I regretted my escape, and I felt all the horror of my situation." After saving her from her escort, the cab-driver left her at a disreputable inn. She ran away, and would have returned to the convent, if it had been within walking distance. Finally she found work in the miserable place from which she writes to the Marquis de Croismare. She fears discovery, and dreads the arrival of someone to take her back to the convent, although, a short time before, she would have sought shelter there in her despair. Now she would kill herself, if that alone could save her. She gives herself away in a hundred gestures and habits learned in the years of her imprisonment, but it is thought that she is mockingly imitating the manners of nuns, and she is laughed at.   The truth will be known before long, and she will be lost.

That conditions such as Diderot described in *La Religieuse* existed in the eighteenth century is a part of the history not only of convents but of monasteries and other religious institutions.   Octave Mirbeau's *Sebastien Roche* gives an account of experiences some of which were personal, in a nineteenth-century religious school; and it is not surprising to find that cases of perversion exist in an environment in which the tendency would most easily be developed into habit.   But Diderot's facts cannot be called typical of the eighteenth century, or of any other time. They existed, and it was right that they should be exposed and denounced, whether exceptional or usual.   Suzanne Simonin's life is rather a combination of special cases, and a record of accumulated miseries, than a typical or average example.   The main point is that such an intensified tragedy was altogether possible, and that a system in which such injustice and cruelty could exist, was radically wrong, in spite of all other considerations.

The destruction of the convents and monasteries in 1790 was far from being the result of an altogether righteous aim.   Great numbers of monks and nuns considered themselves deprived of liberty, rather than set free,[37] and there

---

[37] A. Sicard, *La Vieille France Monastique,* in the *Revue des deux mondes,* LIV, pp. 424, 872 et seq.

were political reasons for their enfranchisement of which many were not ignorant. The abuses of property belonging to the clergy or to monastic orders, and the fact that revenues intended for religious purposes often fell into the hands of laymen who spent the money in other ways, and the question of loyalty to the Revolution, were useful excuses for the Assembly to deprive the clergy of their possessions, and to suppress priories, abbeys and convents; [38] but these measures were taken primarily because the new government needed money, not because religious institutions deserved punishment for their acts and methods. Taine [39] has written of the zealous devotion of the nuns, and of the fact that many of the convents and monasteries were unjustly persecuted, and these considerations are specially necessary as qualifications of the historical significance of Diderot's novel. *La Religieuse* [40] is a drama, an example, and a warning. If it had been published before the Revolution it could have been the cause of no more extreme action than that which was to take place in the inevitable upheaval of France.

---

[38] July 12, 1790.

[39] Taine, *La Revolution,* I, ch. II, pt. LV.

[40] Blaze de Bury, in the *Revue des deux mondes,* March 15, 1882, compares the nun of Diderot's novel with that of Schubert's composition, and finds the latter a general, and the former a special case, in that Diderot's story is of one whose objections to convent life are those of reason and nature, whereas that of the other is the fact of her being in love.

CHAPTER VIII

Restif de la Bretonne

FROM his poetic boyhood in the first half of the eighteenth
century as a shepherd in the fields of central France, to his
disappointed old age in the Paris of the First Empire,
Restif's story is a tragi-comedy of contradiction, shamelessness, honesty, naïve frankness, absurd egotism, loud self-
condemnation, excessive sensitiveness, semi-callousness,
cowardice, occasional courage, desire for justice tempered
by fear of tyranny, extremely bad taste, complete absence
of deliberate cruelty and of real sordidness. It includes an
extraordinary series of love affairs, intense, frequently of
no duration, often unforgettable. Restif had more experience than knowledge, more energy than judgment, and innumerable good intentions. Although his genius was
neither great nor sane, he had genius.

He wrote [1] literally hundreds of mediocre or worthless
volumes, an admirable biography of his father, and an
amazing autobiography, not burdened with accuracy, nevertheless, in the main, true to his peculiarities and his sufferings. It is called *Monsieur Nicolas,* or *The Human Heart
Revealed*—an ambitious, but, as Saintsbury says, not a
fatuous title, for Restif kept this purpose of telling the
whole truth as constantly in mind as it was possible for him
to do, and the results were frequently worthy of the effort.
All his writings, except a very minor few, are reminiscences,

---

[1] Of all his writings, his poetry is the worst.

and, for this reason, though Restif is called a novelist, it is specially necessary to study his life and literature together. He was at his best when he wrote of his own life, or of the lives of those he knew.

His style reflects the inconsistencies, the bungling sincerity, the flashes of power and beauty, the platitudinous philosophy and the false eloquence which were dominant in his nature. He had no faith in art for art's sake, and he tried to look down on writers who spent much time in polishing their work. His idea of truthful writings was to strike off pages of emotion and sentiment and dramatic intensity. The difficulties of fine phrases and composition he always expected to conquer in the future, but he found so much that he felt should be written that he hastened on and on and never had the patience to correct and arrange, nor could he ever really persuade himself that these things were of great importance. The pleasure that reading gave him was seldom critical, and he usually gathered ideas and impressions without noticing the beauty of the forms in which they were expressed.

The one efficient performance of his life was the manner in which he wasted it; but though he drifted energetically from childhood to old age in the direction of insanity, it was one of his failures never to reach the furthest limits of that destination. He preached moral reform, and his life was a muddle of misconduct. He wrote tales of the poor people for their benefit, and sometimes these stories caused him to be hated as a meddler by those whom he had wished to aid. He loved too often, or too well, or too badly to love wisely. His passions were the obsession of his life; their control of him was complete, and their results were tragical, comical, or both. Although he was noted by the critics of his time for the immorality of his life and of his books, a Catholic society in 1848 printed his *Life of My Father* [2] as a "Christian" novel. There is almost no end of such contrasts in connection with Restif. After having been in love with a charming girl whom he never knew, he married the worst of women, and spent the rest of his days, until divorce released them both, in regretting the act and ignoring the vow.

There was much in Restif of poetry, eloquence and deep emotional intensity; and he failed, characteristically, to develop these qualities, or to turn them to any lasting account. "There was in him," [3] says Saintsbury, "a kind of dream-quality," and yet this worked against him, diverting his course from that of real achievement, instead of proving to be a source of poetical production. In the last years of his life, he became cynical in all but one respect. He believed in good intentions and motives which a deeper penetration, in certain cases, would have doubted. He lacked, disliked and misunderstood wit and irony, and when he thought himself profound he was most apt to be stupid. The tragedy of his life he recognized, but he seems never to have suspected the comedy. When he appeared ridiculous he was usually unconscious of the fact, and he attributed to malice or bad manners the laughter which he brought upon himself.

Restif has been called a "monster of originality rather

---

[2] *La Vie de Mon Père.*
[3] Saintsbury, *History of the French Novel,* I, p. 456.

than an original genius," [4] or it may be said that he had an
undeveloped genius rather than a trained talent. His writings are neither intellectual nor thoroughly intelligent.
There are few records of a life in which so much emotion
is expressed and so little understood, even within the limits
of human understanding.

Restif was not without a definite value to literature and
to the time in which he lived. In 1798, Schiller wrote to
Goethe: [5] "Have you read Restif's singular work, *Monsieur Nicolas?* In spite of its platitudes and of certain
revolting descriptions, it has greatly amused me. It is impossible not to be interested in the great number of men
and the greater number of women which he describes in
characteristic groups and occupations that bring before the
reader a vivid picture of the life and manners of the time.
I have seldom had an opportunity of studying such a can-
vas, and it seems to me an invaluable work." Taine
wrote: [6] "Restif lived more constantly and observingly
among the people than any other writer in Paris in the
latter part of the eighteenth century."

Restif's autobiography has never been translated as a
whole, nor has the only other lengthy account of him, a
German biography [7] which refers to *Monsieur Nicolas* as
the most extraordinary of all biographies, and to Restif
himself as the first noteworthy writer "of and for the

---

[4] P. LaCroix (P. L. Jacob), *Bibliographie et iconographie de tous les
ouvrages de Restif de la Bretonne,* preface.

[5] Humboldt, when he went to Paris, described Restif, at Goethe's request.

[6] Taine, *Les Origines,* V, p. 236.

[7] Dr. Eugen Dühren, *Restif de la Bretonne,* Berlin, 1906.

people." Charles Monselet[8] wrote, in 1858: "This novelist with his sleeves rolled up, was the last literary expression of the eighteenth century, and an inevitable reflection of the life and of many of the conditions of that time. *Monsieur Nicolas* is the most important of his writings, and, in general, a résumé of most of his other works. As a phenomenal production I do not hesitate to place it in the same rank with the *Confessions* of Rousseau and the *Memoirs* of Casanova."

Of all the writers that influenced Restif, the most significant and keenly felt was Rousseau, and Restif will be seen to have admitted this, though with characteristically egotistical reservations. "Restif," writes Saintsbury,[9] "was a sentimental philanthropist of all but the most genuine kind, tainted with the vanity and self-centredness which had reached their acme in Rousseau, but very much more certainly sincere, and of a temperament as different as possible from what is usually called cynicism. . . . In comparison with Rousseau, Restif is almost a gentleman, and he could not possibly have been guilty of Rousseau's blackguard tale-telling in the cases of Mme. de Warens or Mme. Larnage. The way in which he speaks of his idealized mistress, Mme. Parangon, is almost romantic." Elsewhere,[10] Saintsbury refers to Rousseau, as a "hopeless cad, in spite of his genius," but he leaves Rousseau, as well as Restif, out of a list of men including Diderot, Laclos, Louvet and, possibly, Crébillon *fils,* who took to pornog-

---

[8] Knowledge of Restif's writings was largely due, in the nineteenth century, to Monselet and Assézat.

[9] Saintsbury, *History of the French Novel,* I, 454–5.

[10] Saintsbury, *The Peace of the Augustans,* p. 180.

raphy for money. Restif was called, in his time, "the Rousseau of the gutter," and Laclos "the Restif of Society," and though these descriptions are partly justified, they are by no means adequate or complete, especially the latter comparison.

That the popularity and influence of Rousseau were immeasurably greater than those of Restif is no less clear than the many points of personal resemblance and contrast between them. They try to excuse themselves for many things which they attribute to their sensitiveness and to the misunderstandings and indifferences of others. Restif admits his faults more frankly; Rousseau twists and turns to free his conscience. Restif's chief aim was to show how he got into trouble, and how his misfortune might be avoided by others. Rousseau always blames his friends more bitterly than himself. They seemed to him deliberately cruel, and altogether incapable of understanding his character and disposition. Although there was a certain justification for this, there was more truth in Diderot's remark: "Rousseau is in the wrong, for, otherwise, too many sensible people must be so." Both Rousseau and Restif felt that the painful thoughts with which they could not but remember the wrongs they had done to others, were proofs that they themselves were rather the victims of circumstances than persons whose conduct could not be forgiven. These feeble arguments have, in Restif's case, a naïve quality, a sincerity which Rousseau often lacks in his most tearful effort to be natural and confidential. They took themselves far too seriously, but one is apt to be amused by Restif's confessions, and to lose patience with those of Rousseau, for there is nothing more wearisome than a confession less complete than it professes to be. Rousseau regarded the novel as the only remaining means by which instruction might be brought to a people too corrupt to be influenced more directly. Restif's moralizing, like Rousseau's, was too constantly an excuse for self-consciousness, and both laboured under the illusion that their personal experiences and feelings were not only endlessly interesting, but enormously valuable to the world.

In Gérard de Nerval's *Les Illuminées*,[11] Restif is referred to as one of the most important of the precursors of socialism. But Restif's theories were hardly more than an attempted sociology,[12] and he advocated social, not political reform. He thought of the government as an autocracy, and believed in the arbitrary government of the king until the Revolution overthrew the monarchy. It was natural that he should have seen, in the new government and that which immediately followed it, simply another form of oppression, although he had no idea of the principles of democracy.

The criticisms which Restif's writings first encountered were chiefly the result of dislike or indifference, or of a questionably flattering curiosity. La Harpe's conventional point of view prevented him from finding any significance in Restif's best work, on account of the formlessness and exaggeration of which Restif was often guilty. Grimm,[13] whose sympathies were also for a totally different manner

---

[11] Chapter on Restif.

[12] According to the article in the *Grande Encyclopédie* on the Emperor Joseph II, that monarch actually adopted some of Restif's ideas for the revision of criminal law in Austria.

[13] Grimm, *Correspondance*, I, p. 414.

of writing, was a more discerning critic than La Harpe.
"Restif has neither the taste nor the true eloquence of
Rousseau, but he has the force and the originality of that
writer. The general plan of Restif's *L'École des Pères* is
extravagant and absurd, but at the moment when one is
ready to fling the book away in disgust, one comes to a
really fine description, or a bit of dialogue of a natural,
rare simplicity. It is almost impossible to imagine a
stranger complexity than the mind of Restif, with its extraordinary mixture of platitude and genius, of ignorance
and knowledge, of wisdom and folly." Sainte-Beuve expressed his surprise that Mlle. de Lespinasse's broadness
of sympathy could carry her so far as to find excellent
qualities in the *Paysan Perverti* of that "ignoble" Restif,[14]
and he quotes [15] Benjamin Constant as mocking the century
that could stoop so low as to admire such an author. Constant wrote elsewhere [16] of his enjoyment of some of Restif's novels, in which, however, he noted the lack of selection of details, and the platitudes of Restif's philosophy
of life.

Victor Hugo [17] sneered at Pigault and Restif indiscrimi-
nately. "Of all the writers of the eighteenth century, he
who dug the most unhealthy passage in the underground of
the masses was Restif de la Bretonne." To Hugo, Pigault
and Restif were equally vulgar. On the other hand, Saintsbury [18] wrote: "There is no vulgarity in Restif. If he

---

[14] Sainte-Beuve, *Lundis,* II, p. 127.
[15] Sainte-Beuve, *Portraits Contemporains,* V, p. 283.
[16] Sainte-Beuve, *Portraits Littéraires,* III, pp. 214–16.
[17] *Les Misérables,* Part IV, Book VII, Chapter III.
[18] Saintsbury, *History of the French Novel,* I, p. 453.

had had a more regular education and society, literary or other, and could have kept his mind, which was to a certainty slightly unhinged, off the continual obsession of morbid subjects, he might have been a very considerable man of letters and he is no mean one, as it is." In these cases, the use of "vulgar" is largely a matter of definition. Restif was not vulgar in the sense of commonplace, ordinary, or boorish. He had not the vulgarity of pretentiousness, or of affectation; but he had neither elegance nor refinement of taste. To Michelet,[19] the novels of Restif were vulgar and indecent, and he was surprised to find some of them in the list of books that had been in Marie Antoinette's library, and took that occasion to compare the queen's taste unfavourably to that of Mme. de Pompadour.

Baudelaire,[20] whose appreciation of eighteenth-century writers was usually discriminating, wrote to someone who had left Restif out of a book on the literature of that period, and told him there were many excellent portions of Restif's writings which should be included or mentioned. Sainte-Beuve,[21] in an essay on Eugène Sue, pointed out, in the work of that writer, the probable influence of Restif. It should, however, be noted that Sainte-Beuve's criticisms are more profound when he deals with another class of writers. He compared Sue to Balzac, not altogether to the advantage of the latter, in his essay on Balzac, and this is a sufficient indication of the tendency of some of his preferences. Charming as are Sainte-Beuve's essays, they were

---

[19] Michelet, *Histoire de France*, XVII, p. 281.
[20] Baudelaire, *Œuvres Posthumes*, 1887, p. 154.
[21] Sainte-Beuve, *Portraits Contemporains*, III, p. 116.

written from the point of view of a man whose exquisite taste, whose sensitiveness, was too easily wounded for a great breadth of literary sympathy. Though born at the beginning of the nineteenth century, Sainte-Beuve belonged essentially to the seventeenth. Balzac wounded him, and his reaction to Balzac's genius was thereby made to weigh more heavily on the side of qualifications and conditions than on that of the power of a great genius. Restif's originality and his inferior genius, hampered by more serious blemishes, could, therefore, be merely "ignoble" to Sainte-Beuve.

CHAPTER IX

La Vie de Mon Père

THE family of Restif had various traditions as to its origin. The name of *Restif* was said to have been added to that of Monroyal in the person of the Templar Jean de Monroyal when he defended the Order of the Temple in 1309, at the time of its destruction. In 1582, Charles Restif is mentioned in a history of Auxerre. "But," says Restif, "all our titles were lost in the religious wars, our ancestors having embraced the reformed faith." All of this is dubious. A joke in connection with his ancestry appears in *La Vie de Mon Père* and elsewhere in Restif's writings. Pierre Pertinax, otherwise Restif, was descended in direct line from the Emperor Pertinax, successor to Commodus, and to whom succeeded Didius Julianus, elected emperor because he was rich enough to out-bid everyone else in the auction sale to which the soldiers had subjected the high office. The genealogy is traced through Merovingians and Carlovingians to a Comte d'Auxerre, some of whose descendants were a shepherd, a swine-herd, a mule-driver, a jockey, a doctor, and a good-for-nothing. Restif asserts that this line of origin was facetiously concocted by his grandfather, who thought it would be amusing to improvise a family record beginning with a Roman emperor whose name resembled that of *Restif,* and, in fact, *Pertinax* and *Restif* [1]

---

[1] The name is sometimes spelt *Retif,* or *Rectif,* but usually, and by the author himself, *Restif.*

both mean stubborn. The list of names was written out on parchment, and had an old authentic look which convinced some members of the family. The idea resembles Oscar Wilde's on the subject of his middle name O'Flaherty: "The O'Flaherties were kings in Ireland. I am descended from them."

Among the villages near Auxerre, capital of the department of Yonne in the region of Burgundy and less than forty miles south of Paris, are Sacy, belonging to the ancient bishopric of Auxerre, and Nitry and Vermenton, closely associated with Restif's childhood and the farm-life of his parents. Of the kind of people who lived in this district, La Bruyère[2] wrote in 1689: "One sees men and women who look like ferocious beasts, burned almost black by the sun, and tilling the soil with dauntless determination. They live in caves or huts, and eat roots and black bread, and drink water." In 1703, Vauban[3] wrote of the hard labour of this peasantry, where the land was as rich and valuable as anywhere in France. "These people, useful and despised, have suffered much and are still suffering." It seems, however, that the peasants of Burgundy were less primitive than those of Brittany, at this time.

Restif's picture of life in Sacy is less gloomy than the above quotations would indicate. Edmé, or Edmond Restif, the novelist's father, was a landowner, and the peasants who worked for his family are described in detail. He was born in 1690, in Nitry. His childhood was marked by the cruel manner in which he was treated by his

---

[2] *Les Caractères*, Paris, 1883, II, p. 67.
[3] Vauban, *Dime Royal*, Rouen, 1707, preface, p. 3.

father Pierre, who is said to have frequently whipped him. This severity did not embitter his nature, and he was kind and affectionate to Restif in later years. His greatest fault seems to have been a propensity for delivering long, moral, exhortatory speeches, as impeccable as they were tedious, to his children, whose respect for him was increased by awe.

At the age of twenty, Edmé went to Paris, worked in a small government position, and lived a sober life. He was a "Hercules with the mildness of a girl," and he was always a model of filial piety. Pierre had never been in Paris, and his having sent Edmé there is a problem, for he thought that young men invariably fell into debauchery in that city. He worried over Edmé's conduct there, in spite of good reports, and when he heard that his son was about to be married he assumed that Edmé had disgraced himself, and ordered his immediate return. Edmé at once obeyed. Upon his arrival, Pierre told him to sit down; he ordered some wine which Edmé felt it his duty to refuse, much to his father's delight, and a glass of milk was substituted. Pierre began a "discussion," which could not be distinguished from a monologue, on the subject of Edmé's marriage with a village girl whom Pierre had selected. Edmé foolishly promised to do anything his father might suggest, and in his old age he told Restif the story: "I was so moved by the speech which my father addressed to me, that I would have married and adored the most hideous of monsters, if such had been the wish of my father."

Duty, however, assumed no such revolting shape, and Edmé married and received his father's blessing on the very day of that venerable person's death. His father-in-law was a tryant, but Edmé put up with him for his wife's sake. Soon after Edmé had become the father of seven children his wife died and he remained a widower for seven years. He was a hard worker, he improved his farm and helped the peasants who loved him and willingly served his needs. He was kind to animals. He grew prosperous. "Never was a man more abstemious than my father," says Restif. "Poverty would have been no burden to him, for he loved to work. His usual supper consisted of one egg, a piece of bread, and two glasses of old wine. He never stayed up late, and he always got up early. During harvest time he sometimes slept all night under a tree, on the bare ground, and felt no discomfort." By popular demand he was appointed justice of the peace, an office from which he would have resigned had his conscience permitted, for his farming occupied all his time, and he had to assign much of this to others in order to perform his public duties.

In 1733 he decided to marry again, chiefly for the reason that he needed a housekeeper. Barbe Ferlet was at first a little too vivacious for his taste, but by degrees and with tactful gentleness he taught her the sobriety of thought, or at least of expression and of manner, which he deemed becoming in a good wife. They addressed each other always in the second person plural, and with proper dignity. Restif was the first of another seven children, and Edmé's respectability continued to grow in the eyes of all who knew him. He was the patriarchal head of a large family, esteemed and loved by everyone. His advice was sought, and his charity spread in many directions. His first seven sons and daughters sometimes quarrelled with the second set, but Edmé maintained his benevolent and peaceful authority no less at home than in the village, and there were no serious family disputes.

In *La Vie de Mon Père,* Restif refers to his father as "the head of the house," as he was doubtless trained to do. He gives a vivid picture of the family life, which seems to have resembled that of the previous generation of the Restifs. Such were the arduous occupations of the day that "only in the evening, at supper, could the whole family assemble. The head of the house viewed with satisfaction the large proportions of his household, for there were twenty-two of us at table, including the ploughman, those who took care of the vineyards in summer and threshed the grain in winter, the keeper of the oxen, the shepherd, and two female servants, one of whom helped in the vineyards and the other took charge of the cows and the dairy. We were seated at table in the following manner: the head of the house at one end, near the fire, with his wife at his side, within reach of the dishes of food which she served to all." She passed the plates to the servants, for they had worked hard all day, and she felt that this was her duty as well as her pleasure in regard to them. It does not appear that her sphere of action was an easy one, however, for she had complete charge of the kitchen, and did her share of the operations thereof. The children's places were allotted according to age. Next to the youngest of the family sat the oldest of the ploughboys, and then his fellow-workers; after these, the keepers of the vineyards; then the keeper of the oxen, then the shepherd, and, last of all, the female servants who sat at the other end of the long table, facing their mistress, who kept a watchful eye on them. Everyone was given the same kind of bread. Restif notes with pride that the odious distinction between those who received white bread and those who received brown, was not made in his father's house, and he adds that such discrimination would not have been an economy, for they gave the cows, pigs, and horses the fodder which other farmers turned into brown bread.

The head of the house drank his glass or two of old wine, and the children, even the oldest, were allowed to have only water and milk. The farm hands were served with a kind of wine which was much more agreeable to them than Edmé's would have been. The peasants of Sacy were bigger and rougher than most peasants and they were especially fond of press-wine, which was strong and pleasing, and tickled their throats. Germain, the "first" ploughman, was extremely large and resembled a German; he was very good-natured, and the children liked to play with him, for he seemed to them a giant. "He was more respectfully looked up to than anyone in the house except my father and mother. None of the servants knew what to do, if anything unusual occurred, until he told them, yet he managed to dominate them without appearing to command."

Such were the diverse comings and goings of all the household, that Edmé never succeeded in finding a convenient hour for the morning prayer, which should be said by all the assembled members. At breakfast, at five A. M., almost everyone could be counted on, though during the summer months the shepherd and one or two others always left the house long before this. However, those who were on hand knelt together, and Edmé directed their devotions. After the evening meal, Edmé read aloud from the Bible. Now and then he would make short comments such as he deemed absolutely necessary for the comprehension of the company. Everyone, including the servants, listened with the strictest attention to every word. Edmé always began in this manner: "My children, let us give ear; the Holy Spirit is about to speak." After the reading no loud talking was tolerated.

In writing of these pleasant memories, Restif compares them with other periods of his life, and he sorrowfully admits that nothing in his later years had ever really taken their place. Perhaps, however, he would have been no happier had he always lived in Sacy. He gives many examples of his father's habit of moralizing. "My dear wife," said Edmé in the course of a conversation, "the most dangerous fault in a husband is to be unable to hold the sceptre of conjugal authority, and it is a common failing among Parisian husbands." He further explained that it was not his wish to be a tyrant but that discipline must be maintained. The wife should charm and gladden the heart of her husband and at the same time obey him in return for all the hard work which he constantly does for her sake. Restif never entirely outgrew his father's ideas on matrimony and the conduct of home life, though his actions were an altogether different matter.

Edmé's theories of bringing up his children were rigid. When one of them had done something which his high sense of propriety deemed punishable, he pronounced the just sentence of his displeasure with all dignity: "My child, a week from to-day, at such an hour, you will be whipped to expiate your fault, and serve as an example to your brothers and sisters." The boys were whipped by the father, and the girls by the mother. The severity of the application of the rod was regulated in accordance with the gravity of the offence. Apparently none of the children took advantage of the interim between the declaration and the execution of the sentence to devise means of escape at the appointed hour. They probably realized that deferred pain would be greater. "Once," says Restif, "I received such a whipping that I felt a soreness for a fortnight afterward, but this was for a very serious fault," he does not say what. None of the girls ever had such severe treatment as this. When any of the children had done a praiseworthy deed, he or she was rewarded with the paternal benediction, at supper, in the presence of the assembled household.

The opening sentence of *La Vie de Mon Père* is typical of Restif's oratorical tendencies, and similar introductions may be found in most of his books:—"Humble mortal, virtuous without ostentation, you who have done good for the joy of the doing, and have chosen to live frugally, you, my father! receive the homage that the least worthy of your sons presumes to offer to your memory!" This is the tone of the whole book. The gesture is too elaborate, but there is no affectation in the tribute. It is simply Restif's manner of expressing his deep admiration and affection for his father. He is grateful for an example which he admits his inability to follow.

In 1762, Edmé was remarkably strong and well for a man of over seventy. He had the health of the peasants who carry heavy burdens in old age, and seem to be able to endure as much as their lusty grandsons. Just at the time of the mowing, there was a flood, and the fields were inundated. At the risk of his life, Edmé went into the meadows and worked longer and harder than anyone else, cutting the grass under the water. The weather was extremely cold and the double exposure had its natural consequences. Many of the peasants were laid up, and Edmé suffered with a fever from which he never recovered. "He awaited death serenely, and even with a kind of joy, troubled only by the thought of my mother's sorrow. Heaven bless you, my father, and may you look down from the Abode of the Just with pity and kindness upon your unfortunate son! Amen." If Edmé had known what Restif's life had been in Paris during the years preceding 1763, he would have felt it his duty to whip him. But he never knew; and, on his deathbed, he expressed the wish that his children were established in the capital, as he recalled the days of his youth.[4]

---

[4] *La Vie de Mon Père* was reviewed by the *Journal de Paris*, March 24, 1779, the year of its publication, as the best of Restif's novels and as having an admirable simplicity and naturalness. Assézat, *Restif écrivain, son œuvre et sa portée,* p. 67: "*La Vie de Mon Père* is written in a style with which not even purists can find fault, nor can they object to it on moral grounds. Dignity and simplicity of narrative are to be found in Restif's writings only when he confines himself to the lives of his parents, or to those of the peasants who lived near them."

CHAPTER X

Childhood and Youth of Restif

Monsieur Nicolas, an autobiography, was published by Restif in 1796–7, in sixteen volumes. It is very rare, especially in the first editions, which were never successful; but it is almost equally difficult to find in the more modern printing, that of Liseux (Paris, 1883), the fourteen volumes of which include practically everything that appeared in the original publication.[1] Five years before he published it, Restif issued a prospectus with a list of subscribers including several crowned heads, titled persons and ambassadors. Whether he did this boastfully or simply as advertisement, the performance is equally typical, and, probably, an invention. There follows a long "note" in which Restif declares himself faithful to the truth in spite of all the "prudish" objections which he predicts the book will arouse. He expresses his belief that the work will exercise a good influence; his readers will be warned not to get themselves into the many troubles therein described, and from which he could never extricate himself. He fears that it will be said of him as it was said of another author: "He must be utterly desperate to print such a book"; a statement which Restif admits to be perfectly true of himself. He wrote *Monsieur Nicolas* in his old age, sick and miserable, and expecting death, after which, he thinks, his book will be

---

[1] The latest edition of *Monsieur Nicolas* began recently to appear in Paris: Jouquières et Cie., 1924.

better understood than it could possibly be during his life. His reasons for writing it appear in his *Dedication to Myself,* recalling the opening sentence in Rousseau's *Confessions:* "I am undertaking something which is unexampled and of which the performance will inspire no imitations." Rousseau had not imagined the possibility of a Restif.

The dedication seems to have been written nearly twenty years before Restif wrote the book; perhaps as a note, to keep the project in mind. "Dear self! best of all my friends, most powerful of my protectors, my sovereign lord and master, accept the homage which I offer you in this moral and critical examination! It is a return for all the services you have rendered me, and an encouragement to your performance of still more. Though you have sometimes betrayed me, you are nevertheless the best of all my friends. Your treacheries have operated as a result of error rather than of malice, and consequently I pardon these lapses. With what art have you turned toward me the good-will of certain people! How cleverly have you managed to make me interesting! When your efforts have proved unavailing, there has never been a possible success. Often you have done me untold good by simply tempering the heat of my desires. This is a greater service than the complete indulgence of my passions would have been. Every good thing that I have ever done has been the result of listening to your voice and of working with you. Whenever I have done wrong, the fault has consisted in leaving much to chance, in neglecting to confer with you and with our most intimate friend, our conscience, thereby setting you and this adviser at odds with one another. For many a day you have urged me to write this, my own history, and these have been your words: 'You are well-known, but not understood; evil reports are spread about you. Justify yourself by opening your heart to the public as one opens a book, and by saying to friends and enemies alike: "Read me; I who have written so many books, here I am, myself a book. I have described others reservedly; I present myself without reservation. I picture the ordinary man as Rousseau has pictured the great man, but I do not imitate Rousseau slavishly. The idea of my book did not come from him. It is my own conception.

" ' "I have always been free from the three vices which have so often pursued and wrecked the lives of men: overeating and drinking, gambling and laziness. I have loved my parents, virtue, truth, pleasure. The last I have sometimes loved too much, but I have never loved vice. All my life has been taken up in various labours, and in that noblest of all passions, the only one that is truly interesting —love!" '

"And now, dear self, I publish all this in deference to you. Peace be with you!"

Sainte-Beuve has said that in proper quotation one may find the best judgment of an author, and this naïve confession is a perfect likeness of Restif. The overtones are unintentional; Restif had no idea of causing the smile with which one reads his dedication. The wonder is that he could have written as he wrote without this smile on his own lips, and this fact is one of the most important lines in the picture. It is drawn as if by accident, but it is exactly in its place. There is the pathetic side of this humorous trick which sincerity played on him, and this aspect of his nature is a true and typical one to observe.

To return to Restif's debt to Rousseau, it seems that the *Dédicace à Moi* was written in 1777—five years before the *Confessions* of Rousseau appeared; in which case Restif's statement of his originality must have been added later. He fears that his Mme. Parangon, who appears in the first half of *Monsieur Nicolas,* may be taken for an imitation of Rousseau's friend Mme. de Warens, and he denies the imaginary imputation with a great array of evidence. There are quite enough differences between the characters of these ladies and the treatment which they received from their respective lovers, to lay his doubts at rest, and it is the general idea, again, rather than the details of the stories, which Restif at most may be said to have borrowed from Rousseau.

Restif mentions his habits of keeping old letters and innumerable other memorials as being a great help to him in giving the full account of his life. He wrote from memory only up to his eighteenth year, and from that time he depended upon "documents." And why should he invent when his life is more absorbing than the figures of any fancy? This is the serious question which he puts to his readers.

There is a suggestion, too, that Restif thought the admission of blame for his sufferings might plead in his favour at some future tribunal. And, more practically, he hoped for financial gain of which he stood in great need, and which the publication of such a book might easily be expected to bring.

In still another preface, Restif quotes Montaigne to the effect that one always loses by talking of oneself: no one believes any of the good, and everyone believes still more of the evil. Again he returns to the question of sources, admitting this time, that the *Confessions* of Rousseau and those of St. Augustine were the "models" for *Monsieur Nicolas.* "I have much of the character of Augustine, but little of that of Rousseau. I can prove that Rousseau romanticized his life, and as for Augustine's *Confessions,* they are simply a fable." Unfortunately Restif did not mean to use the word *apologie* when he wrote *apologue.*

And now the final prefatory fling: "Depart, Nicolas-Edmé, and let the man alone appear! Here is a book of natural history which places me higher than Buffon; a book of philosophy which ranks me with Voltaire and Rousseau and Montesquieu. I have feared naught but falsehood, in my history. I leave it as a model to future ages!"

When Restif wished to show how little the eighteenth century understood its great men, he praised Voltaire. The above quotation, however, is a case of a very false modesty. Restif never really thought of himself as on a level with Voltaire. He was sure that his proper place was a far loftier one. His self-satisfaction proceeds:—"This is no pretty little twaddle in the manner of Marmontel or La Harpe or d'Alembert, but a useful supplement to Buffon's *Universal History* and to Montesquieu's *Esprit des Lois* and to Montaigne's works."

Restif was born in October or November, 1734, in his father's farmhouse in Sacy. This building, and several of those that stood in the neighbourhood were owned and kept up in the traditional manner described in *Mon Père,* for over a hundred years by the descendants of the Restifs, with the same furniture and household goods. Part of the

original house is still to be seen with later additions form-
ing a square courtyard typical of French farms.   One
of the Restif descendants was living there in August,
1924, and she possessed a picture of Restif which she trea-
sured, the same that is used in this volume and also in the
Liseux edition of *Monsieur Nicolas*.   The farm in 1924
was prosperous and well-kept.

Restif was christened Nicolas-Anne-Edmé, but his father
decided to leave out the "Anne," and decreed that he
should be called Monsieur Nicolas; and his father's friends
and dependants almost always addressed him thus.   His
literary "title," Restif de la Bretonne, was derived from the
collection of farmhouses which his father had owned, and
which formed a part of the village of Sacy, called la
Bretonne.

Restif calls attention to the fact that the name Nicolas
comes from two Greek words meaning *victory* and *people,*
and he proudly infers that he was born to rule over many.

Restif rejoices in the fact that his father and mother,
after long effort, succeeded in conquering the slight irasci-
bility of their natures, for if he had inherited this quality in
a marked degree, his passionate nature would have turned
him into a monster, whereas the ardour of his disposition
was happily tempered by a purity and frankness which were
altogether essential to his salvation.   In addition to these
"amiable" gifts he was generally considered a most beautiful child.

He remembers a very early tendency to notice pretty
girls, and he recalls the permanent influence of certain
scenes which were bound to present themselves to his young
eyes in a village where boys and girls frequently shared the

THE FARM OF THE RESTIFS AT SACY AS IT APPEARED IN 1924

manners of the animals which were their property or
their charge and almost constantly their companions.   He
was worried by sex-phenomena which he could neither understand nor forget.   The shameless bad habits of boys
who were older than he, were often impressed upon his
memory, especially as these fellows made no effort to hide
from each other, or from the passer-by, the indulgence
which they practised.   Their behaviour revolted rather
than attracted him and this reaction operated later on,
when he was old enough to imitate them and saved him,
always, from this danger.

He had been told by his parents that the Virgin whose
picture hung in the house, would weep when he did wrong.
When he said he believed this, his older brothers and sisters
laughed at him.   One day he examined the picture, and
persuaded himself that it could not weep.   "Thus," says
Restif, "I lost my faith before I learned to reason."   He
suggests that parents tell their children the truth.

He was a very sensitive and nervous child.   "Between
the ages of fifteen and sixteen I should have died if I had
had to pass a cemetery at night.   I took a fearful pleasure
in listening to the stories that were told in the evening,
before the fire, while scutching the hemp.   When I had to
go out in the dark, after this, my hair stood on end.   In
the yard I saw hideous monsters with eyes of fire, with
mouths that vomited flames through gleaming teeth.   I
rushed back into the house, and everyone burst out laughing.   When others left the room I was seized with pity and
respect for their bravery in facing what I had seen."   As
he lay in bed he imagined that strange creatures with horned
heads appeared before him, and made faces that terrified

him. His father and mother slept in the same room. He wakened them with loud cries. Then when they thought he had gone to sleep again, he heard them discussing his abnormal timidity; he felt that they were mocking him, and his wounded pride could soothe itself only in sorrow and loneliness.

Things that had little or no effect on the children that he knew, were a torment to him. "I fainted when I saw my own blood or that of others, and, sometimes, when a sickness was described. I have been unconscious for more than an hour as the result of a light blow. But, later on, I combined the sensitiveness of a woman with the strength of a man." Except for frequent attacks of colic, he seems to have been little afflicted with the sicknesses that are common in childhood. He never forgot the terror with which he saw his father shoot a mad dog; a double shock, for he had just been bitten by one of his father's dogs, an old friend with whom he had always played, and whose affection for him now seemed a bitter illusion, though of course the dog had meant no harm, and, fortunately, was not mad.

Always, as a child, he feared men, with the exception of his father. They seemed to him cruel and domineering and too fond of mocking those about them, and each other. This love of irony repelled him, and he never ceased to hate it. Women were much gentler and more sympathetic, and he liked to be with them. For the most part he was very lonely, and he convinced himself that he was not made for companionship. Looking back on his childhood, Restif pictures himself as a little savage, conscious of inability to think and act and feel as other children do. His pride prevented him from enduring their superiority, for so he

called it, and he sought comfort in solitude. His older
brothers, then divinity students, frightened him because of
a severity of manner which he later attributed to their
zealous Jansenism.

One day, when he was still very young, the family was
displeased with him on account of something he had done,
and he was asked if he would thrust his hand in the fire to
save his mother, if she were in danger. He at once did so,
and would have put the other hand to the same test, but
of course he was pulled back by the pacified inquisitors.
At school he was teased and bullied by his companions and
misunderstood by his teachers who were stupidly untactful
and frequently embarrassed him. At the age of five he
visited his sister Anne and her husband who lived in Vermenton, not far from Sacy. Here he had to listen to a
great deal of loud and angry talk on the part of his
brother-in-law, whose sentiments in regard to Restif's
father were as insolent as they were false. Restif went to
school in Vermenton, but he hated his life there, and was
glad to go back to Sacy. His father was persuaded by
Collette Collet to send for him. She was considerably
older than Restif; she liked him, saw that he was homesick,
and, as the daughter of an old friend of Restif's father,
did not hesitate to suggest the boy's return. She was to
become the adored Mme. Parangon.

Soon after this, Restif had what he calls the first bad
attack of that terror which always haunted him, during
these early years. He was walking down a street in the
village when he saw a threatening-looking dog and an
"equally terrifying" caterpillar. He stopped, trembled,
dared not go on. A "heroic" girl of little more than his

age, arrived upon the scene and stepped upon the caterpillar. Taking Restif by the hand, she led him safely past
the dog, without laughing at the poor boy; and yet, under-
neath his gratitude, he felt horribly ashamed, and despaired
of ever being like other children.

One day he was playing with some boys who began to
tickle him as well as each other. At once he fainted. His
father and mother found him unconscious, and thought he
had been struck. When they discovered what had happened, they were deeply concerned, and decided that such a
child would surely die in early youth. On the contrary,
however, he seemed not at all inclined to die, and his
strength increased in all but nerve-balance. He resisted his
playmates, who were older and more sophisticated than he,
when they did not confine their attentions to tickling.

His first friendship began when he was six years old.
The boy was of the same age, and bore one of Restif's many
names, but he was known in the village as "M'lo Bérault."
He was a coarse little peasant, and, at first, Restif found
him unsympathetic and incapable of understanding him.
However, Restif learned to like him, though solitude still
exercised a stronger appeal, soothing his sense of inferiority
and backwardness. He distrusted all young people except
M'lo, and all men except very old ones. Old men and
women did not tease or mock him. They treated him
kindly, and spoke gently and often affectionately to him.
When he was teased about liking ugly old people, he said:
"I do not like them because they are old, but because I do
not fear them."

Restif and M'lo played together nearly every day.
They selected a corner of the yard where they built a bench

and several shelves, and they got provisions for the establishment from Restif's mother. The furnishings increased in number; they also collected a lot of toys, and, eventually, a crucifix was hung on the wall and a *Prie-Dieu* installed. When it was time to eat, M'lo smacked his lips as he munched better bread than he ever got at home. Stray peas and beans, which they left on the ground, sprang up after a rainy week, and this haphazard vegetable garden was destroyed one night, much to Restif's sorrow.

He speculated on many aspects of life, and his conclusions were not immeasurably more inaccurate than his later explorations in what he imagined to be the field of science. One of his brothers was born about this time. "I noticed that my mother seemed to be quite ill, but that my father was perfectly well. I imagined that they had made the child with pieces of their flesh and drops of their blood, but I failed to come to any conclusion as to how they could have done it."

The friendship with M'lo declined on account of his stinginess and reluctance to do his share of the work in their establishment. Restif made other acquaintances, among them a girl named Fanchon Bertier. Up to this time he had always avoided girls, for such was his shyness and fairness of skin, in contrast to the other boys of the village, that he was considered an effeminate, pretty little fellow. The girls gathered in a circle around him, kissing him with intermittent bursts of laughter, and succeeding, by a force of ten to one, in subduing all his efforts to escape. He decided that all women, especially young ones, liked men, no matter how ugly, if they were rough and domineering, and he wished that he were not good-looking, so that he might be loved.   His parents thought he really disliked girls, but on the contrary he was much attracted by them. The dilemma of his not daring to kiss them, and his hatred of being forcibly kissed by them, had escaped the parental eye.   "My elders failed to observe that my morbid sensitiveness resulted from an excessive interest in the mysteries of sex, instead of an abnormal indifference to these things" —excessive, he admits, for his tender years.

At the age of ten he thought himself in love with Suzanne Colas (a lovelier and more delicate creature than the girls of Sacy) whom he met when she came to the village for a short visit.   He promptly forgot her when she went away, but he was interested to observe that many of his ideas had changed during her stay.

There was a girl named Nanette who worked in the hayfields near Sacy, and had heard much about Restif before she saw him.   She determined to capture the strange, elusive youth, but found to her surprise that his alleged shyness was altogether legendary.   Restif solemnly reports his discovery, many years later, that at the age of eleven he had been a father.[2]

He preferred solitude to Nanette; he preferred solitude to school, where he seems to have learned much less than in her company.   As yet he could not read.   He wandered far in the fields, where every glimpse of bird or animal life fascinated him, particularly the discovery of a bird's nest.   He preferred solitude to the friends of his

---

[2] "In a number of studied cases, thirteen is stated to be the earliest age at which boys have proved able to beget children. . . . Boys are never capable before thirteen."—Havelock Ellis, *Studies in the Psychology of Sex,* VI, pp. 35, 637.

family, unless they were poor, simple people. Sometimes he could be induced to join in the games that were played in the neighbourhood of Sacy, and in the majority of the villages—a custom which Restif believed to have declined in the later eighteenth century, though village games, of one kind or another, have always had a varying popularity. Some of these games (apparently not those which were to lose favour) were not altogether decent, but after he became accustomed to them, Restif reversed the precedent established by the girls of Sacy who had formerly pursued him. It appears also that the zeal with which they avoided him was not excessive.

An idyllic prose poem, a charming picture of the happiest days of his life, a time to which he often looked back with a longing for joys irrevocably lost, comes as a close to the comparatively short period of his childhood. Jacquot, the shepherd of the various flocks and herds that belonged to the Restifs, was a simple lad whom Restif found most congenial, and for whose stories and legends he would spend day after day in the fields, as well as for the fascination of watching the pigs and cows thus escorted, and for the sights of birds and beasts which marked the way. There were views of hills and valleys, far and near, tinged with the soft colours of morning and evening, or sleeping calmly in the hot sun. The appearance of the country in the neighbourhood of Sacy is wilder than the typical French rural scene. The hills are rockier, the slopes are steeper, the colours of the landscape are more vivid and present a series of contrasts to what may be called the general smoothness and softness of central France. To Restif, Jacquot was a person whose vast knowledge called for a respect which his good-fellowship made easy tribute, and, when he went on a pilgrimage to Mont-Saint-Michel,[3] Restif lived in a blighted world. This journey was incumbent upon all boys of fifteen or sixteen, and not to go was to be regarded as a poltroon and an unbeliever. There was no one to take Jacquot's place, and Restif asked his father to let him fill the gap till Jacquot's return. This seemed too big an undertaking for Restif's eleven years; however, he was allowed to go on one condition— that he venture no further than the outskirts of the village, for fear of wolves. This injunction was at first scrupulously obeyed, and he was satisfied. The sunlight soothed him as it shimmered on green meadows in the wind, but he longed for Jacquot, and sometimes he wept or voiced his loneliness in an improvised ballad which he set to an old tune. This kind of relief became a habit, and in later years disturbed the residents of the Île Saint-Louis in Paris.

> *"Jacquot est en pèlerinage,*
> *A Saint-Michel;*
> *Qu'il soit guidé dans son voyage*
> *Par Raphaël!*
> *Par ici nous gardions ensemble*
> *Les doux moutons;*

---

[3] There have been pilgrimages to Mont-Saint-Michel throughout the centuries of its history. Louis XV is said to have been the first king of France who neglected the custom. (See L'Abbé Bosseboef, *Le Mont-Saint-Michel*, p. 463.) Restif does not explain why he himself never made the pilgrimage, though he calls it a recognized duty on the part of the boys of a certain age. Many distinguished persons, as well as peasants, made the journey in the eighteenth century. Bosseboef, p. 146.

Jacquot va par le pont qui tremble,
    Chercher pardons."

Restif failed to invent other verses, so he sang this one
again and again. Jacquot prolonged his absence, and his
stoical father coldly reported that the boy had perished
in recklessly trying to regain the mainland while the tide
came sweeping in, around the island. In those days no
roadway stretched across the sands. Restif shed more
tears, and continued to tend the flocks, for shepherds
were scarce, and his father could not find another. The
young shepherd was now given permission to go as far as
he pleased with three big dogs to help him, and to drive
away the wolves.

His favourite pasture was some distance from Sacy.
There were grapes and other fruit to be picked along the
way, when the proprietors had their backs turned, or when
they had gathered their grapes too hastily, and took no
precautions against wanderers or sheperds like Restif who
might find rich clusters on the vines.

Of the gathering of the grapes there is an account in
Les Contemporaines (the story of the wife of the bailiff
and the wife of the public prosecutor), a recollection of
scenes of this kind which Restif remembered from childhood. He tells of a girl whose father owned a large
vineyard. He had called in, according to custom, a lot of
boys and girls from the neighbouring hills to gather his
grapes for him. The girls were large and healthy and
extremely free of speech. The boys were equally frank,
but not so good-looking. The vintner's daughter was only
fifteen; she had been in a convent-school, and she was sent

out by her father to supervise the work of the grape-gatherers, while he attended to the wine-presses. Two older women, for whom the story is named, were to help the girl. The workers scattered themselves in pairs over the field, and picked the grapes rapidly and silently in the cool of the early morning. Animated conversation developed with the heat of the day, and the two older women talked to the girl in charge to prevent her hearing the remarks of the workers. One of them explained that these boys and girls talked as animals would talk if they could, but that they were good-hearted and not to be despised. At night they all slept in a barn. They were so ignorant that the bailiff's wife promised to tell them stories in the evening if they would restrain their tongues during the day. This they promised to do, for they were particularly keen to hear ghost stories and tales of superstition and mystery. They grouped themselves around the fire in a big room, after supper; now and then they interrupted the story-teller and asked foolish questions or sometimes made intelligent comments. Their friend infused as much instruction as she could into the kind of narrative they liked, and she felt, after the grapes had all been brought in, that these young creatures went away in a better frame of mind than they had come.

The most memorable of Restif's days as a shepherdling is worthy of his long account. "At first I had not dared to explore a solitary valley which lay beyond the vineyards, for the outskirts of the forest at the entrance of the valley had always terrified me. At last I ventured among the trees with all the flock. Down in the valley there was a pasture for the sheep and goats. When I found myself in this place I felt a secret horror, increased by the stories that Jacquot had told me of men excommunicated from the church and turned into beasts. My various flocks seemed to like the valley; the pigs found a kind of wild carrot which they dug up. Under an old oak tree I saw a huge wild boar, and then a hare and a deer. I seemed to be in fairyland, and I hardly dared to breathe. I cried out when a wolf suddenly appeared, and I set the dogs on him, for fear he might attack the flock, otherwise I should have loved to watch him. The dogs frightened away not only the wolf, but the deer and the hare and the boar; but the charm of the place remained, and was enhanced by the arrival of a hoopoe bird which perched on a pear-tree the fruit of which is called the honey-pear by the peasants because it is so sugary that when it is ripe the wasps and bees eat it. Then an idea occurred to me: 'This valley belongs to no one. I shall take possession of it—my little kingdom. I must raise a monument, as they did in the Bible, to establish my title to the land.' When I had piled up my mound, I stood upon it and surveyed my empire, for, seeing no one, I found myself in possession, and I pictured to myself the state of man before there were any kings or laws or bondage. This happy day ended all too soon. When I reached my father's house I was sad and silent. The bustle of housekeeping and the restraint of authority weighed upon me. My mother thought I was ill. Then I told my parents about the valley, and they were so pleased that they told me I could go there as often as I liked. The next morning I started out very early. I carried food and drink, and a piece of steel from which I could strike sparks to light a fire, as Jacquot often did,

to warm himself or to cook birds' eggs which he found, or
animals that he killed.   I reached my valley and saw my
monument with transports of joy.   I built a kind of altar
on the heap of stones, and lit a fire, for the air was cold.
Suddenly I saw a hawk swoop down and disappear in a
thicket where I found him with a lark in his claws.   I
killed the hawk with a blow.   The lark died soon after.
I remembered the story of Abraham's sacrifice which my
father had read me from the Bible, and I thought that, as
king of my valley, I could also officiate as priest, for I
was a free sovereign and could assume any rôle.   I considered the hawk a criminal that had disturbed the abode
of innocence; his crime had merited death, and I determined to do homage to God in sacrificing the bird.   Just
then I heard, at a distance, the voices of boys and girls
who were also in charge of flocks.   'Come and see this
wonderful place,' I cried.   I received them as a host, but
they did not find my valley quite as charming as it was to
me.   I explained my right of dominion, and invited them
to view the sacrifice.   I built up the fire, and threw into
it the entrails of the hawk, as Jewish priests do.   I chanted
psalms as the smoke and flames arose, and I stood gravely,
deeply impressed with the grandeur of my ceremony.
Then I roasted the bodies of the hawk and the lark, and
divided the meat among my companions and assistants.
The dogs received their share."   He showed his friends
the boar, which luckily appeared at the right time, and
calmed their fears when they showed signs of terror.   The
justice of the reign of Restif was soon marred by the
pleasure with which he saw one of his dogs catch the hare
and bring it to his feet.   When he showed his wondering

young companions the various parts of his kingdom, he thought: "What a pity that the deer and the wolf did not come to show themselves off! . . ."

"This great day was the last of my good luck, for that year, at least. Jacquot had returned, when I went home! Ah! what plans had been made against my peace, in view of Jacquot's arrival." Restif was to go away to school. He discussed this sad decision of his parents with the boys and girls whom he had introduced to his kingdom only the day before. All possible marriage arrangements among them were considered, and it was voted a great shame that Restif could not remain and marry the shepherdess who had been chosen by and allotted to him. They bitterly complained of the boredoms which constituted one's life at school. Here, all together, living in the fields, they could be quite happy. Besides, they could learn all they wanted, or needed to know, at home and on their farms. By this time Restif had learned enough to feel that he could teach his younger brothers and sisters, and he found the occupation a pleasant pastime.

And there were memories of other good times which added to Restif's regret at the thought of a change. He and his friends were fond of holding services in an improvised chapel. Jacquot assisted them in their ceremonies, and advised them how to make their costumes. The altar was elaborately adorned, and Restif was chosen for high priest. A difficulty arose as to the manner of representing God. Jacquot was disappointing; he told them he had never seen God. Finally Restif provided a stone shaped like a wheel, and this image was placed in the chapel. Restif explained that a wheel went round and round forever, and thereby resembled God's eternity, though, of course, God was infinitely larger than the wheel. His eyes were the sun and moon, and the stars were his angels. The emblem, and the interpretation thereof, met with unmixed approval, and Jacquot especially hailed the marvellous ingenuity of the idea.

Not even these religious duties were allowed to interfere with his departure for Joux, where he was to attend school. Though only a short way from Sacy, Restif suffered from homesickness. Little things which other boys easily passed over, weighed heavily upon him, and if he had not found a friend in a young girl named Julie, his depression would have been intolerable. "I appealed to her," he explains, "through my ability to learn quickly, and on account of my extreme sensitiveness." She was also a student, older than he, and often helped him with his lessons. She became the mother of his second child. When Restif had been but a short time at Joux, he was sent back to Sacy with a bad case of smallpox, which "utterly destroyed the beauty of his complexion." He could hardly bear, now, to look at himself in the glass, and he dreaded the effect of this alteration upon Julie, to whom he was devoted, and who had given him every attention during a previous illness. He imagined, in a delirium which lasted three days, that he was pursued by dogs and that snakes were twining themselves about him. He struggled so violently that his father could hardly hold him, and gave up hope of his survival. His mother nursed him, and he recovered in a few weeks, after which he did not go back to Joux, but spent his time reading and writing at home.

At the time of the harvesting, Jacquot thought he could
profit more by gathering the crops than watching the
herds, for the labourers were paid in grain, instead of
money, and he could provide himself for the winter as he
could not otherwise do. Restif was delighted to find that
the post of shepherd was again open to him. At first he
could not go to "his" valley, for the way was barred by
the fields of uncut grain, so he took his sheep and pigs
to a place not far from home. "There was an old wild-
apple tree religiously venerated by the owners of the land.
The branches came within two feet of the ground, and it
was easy for me to climb. . . . In the cool of the evening,
after a hot day, I let my flock graze peacefully, while I
rested at the foot of the tree in which I had sat all day.
Suddenly I heard the shrill squeals of one of the little
pigs. I was frightened, and hastily got up again among
the branches. Then I saw a remarkable battle. A wolf
had attacked the pig, and the old sow came to the rescue
of her offspring, giving the wolf a thrust with her snout
that sent him flying. I was overjoyed, but I dared not
come down from the tree, for another wolf stood below
me, with flashing eyes. 'A wolf! a wolf!' I cried, as
loudly as I could, and they heard me at home. The dogs
arrived first upon the scene (they had gone back for
water), and one of them attacked the wolf under my tree.
The other wolf was watching, at a distance, and he ran
when two of the dogs started for him. I came down from
the tree; my father arrived with a gun, and some of the
ploughboys with pitchforks. The wolf that had been under the tree escaped from the dog, but my father shot him
in the leg, and the ploughboys killed him. My father said

that the wolf was a man-eater, older and wiser than the other, and had sent the young wolf to attack the flock. If he had selected one of the lambs, he might have got away with it. I must not forget the scene which had taken place when the sow saved her little one. All the thirty pigs in the flock, the smaller ones encircled by the larger, surrounded the little pig, and replied to its cries with a chorus of grunts that sounded like a general conversation. I was greatly struck by it. I did not doubt that they were trying to console the little one. The sow was outside the circle, bristling frightfully, and sighing, from time to time, in a peculiar and terrifying manner." The people of Sacy believed that Restif himself had killed the wolf until he told one of his friends what had happened. His mother was frightened, and determined that Restif should not go into the fields alone. A young peasant named Courtcou was hired, and Restif went with him, as he had gone before with Jacquot. Courtcou's character left much to be desired, and Restif found his influence bad. His stories were such as Restif had not heard before, and they sank too deeply into his memory. Courtcou said, with great pride, that he had violated several girls, and told Restif many of his adventures. He knew how to conjure up the devil and persuaded Restif to perform the lengthy ceremony, under his direction. There was much mixing of potions and sacrificing of birds, and when these preparations were in order, Courtcou vowed he saw the devil, but Restif neither believed him nor witnessed the apparition.

One day Restif was taken to Nitry to see the celebration of the "Patron Saint's Day." "The attack of smallpox had made me less handsome, though I was still good-looking at a distance, especially when my mother had arranged and curled my hair, which had begun to grow again. I was dressed in my best, and I noticed that I made a good impression, and that flattering remarks were made about me as I walked to church with my aunt." It was the custom, on "Patron Saint's Day," for all the girls of fifteen years to present themselves in the church at the time of the offering, to which each one contributed a farthing. The girls assembled in the nave of the church, and the men in the choir and transepts, where they could watch the girls marching in a long line to the altar. Restif asserts that the purpose of this ceremony vaguely resembled that of the Spartan custom of collecting the girls of a marriageable age in a public place to dance before the young men of the city, who were expected to select their future wives from the group. Restif was interested in the ceremony, but seems to have seen no particularly attractive person in the congregation, though he could imagine himself a judge.

His happiest days were nearly over. "When I think of them, I realize that later years have brought me no such blissful experiences. In my advance through life I have always lost in joyousness and hope. Unfortunate mortals! You are happy when you cannot appreciate your happiness; when you learn to value it, you have passed beyond its sphere." One day Restif heard his father discussing him with someone. " 'What is your opinion?' asked my father. 'Shall I make him a labourer?' " "No," was the answer. "That reply," wrote Restif, "that word decided my fate. It re-echoes in my heart, that 'no,' which had been suggested by kindness, but which was to cause me so much pain." Restif's father had been told that his son gave promise of ability as a student, and he had determined to give him an opportunity for further study.

Of the last day with his flocks, Restif wrote: "I returned to reign in my valley, but I had lost the former ecstasy, the serenity of spirit. Instead of being conscious only of the charm of the present, as in other days, I brooded over the past. I traced in my mind all that had happened in the year. The thought of Julie Barbier at Joux, of her charms, of her good qualities, of her friendship, plunged me into a profound melancholy. There were other sad thoughts. I expected each day to hear my father's decision to send me to Paris under the care of my brother, the Abbé Thomas. These thoughts disturbed my peace, ruined my blissful isolation in my valley, for I was no longer alone. My thoughts pursued me, and blighted the spell which the place had formerly cast. But I rebuilt my pyramid (feeble work! Image of the works of man!) and when I had finished it, I said good-bye to my cherished solitude, as if by instinct, for that very evening I found, at home, the girl who would take my place in the fields next day. In the morning the good Marguerite Paris, housekeeper for my brother, the vicar of Courgis, arrived on her donkey with a letter from the Abbé Thomas, fixing the day of my departure. I considered this a misfortune, and now I know that I was not mistaken. Reader! the happiest days of my youth are over. When innocence departs, the purity of joy is bound to disappear. Like Icarus, I fly imprudently into danger!"

"The Abbé Thomas was a thin, intense, hot-headed, passionate, lustful man who had become master of himself by means of prayer and devotion." Restif never cared for him, and he never understood Restif. However, his father's will was law, and in 1746, when Restif was twelve years old, Edmé took him to Auxerre (a journey of sixteen miles) where the Abbé was visiting. He lived in Bicêtre, a suburb of Paris, where he directed a company of choirboys in which Restif was to be enrolled. At Auxerre, the Abbé asked Restif what he had read, and Restif replied: "The lives of the saints, and the Bible." His memory was tested, and found to be phenomenal. Not only could he give the list of the books of the Bible, but he recited, word for word, the first chapter of Genesis, and, as he naïvely reports, "the whole of another book, not so long as the Bible." The Abbé was delighted, and said that Restif gave promise of great learning, and that he must settle down to hard work.

Auxerre seemed to Restif a most wonderful city, and he imagined that all its inhabitants were rich and that all the women were handsome. The visit was not long enough to break these illusions, for the journey to Paris was promptly undertaken, and Restif became absorbed in the changing scene. The roughness of the road and the swaying of the stage-coach made Restif sick, and his father gave up this mode of transportation. The next conveyance was a light carriage which jolted so violently that another change proved necessary—"to save my life." Poor Edmé found himself obliged to proceed on foot, but he made no complaint, and Restif was touched by his father's kindness and cheerfulness.

Days had to be spent on the road, at this slow rate. Just outside of Melun, Restif was startled by a rumbling sound, like distant thunder. "Father," he cried, "a band of robbers is coming." "No," said Edmé, "those are the great coaches bound for Fontainebleau, where the king holds his court." Now ensued a series of questions and answers about the monarchy and the government which served to confuse rather than clarify the mind of Restif. He was much impressed by the information that all France would have to fight for Louis XV, if the king so willed. During the nights that they spent in towns along the way, Restif cried when he thought of his valley and the days of his shepherd-kingship. He feared the great world which was opening before him, and, at the same time, he imagined that he would like to go to America and live an untamed life in the woods; he, poor child, who shuddered at shadows! In conflict with his love of solitude was the idea that he would do great things, control many people, if opportunity would but present itself. Then, when the dark mass of Paris appeared before him, he could think of nothing better than to live there always. The immensity of Paris amazed him, yet he was astonished when his father told him that not all the people who lived there knew each other as they did at Sacy. It was some time before he could become accustomed to walking in the streets of Paris without saying, at least, *bon jour* to everyone he passed.

When Restif and his father reached the southern outskirts of Paris, where Bicêtre extended its drab, monotonous rows of buildings, they went at once to the house of Abbé Thomas, near the church, which they visited later on. Restif mistook the choirboys for little priests. They reminded him of his brothers and sisters, dressed for the ceremonies in their toy chapel. The choirboys welcomed Restif warmly, and showed him his bedroom which he was glad to find high up, commanding a wide view of Paris. One or two of his relatives who were living in the city, and who had not seen him since his illness, were hardly able to recognize his pock-marked face; and the fair hair they remembered had turned brown.

The Abbé told Restif that the choirboys called each other "brother," but that one among them had the name of Nicolas, and another was called Edmé; so he suggested that Restif be called brother Augustin—"a fine name, borne by one of the greatest men in church history." Restif was more than satisfied, and said that "brother Augustin" was just as good as "Monsieur Nicolas."

Restif's father stayed in Paris for several days, and saw that his small son adjusted himself to his new environment without any preliminary objections to the mediocrity of food and wine. When Edmé left, however, Restif had a severe attack of homesickness. His "brothers" did all they could to cheer him, for which he showed deep gratitude, though he could not always force back the tears. The Abbé noticed this, and sent him to the hospital, so that he might not depress the other boys, but his two chums were allowed to go with him. "The secluded room was extremely neat and clean. On the mantelpiece was an object of devotion, the most touching that could be imagined—a statue of the Christ child, stretching out his arms. This verse was written at the foot of the statue: *Venez, mes enfants, écoutez-moi, et je vous enseignerai la*

crainte du Seigneur.   I was touched; I wept bitterly; and
this was a step toward consolation.   Homesickness is a
cruel malady!   Thanks to my two comrades, I gradually
became more calm."

An unexpected and vivid reminder of the shepherd-life,
however, brought on another attack of homesickness.
"Each dormitory bore the name of a saint, and, consequently, celebrated a patron saint day, by the performance
of an elaborate service.   There was the saying of mass, in
the chapel, followed by a sermon.   On the day of the
fête of Saint-Mayeul, the walls were hung with tapestries
representing forests, wild animals, birds.   There were no
hunters, and everywhere there was peace and happiness.
The choirboys were singing.   I looked at the tapestries,
and I seemed to see my valley, painted as I knew it.   After
the service I could not eat, for I wanted to return to the
chapel.   There I sat for hours, entranced.   I wept without knowing that my tears were falling.   A sermon was
preached in the chapel while I gazed at the animals and the
birds and the forests, and my sobbing almost choked me.
I seemed to be, once more, in my valley.   It was thought
that I had been moved by the sermon, but I had not heard
a word of it.   Oh! love of the forest which I lost with
my youthful innocence!   I had cause, indeed, for tears!"

One of Restif's two friends became so fond of him that
he could not bear to see him pay the least attention to the
other boys.   This absurd jealousy was something of a
strain, but he managed to avoid causing unnecessary pain
without surrendering to this tyranny of affection.   With
the help of his friends, Restif was soon in a frame of mind
in which he could begin his studies.   His first task was to

learn to read, and this he accomplished with great rapidity.

A day under the strictly ordered Jansenist régime was very like another. As soon as the boys got up they said their prayers. They rinsed their mouths with water and vinegar before breakfast, a process which Restif blames for the decline in the whiteness of his teeth. After breakfast, the boys wrote or studied till ten. Reading aloud, half an hour of singing, and lunch at noon, were followed by an hour of recreation. A period of study preceded the three-o'clock recitations, and a light repast was served at four. Another time for reading aloud was succeeded by three hours of much appreciated reading *ad libitum,* from a set of selected books. Supper at eight, recess till nine, usually consisting of a walk under the escort of one of the older brothers, brought the boys to bed at nine-thirty. A half-holiday came every Thursday. Restif continued to suffer from homesickness, now and then, and sometimes a special indulgence was granted for him to play checkers. This remedy seldom failed.

Before Restif had been long at Bicêtre, the school broke up and the boys were sent home, due to the growing religious disputes into which the Jansenists were plunged throughout the eighteenth century. The opposition to Jansenism got on the Abbé Thomas' nerves, and he decided to resign. For a time Restif stayed with his half-sister in Paris, a visit which he filled with much reading:—parts of *Gil Blas,* and many other books of a kind not likely to be found in a religious school. From Paris he was sent to Courgis, near Auxerre, where another of his half-brothers was a vicar, whose peaceful career was inter-

rupted, in 1794, by the Robespierrists, who drove him
from his parish, and shut him up in Auxerre.   When he
escaped, he was the first priest in the department of
Yonne to accept the civil constitution of the clergy.   The
Abbé Thomas also moved to Courgis, whither Restif was
conducted by Marguerite Paris, the vicar's housekeeper.

Restif bewails the fate that drove him thus from place
to place.   No sooner had his shy disposition been sufficiently conquered to enable him to make friends than he
had to leave them.   Already his life seemed to him a
series of untimely and needless farewells.   Strangely
enough, when he left Bicêtre, he felt himself to be a religious martyr, driven before the wind of hatred that blew
against the Jansenists.   In this glorious sensation he found
more satisfaction than he had faith in any of the teachings
or practices of the Jansenists under whom he had studied.

"Courgis was to be my second home, Auxerre my third,
and Paris my grave."

Before he began his studies at Courgis, he spent a day
with his parents at Sacy.   The Abbé was there, and Restif
took him for a walk, showed him his valley, and tried to
explain what it had meant to him.   The Abbé, however,
was not interested, and in this way he resembled Restif's
other half-brothers, who were not only considerably older
than Restif, but seemed incapable of any real companionship with him, or of entering into the thoughts which
made him, in part, a stranger to the ordered and ordinary
lives of the rest of his family.   Restif, with his fourteen
years, was more than ever in need of sympathy and guid-

ance, and seemed less likely than ever to get the former
or to follow the latter.   His father and mother were glad
to see him, of course, but they made less of him than of
the Abbé whose air of knowledge and whose serious talk
impressed them.   Restif, though not exactly slighted, felt
as if he hardly belonged among his relatives, and as if they
would always be bound to laugh at what meant most to
him.   He walked about the place, looked at the animals,
noticed the new members of the groups, and found his
usual solace in the fields and woods.   Early next morning
the Abbé, who was restless for reasons other than Restif's,
conducted him to Courgis, where he was to study Latin
and other subjects, with the help of his two brothers—a
privilege upon which Restif's parents had laid great
weight.

It was not long before Restif fell deeply in love, perhaps more deeply than at any other time in his life.   One
day, in church, he saw Jeanette Rousseau; one glance at
her was enough to completely extinguish his interest in the
girls he had seen at Sacy.   She was three years his senior,
tall and modest and charming, with an air of innocence
and a delicate complexion.   "At the age of fourteen, my
soul awoke to a greater impulse than the physical attraction of love.   Her pretty little foot was irresistible to me.
I resolved to be worthy of this girl at all costs; I worked
as I had never worked before, and prayed that I might win
her.   Even now, after nearly fifty years, I cannot write of
her without emotion.   Yet I never knew her; once, by
chance, I spoke to her.   My feeling for her was as pure
and tender as it was intense."   If he could have been with

her always, he thought, he would have become a very great man! He writes of her in his "calendar," in which he consecrates March first to her memory: "I have never ceased to love her, and now, in my old age, I love her more than ever. At Courgis I loved her with a delicacy which I have never been able to feel for anyone else. When I knew Mme. Parangon my sensibility was still exquisite, but not quite so pure as at Courgis, and since that time it has gradually grown less delicate. In 1788 Jeannette was still unmarried, and in 1794, after my divorce, I tried to find her, but in vain." Later in that year he writes: "I know now that Jeannette has been dead for several years." These chronological confusions are neither rare nor surprising in the records of the loves of Restif.

The one great moment when Restif spoke to Jeannette marked the day when she came to the house in Courgis in which Restif lived. She rang the bell, and Restif opened the door. Such was his emotion, as he saw her there, that he could scarcely answer her simple, impersonal inquiry as to someone, not Restif, who lived there. When he at last told her that the person whom she wished to see was not at home, she thanked him and turned at once to go.

In spite of the heroic resolutions which he had made, his purpose of making himself worthy of this "heavenly creature" did not prevent his conduct from belying the vow. He had not the excuse of loneliness, for some of the boys he had known at school in Joux and Vermenton were now at Courgis, and helped him to pass the time when he was free. None of the other girls at Courgis were as lovely as Jeannette, but they were attractive, and

Restif found them less unreal than his dream of her who seemed beyond his reach.

Nor could he say that no older, wiser person took the trouble to advise him and sympathize with his longings. Marguerite Paris, who brought him home from Bicêtre, had taken a great liking to him and loved to talk to him and give him the benefit of her experience and good sense. She appealed to him strongly, he listened to her, and when she told him he must control himself if he wished to win Jeannette, he promised to be faithful. Her concern for him grew as she watched him drifting and falling into bad habits. She told him that, at best, his chances in regard to Jeannette were slim, for her parents were ambitious, and would no doubt object to him as a son-in-law for even stronger reasons than that of his tender years. Marguerite realized that Restif's brothers could not understand his character, and that the severity with which they had begun to regard him, would in all likelihood drive him further and further from the path into which they had resolved to draw him. She was to see, however, that her kindness and gentleness could do very little good, and she despaired of hitting upon any means of curbing his constant self-indulgence and his deplorable facility for breaking his word. He would kiss her hand, his tears would flow, he would promise earnestly to be worthy of her affection. Marguerite discovered, however, that she herself was the immediate temptation that he found most difficult to resist. She had succeeded in restraining him until one night of which Restif wrote: "I made a bold resolution, and determined to accomplish my purpose . . . I was beside myself. . . . Late at night, when I knew that every-

one in the house [4] was asleep, I got up quietly, without
regard to the danger of discovery, and entered Marguerite's room. I listened. She was asleep. . . . She
was dreaming. . . . She awoke too late. . . ."

The next day he found her weeping bitterly, and he
again determined to mend his ways. Marguerite went
away on a visit, and Restif swore that he would observe
her warnings, for she had told him that he would suffer
grievously if he continued to give himself free rein. But
his acquaintances at Courgis were as determined that he
should go their way, as Marguerite was concerned that he
should change his course. He followed the examples of
his friends; he began to write poems to girls other than
Jeannette and Marguerite, and the sentiments therein expressed were "objectionable" in a high degree. The
vicar developed a habit of looking about in Restif's room,
and here he found the manuscripts in question. He lost
no time in summoning the culprit, and burned the papers
before his eyes, telling him to destroy, in future, and in
this manner, all documents which he would be ashamed to
read to anyone other than the person to whom the verses
might be addressed.

From this time on, the Abbé and the Curé [5] were suspicious of everything Restif did and said, nor were they
always convinced of the validity of his plausible and clearly-
stated explanations of tardiness or failure to keep appoint-
ments. His reputation hung solely upon the excellence of
his recitations and the accuracy of his memory, which far

---

[4] Restif slept in a large room in which were four beds, one of them occupied by the Abbé. Marguerite slept in the next room.

[5] The Vicar.

surpassed that of any of his fellow-students. He could still repeat whole chapters or even books of the Bible, "word for word," though he does confess to putting in occasional synonyms which were called errors, and for which he got no credit.

He reproaches himself for his misconduct, but the burden of his sins was never intolerable. He is sure that his affairs are not vices, or, if they are, they constitute his sole vice. This specialization clears his conscience, for who can be perfect in this world? How much better he is than those who drink and gamble! This is not too simple, but too sincere for a confession of Jean-Jacques. The *type* may have been borrowed, but not the *tone*.

In due course of time, Marguerite returned to Courgis for a few days, mainly to tell Restif that she would give the child which was to be born every possible advantage under the circumstances, and that she would never reveal that its father's name was Restif. He was deeply moved by her affection for him, and he asserts that he surely would have married her if she had consented. He tried to persuade her, and failed. He was too young, she said, and she would be a burden to him, more and more. They parted with many tears, never to see each other again.

Although the complications of this incident seemed to be fairly definitely solved, the difficulties with which Restif had begun to beset himself were gathering their forces for attack. He failed to conceal the objectionable verses which he continued to produce, and his father was told of their unsaintly qualities. He hastened to Courgis, where he delivered one of the sermons so lengthily and impressively embodied in *La Vie de Mon Père*. A sense of the deepest and most righteous indignation burned in the soul of Edmé, and Restif decided to leave Courgis on his own account, and thus escape the enforced departure which threatened him. He wrote to someone at Bicêtre, asking if the school had been re-established since the withdrawal of the Abbé Thomas, and if he might return there. This letter frankly criticized and complained of the manner in which the Abbé and the Curé exercised their authority at Courgis, nor were the names of these reverend brethren withheld. The inconsiderate person to whom these confidences were addressed replied by sending Restif's letter to the Abbé, who promptly wrote to Edmé, advising that Restif be removed at once from the school at Courgis in which he had so thoroughly disgraced himself. No business or profession could be less suited to this boy than that of the study of theology.

Edmé felt that his son should have another chance, that he had been judged too hastily, and that he must be forgiven on account of his youth. To pardon Restif was the least attractive of all possible attitudes that could have been suggested to his orthodox, Christian brothers, for they had grown to dislike him heartily, and his letter had almost turned their inclinations into hate. Worse than this, their anger found vent in hurling insults at Edmé's wife (their step-mother) in explanation of the marked failure of Restif to inherit the qualities of her husband. These were the men whom she treated with such respect.

Restif continued to progress in his studies, through the inspiration of his thought of Jeannette. One of his brothers adopted an extremely cold manner of addressing him, and the other refused to speak to him at all. The

situation would have been intolerable, had not Jeannette
lived at Courgis. Restif decided to wait for his father's
summons instead of making further efforts to escape from
his brothers. Having spent many days longing to go, he
wept copiously when his father finally sent for him. He
went into the church where he had first seen Jeannette, and
knelt on the spot where she habitually prayed. Someone
saw him there, and the rumour spread in Courgis that
Restif's religious zeal was pure and high, for one so young.

He remained at Sacy for some time while his father tried
to make up his mind what to do with him. Neither M.
nor Mme. Restif wanted their son to be a labourer or to
go into business, although all their efforts to uplift him had,
so far, been bewilderingly ineffectual. Restif read and
studied a great deal during these weeks. How could he
care for this kind of work and at the same time ignore the
proprieties of conduct? All his father's friends were certain that he would never be a student worthy of the name,
and they advised Edmé to keep him busy on the farm.
What else was he good for? Meanwhile Restif read
Terence and Ovid by the hour, occasionally interrupting
this pleasure by working in the garden with his mother, or
taking care of the animals on the place.

Jeannette was still uppermost in his thoughts, especially
when he was alone. Sacy, like Courgis, provided other
feminine resources, and, after all, he said to himself, what
other way was there of forgetting Jeannette? His love for
her seemed hopeless, and no doubt it was his duty to put her
out of his mind as much as possible. This kind of argument
developed steadily into a fixed habit, but his mental vision
was never sufficiently clear for it to become a hypocrisy.

CHAPTER XI

The Apprentice at Auxerre

THE most important period of Restif's life began in July, 1751, when he was sent to Auxerre to begin an entirely new experience, under different conditions, with companions of a type he had not known. The tendencies which asserted themselves at Courgis, hardened into character at Auxerre, and completed their operations in Paris.

Mme. Parangon had remembered the day at Vermenton when she met Edmé's son. Her husband owned a printing-press at Auxerre, and she suggested that Restif live at their house, and learn the trade of printer. Edmé had long known and respected her, and this offer came as a happy solution of the puzzle of the boy's future. Mme. Restif welcomed the thought. She borrowed a donkey from one of her relatives, and advised her son to start upon his journey early in the morning, thus avoiding the heat of the day. She added, with a peasant's solicitude for the care of animal-property, that the fatigue of the donkey, no less than that of the rider, would thereby be lessened.

Before he could go, Restif was bound to listen to another of his father's orations, full of the most excellent advice, and consequently predestined to neglect. He spares his readers no more than his father spared him, and the paternal exhortation appears in full in his autobiography.

He and the donkey arrived safely at Auxerre. When he began his apprenticeship at the shop of M. Parangon, he became at once the object of the ridicule of the other employees, and, as usual, he attributed to malice much that doubtless sprang from harmless humour. "Such people," he says, "would mistake the *naïveté* of my manner for silliness," and he assumed that his fellow-workers were jealous of the favour shown him by the Parangons in opening their home to him.

At first, his duties consisted in picking up scraps under the printing-presses, in sweeping and cleaning and running on errands. Being merely an apprentice, he had to take orders from anyone in the establishment, and there was nothing too unimportant or useless for him to be called upon to do. Sometimes he had a right to be resentful. It was discovered that dogs terrified him, and one evening it was arranged for him to be decoyed into a dark street where several rather savage dogs lurked. Restif could run with amazing speed, and he managed to escape. When his tormentors found him they examined his legs and were disappointed to observe that the dogs had not bitten him. He concluded that an apprentice was lower than a slave, and it was doubly painful to be subjected to people who were ignorant and even illiterate. His knowledge indeed seemed vast in comparison to theirs. How strange that his father should have seen fit to reduce him to this bondage!

His sufferings in the factory were augmented by the absence of Mme. Parangon who was making a visit of several months in a distant town. The complete disorder of the Parangon household proved the need of her return. A distant cousin of Restif, Mlle. Gauthier, who disliked him intensely, reigned in Mme. Parangon's stead. She was soon replaced, not for her marked incapacity, but for per-

sonal reasons. Her successor brought no order out of
chaos, for M. Parangon, in spite of Edmé's high regard,
lived in a slovenly manner, and demanded nothing better
than to be allowed to indulge in undisturbed infidelity to
his absent wife.

Restif made several congenial friends, and, in spite of
all annoyances, he began to like Auxerre, though it was
anything but the city he had imagined when he stopped
there on his way to Bicêtre. At any rate, it was more
stimulating than the quiet life to which he had been accustomed. His initial shyness soon wore off, and he
adopted the gaiety of his companions, though their immorality shocked him to such an extent that for a long time he
was regarded as a model of virtue. The shamelessness of
his acquaintances, however, surprised him less than the discovery that M. Parangon's conduct closely resembled
theirs.

The office of housekeeper changed hands several times
before Mme. Parangon's return. The installation of a
girl named Toinette was a pleasure to Restif. Her manners were far better than those of Mlle. Gauthier, but they
made her the object of many jokes which carried humour
to the point of insult. On several occasions Restif cham-
pioned her cause, and gloriously rescued her. Although
Restif objected to the manners of the Auxerrois, he leaned
more and more toward the kind of life which he saw all
about him, and his sensitive scruples began to give way.
He persuaded himself that his disposition required a certain
laxity of conduct, and his obsession for women seemed to
him only natural. When he met Mlle. Servigné, who reminded him strongly of Jeannette, he argued that his atten-

tions to her were directed at the same time toward the great object of his devotion. He did not enter into all the vices of his friends, and this balm of self-denial always calmed his conscience.

"My heart never became entirely corrupt, for the charms of friendship never left me cold!"

The point of view of the youths of Auxerre weighed on him when he was not enjoying the freedom of an evening spent in their carefree company, and at such times he sought relief in books. The novels of Mme. de Villedieu occupied many spare hours, and he thought they helped him to understand the charm and mystery of Mme. Parangon's character, and gave him the patience that he needed in awaiting her return.

Incidentally he began to be more popular. His fellow-workmen learned to respect him as they had not done before. They appreciated his good manners and his willingness to work, and to do his share of all that he knew how to do in the routine of the printing-house.

At last Mme. Parangon arrived. Restif, at work in the shop, heard someone call her by name. All the workers at once ran down to see her. Restif timidly followed them, at a distance. She seemed to him even more charming than Jeannette, and this impression astonished him, for he deemed himself a connoisseur of good looks, and he had not dreamed that anyone could rival Jeannette in his eyes. Mme. Parangon's gracious smile and kind words made no distinctions until she summoned Restif. He advanced modestly, saying with quaint gravity: "Madame, I have the honour to congratulate you upon your joyful return to your home." He immediately retired in some confusion,

only to be called forth again.   Toinette had filled her
mistress's ears with complimentary reports of Restif's behaviour, and had convinced her that he would do well, and
be an honour to all his friends.   Mme. Parangon drew him
aside, told him of her great expectations, and presented
him with a silver watch, for which his gratitude could find
no proper utterance.   His pride in her gift grew in proportion to his knowledge of how fondly everyone regarded
her.

Mme. Parangon managed in an amazingly short time to
put her tumbled household in order; and even the printing-
presses seemed to run more smoothly.   Heretofore, Restif
had eaten in the kitchen.   Now he sat at the table with the
family.   Mme. Parangon discovered that Restif had been
set to tasks that she considered beneath him.   "I had
thought," she said to her husband, "that you would show
more consideration for the son of my father's friend."   M.
Parangon replied: "I have followed the usual custom in
regard to apprentices, and Restif has never complained."
He had noticed, however, that M. Parangon took the
trouble to do for others of his workmen things that he
would never have done for him.

Restif makes extraordinary remarks about the reading
which he managed to accomplish: "After having finished
all the novels of Mme. de Villedieu, I plunged into Molière,
Corneille, Boileau, La Fontaine, Racine—Racine above all!
Yet Racine has done me more *harm* than any other writer.
Everything connected with Jansenism has proved fatal to
me."   The effect of Mme. Villedieu's books was to stimulate good conduct; Corneille's, even more; Molière's, sometimes; but Racine discouraged him.   When he had read

and re-read the poetry of Racine, he wrote: "I felt a keen and humiliating admiration. When I compared my verses to his I found I was setting up those of a man against those of a god! Racine destroyed the audacity which I gained from Molière. I became jealous of Racine; I hated him as an imperious and too perfect master. After reading him over and over, I became disgusted with my work, and especially my poetry. I tore up every page that I had written, and thereby lost much valuable material for my autobiography. If love had not continued to inspire me, I would never have produced another verse. Love triumphed over my critical decision, and I attempted a translation of Terence. Then I made rhymes to soothe my heart."

His affection for Mme. Parangon steadily grew, and developed, on one side, into scorn and jealousy of M. Parangon, whose sordid character seemed a sacrilege in connection with his wife. How he, Restif, would have loved her, and what an inspiration they would have been to each other! He advanced in her good graces, and observed that her attitude toward M. Parangon was not one which should lead him to despair of her ever falling in love with him. Yet she gave no indication of the least unfaithfulness to her husband. "My taste for reading, and the fact that I did not gamble or drink like most of the young men of my age, increased her esteem for me. I was an exceptional youth, destined for high achievement, she thought, for I seemed to have conquered the follies of youth at an age when they usually hold full sway. She did not know that my exclusive interest in one indulgence diverted me from others, nor did she notice how she herself affected me. She liked to hear me read to her, and to discuss my studies and writings with me. She advised me not to read the *Contes* of La Fontaine, and other such books. She asked me to show her my translations of Terence." She did not know that Restif secretly wrote verses of the kind which he had composed in Courgis, nor that he addressed them to different girls whom he knew in Auxerre, just as he had formerly done in the theological school. He asserts that some of his poems were received as graciously, by those to whom they were sent, as if they had been written by Voltaire. Restif defines the immorality of these productions as "bad taste." If he had read *Tom Jones* he would have found "true virtue" described as "nothing else but true taste." But he did not read *Tom Jones,* and he would have taken issue with Fielding if he had. He once wrote such a censorable "poem" that he thought it best to send only the better half of it to her whom he thus honoured. This restraint he calls a proof of his finer feeling.

It was a part of his peculiar nature that he seemed to feel, personally and intensely, more and more, in proportion to the growing number of the objects of his affection. He could be in love with several girls, and suffer more cruelly if he lost any one of them, than might be supposed. The fatal day of March 11th, 1753, brought him woe "from which," he says, "I have never entirely recovered." The girl in question was snatched from him by death, and he "wept for many days." He refers to her as his wife, but this is merely a term of endearment. Such was his grief that he promptly fell in love with other girls, or drowned his sorrow in their company. He was told a story about the dead girl which was not to her credit, and at first he

said nothing.   Then he awoke to the realization of the ap-
palling fact that he had not denied the slander, and he
bitterly reproached himself: "Miserable wretch, unfit to
live, you did not defend her memory.   Oh! monster! what
has become of your heart?"   His sobs nearly choked him;
finally in exhaustion he fell asleep, and, in his dream, the
dead girl came to him, pardoned him, calmed his affliction.
He told Mme. Parangon of this experience, and she said
"You are specially blest by heaven.   You are not an ordinary man."   He believed her.

When he had been in Auxerre for about three years, he
began to take dancing lessons, and learned the minuet, the
*passepied la Bretagne, l'ancienne allemande, matelote, sa-
botière,* and other popular dances.   He describes them as
variations on the minuet, for the most part, and no doubt
much less formal than the dance which graced the circles
in which Restif did not move.   He affirms that he was one
of the best and handsomest dancers in Auxerre, and that he
easily succeeded in distancing many who had practised the
art much longer than he.   Apparently the ravages of small-
pox did not hinder his popularity.

Mme. Parangon did not dance, and consequently this diversion helped him to keep his mind from brooding too
constantly upon her charms.   She noticed and appreciated
his effort to keep his passion within bounds, only to experience, before long, the trouble he had caused Marguerite.
He knew and admitted that every shade of fault had been
his.   Her confidence in him was hopelessly shattered, but
she continued her kindness to him, talked to him, tried to
influence him without letting him know she thought him
lost, and though her fondness for him survived, she suc-

ceeded in setting rigid limits to their intimacy, which could never again be put upon the basis of trust. M. Parangon eventually found out what had happened, and his vengeance was to come. Restif mingles his usual conceit with the humility of one of his confessions: "Do not pity me, you whose lives are those of insensible machines! Do not pity my miseries that resulted from my blameworthy conduct. I languish now, in old age, without hope, without consolation. I would a thousand times rather have had brief spells of happiness than lived your dull lives. It is blasphemous to pity the happiness that results in despair, for it was happiness, if only for a moment."

On the day of Mme. Parangon's departure from Auxerre for the same reason that had induced Marguerite Paris to leave Courgis, Restif was about to celebrate the anniversary of the death of the girl who had come to him in a dream. This ceremony he postponed in dutiful and affectionate regard for Mme. Parangon. When they had said good-bye in the manner in which Restif and Marguerite had parted, Restif went on with his memorial rites. He had already caused many people who had loved him much unhappiness. He knew this, he hated to cause pain, but he continued to be a source of grief, in spite of what seemed to him conscientious efforts in the opposite direction.

During Mme. Parangon's absence, Restif fell in love with Toinette. He told her that if ever he became a "master printer" and wrote a book, he would include therein the following sentence: "Colette (Mme. Parangon) was the most adored of women. Her servant, Toinette, was the prettiest, the most likeable, the best of girls. I, Nicolas-Anne-Edmé-Augustin-Restif-de-la-Bretonne-près-Sacy, have had the honour of knowing them both." There is the sentence, written in his biography, proving him to be a man of his word. One sees him pausing to gaze at his own faithfulness.

While Mme. Parangon was in exile, she added to the sorrow of her knowledge of Restif by meeting Marguerite Paris, and hearing her story. When she returned to Auxerre she discovered his affair with Toinette. She felt called upon to deliver a warning admonition to her wayward young friend, and as she did so, he knew her deep affliction: "I know that in your heart you have no wicked intentions or corrupt motives, but that you have never been able to conquer your passions";—a verdict which this caricature of Tom Jones was ever ready to admit and to continue to prove. Mme. Parangon advised him to devote himself to reading and study, as much as his other duties would allow, in order that he might make a favourable impression on her father who was shortly to arrive in Auxerre. He was to bring his younger daughter, Fanchette, with him, and his intention was to procure for her no less a husband than Restif himself. He had been led to take this step in recognition of his regard for Restif's father, and of the flattering reports which Mme. Parangon had sent him in connection with Restif. The latter at once settled down to work, for he had seen Fanchette, and she had pleased him, and he was therefore anxious to appear industrious, having no doubt that in other ways he would appeal to her without effort on his part.

M. Collet and Fanchette greeted Restif cordially when they arrived. Restif complacently watched the development of plans which were presently being made for his mar-

riage to Fanchette.   Friends of both families who heard
of the match thought it admirable for both.   Restif consented to the marriage but hardly persuaded himself that
his love for her equalled that which he had felt for Jeannette or Mme. Parangon.   Meanwhile his amours continued, and he inserts in his autobiography a confession that
he believed himself to be the father of nineteen children,
whose mothers were equally numerous.   He emphasizes his
frankness: "When I am faithful and honest, I give myself
the credit of these attributes.   When I am the reverse, I
admit the facts with equal readiness."   He attempts to
excuse himself for his conduct at the time when his marriage
was being arranged, by asserting that his behaviour, bad
as it was, could not be compared with that of certain other
persons whom he knew.   "It is impossible to guess how
gross, revolting, vulgar are their manners, thoughts and
expressions."   He describes harrowing scenes of brutality
which he witnessed, and in which he never took part, except to rescue the victims of such cruelty.

Though it had been agreed that Restif was to marry
Fanchette, no date was set for their wedding, and the en-
gagement was to be, in all probability, a long one.   The
respective parents of the pair should have realized that if
marriage would save Restif, as they seemed to think, he
must be married at once or it might be too late to save
him—problematical as that salvation was in any case, event
or circumstance whatsoever.   Restif was nearly twenty-
one.   Did they imagine he would be wiser at thirty?

"The eighth of May, 1755, was the last day of my
apprenticeship; I became a journeyman.   Toinette congratulated me with tears in her eyes, for I had to leave

the Parangon household, it being the custom for the class of workmen of which I now became a member to find lodgings in the town. M. Parangon announced my promotion to the workers, and told them to treat me with respect. I give these details to show the customs then in vogue, for printing has since become a lower order of labour. The manner in which a printing-house is now run, no longer resembles that of 1755. With the end of my apprenticeship, my troubles continued to increase."

Restif involved himself in a duel with an old servant of M. Parangon's, who had insulted a woman in his presence. He wounded his antagonist, and was surprised at his own skill in handling a sword, and felt that now, at last, he had established himself as an honourable man. The affair at once raised him in the eyes of the Auxerrois, but he decided to go away for a while, until the gossip on the subject had subsided. His reputation should be brilliant if this talk would but cease. Even gossip could not dim the glory of his departure from Auxerre. A deputation of the girls of the town had decided to present him with a wreath, which was formally offered to him by one of their number, accompanied by the delivery of a short but equally flattering speech. Restif accepted this tribute with becoming dignity, and recognized its suitability.

He went to Sacy, and told his family all about the duel. His father praised his conduct, but his mother said: "What a risk to take. Had you forgotten Mlle. Fanchette?" His parents had set their hearts on this marriage, and, in promising to accept the daughter of M. Collet, Restif gave them what he calls the only real pleasure that ever came to them through their wayward son.

A great change in Restif's life was at hand. On his return to Auxerre, Mme. Parangon told him that she had decided to send him to Paris for a time, hoping that he would profit by this experience and the advantages which it offered in his trade. She gave him the addresses of certain publishers who might be of use to him. During this talk Fanchette was present and when Mme. Parangon had finished, Restif knelt before Fanchette and promised to be true to her while he lived in Paris. She smiled confidently, thinking of the duel, and of Restif's heroism.

Tearful and many were the farewells. Restif did not say good-bye to all the girls he knew, for he noticed that Fanchette seemed a little jealous of them. "This feeling on her part entranced me, and that day I was faithful to her for the only time in my life." His friends expressed their deep regret at his departure. One of the men in the shop said: "A young man leaves the town, and, to me, the town will be empty henceforth."

"I was to go at five next morning. Mme. Parangon offered to kiss me. I threw myself at her feet. My father, who had come to Auxerre to say good-bye, saw me kiss her hand and heard me say to her: 'What would have become of me without your kindness!' When I had risen, at her bidding, she held me in a close embrace. I seem to feel her now against my heart, in its violent agitation. With less intense emotion I threw my arms about Fanchette, and renewed my vows. My father was overcome with joy. Mme. Parangon encircled both Fanchette and me in her embrace, and drew us near the portrait of her father: 'Promise him to marry and love each other always.' We swore to be faithful. I seized my father's hand, and he went out with me. Before closing the door, I said to Mme. Parangon: 'This is the hour at which I have so often returned to this house. Now it is the time of parting.' Again I embraced Fanchette. 'My courage fails me,' I cried, 'I feel that this is an eternal adieu.' Mme. Parangon sighed. I hear her now: 'Go, unfortunate one. Your sensitiveness and your despair are contagious. Go!' This was her last word to me. I left these two most dear of all my friends forever. From this moment I knew that I was lost; and, friendly reader, I had lived but twenty years! As I walked with my father, I sighed grievously. In my dreams that night I saw Mme. Parangon dragged by monsters into deep water. At four o'clock my father woke me. He wished me to go with him to the cathedral to pray, but I escaped, and ran to Mme. Parangon's house. I wept as I kissed the threshold: 'Adieu, adieu, cradle of my youth!' Toinette ran down to the place from which the coach started, and bade me a tearful farewell. My father almost wept. Indeed I was truly loved. Now I am indifferent to the world. Miserable creature that I am, all whom I loved are in their graves. O reader! have you not remarked the charming offer which Fate makes to Youth? We imagine that the chance will come again. Alas, it comes but once! Why did I not make the most of these happy years? Fate which had played with me as with a spoiled, lovable, innocent child, turned a hard cruel face to me, after I left Auxerre. My springtime is over. Now I am to burn in the heat of summer. Autumn will follow, then winter, then death!"

What a picture of bourgeois sentimentality! Another diary might have said: "Tiresome and tearful farewells.

Mme. Parangon's capacity for weeping is endless. We all became hysterical. I would have been no happier if I had stayed at Auxerre and married Fanchette. At any rate my departure was lucky for her. I never loved her; and she loved the totally different person whom she imagined me to be."

CHAPTER XII

The Printer in Paris

RESTIF arrived in Paris in September, 1755, and stayed for a time with his sister Marie. A printer named Boudard whom he had formerly known in Auxerre helped him to get a job in the Galeries du Louvre, the royal printing-press, and persuaded him to share his room at the Hôtel du Saint-Esprit, where he lived with Chambon, a clock-maker whose work kept him there while they were at the printing-house. This facilitated the division of labour in their bachelor quarters. Chambon watched the pot, and their soup was ready when they returned. Their simple meals consisted, in addition to the soup, of meat, bread and vegetables with occasional relishes. Boudard, who knew more about butchers than his friends, usually brought the meat; Restif cooked it, and attended to wood and coal. After lunch (apparently on Sundays only) they washed the dishes.

Their expenses were remarkably low, for they could get along on three francs per week for food. Restif's and Boudard's wages at the printing-house were two and a half francs each, per day, and between them they managed every week to save about twelve francs.

Restif complains a little about the stinginess of the director of the "Galeries," but, on the whole, conditions were reasonably fair, and, at any rate, not those of slavery. He notes that during the Revolution the director was guillo-

tined, after which the workmen became insufferably insolent. The "Imprimerie Royale" became the "Imprimerie
Nationale," and the change appears to have been for the
worse, though the growing tyranny of the director had
merited death. Unfortunately this picture is typical of
many of the first results of the new régime.

It must be said in Restif's favour that at first he made
valiant efforts to resist the temptations which beset him
not only when he went out with his friends, but even when
he visited his sister Marie, whose acquaintances were not
always characterized by a desire to keep Restif in the
strictest possible restraint. Then he found the only altern-
ative took the form of monotony and routine and solitude.
Frequently he stayed in his room at the Hôtel du Saint-
Esprit while his roommates amused themselves elsewhere.
He had never been to the theatre, and he could think of no
way of passing his idle hours. Brooding over memories
of life in Auxerre increased his gloom. Instead of looking
for new books to read, he spent his time going over and
over his notebooks and letters. "I lost the vivacity of my
personality, and became an ordinary worker whose trade
was mechanical and deadening." He reproaches himself
bitterly for this stupid behaviour, and suddenly it occurs
to him to criticize Mme. Parangon: "The chief place in
her heart was ever filled by her love of virtue, and her
regard for me occupied a less important place." If this
had not been so, why did she send him to Paris, even for his
own good, as she had professed to do? When Restif
sought relief from these thoughts in the company of another sister, Margot, her home proved to be a repetition
of Marie's. He met a great many girls at both houses,

several of whom were more or less attractive, but none of them made a sufficiently deep impression to really interest him.

And yet a peaceful happiness and a kind of content marked most of the remaining days of 1755, for Restif, Boudard and Chambon were good friends. With the new year came new troubles. Two women of unquestionably questionable character settled in the Hôtel du Saint-Esprit in a room adjoining Restif's. One of these women was younger and prettier than the other, and Chambon promptly allied himself with her. Boudard and Restif held back for some time, but eventually they were lured into Chambon's way; so much so that a quarrel began, for all three disputed Chambon's choice. Disagreeable scenes of conflict alternated with scarcely less attractive periods of peace, and finally Chambon, in a rage, used domestic chaos as an excuse for leaving Paris, where he had not made a success of selling clocks. He retired to the country, near Auxerre, and spread malicious tales in that city as to Restif's conduct in the capital. Fortunately no credit was given to his accounts, for Chambon had formerly lived in Auxerre, where the reputation of deliberate and habitual mendacity had fixed itself upon him.

Boudard and Restif continued their friendship, but Restif moved to a pension kept by a Mme. Lallemand, and found a better job in the printing-house on the Île de la Cité, near the cathedral.

He discovered that one Jeannette Demailly, whom he had known and "respected" before he came to Paris, lived not far from his pension. It seemed to him that she must be in need of brotherly protection, and, no doubt, she

would be a more congenial sister than Marie or Margot.
This Jeannette was not the idolized Mlle. Rousseau of
Courgis, but Restif's affection for her was real and she accepted his offer, and came at once to share his small room.
They had, at first, only one bed, but Restif arranged for
himself a place on the floor where he slept comfortably
enough.   While he worked at the printing-house during the
day, Jeannette swept their room and prepared the evening
meal.   They were very happy until the Abbé Thomas heard
of this extraordinary partnership, and wrote his objections
at great length.   Restif ignored his brother's ideas on
every subject, but he dreaded the disapproval which Mme.
Parangon would express, and he knew that she would be
told much more than the truth.   Consequently he advised
Jeannette to move to the home of a married woman whom
she knew, and whose husband had deserted her.   This
friend gladly gave Jeannette a room, though she readily
believed in the innocence of the life that Jeannette and
Restif had lived together.   In proof of her faith she could
tell of a family the five members of which had blamelessly
occupied one bed—father, mother, daughter of sixteen, son
of eighteen and son of twenty.   Besides, she had talked to
Restif's landlady, whose suspicions of Restif's conduct had
led her to spy on him.   To her complete satisfaction (or
disappointment, for she was not a respectable person) she
had discovered nothing, though she had managed to see
them often at different times of day and night, without
their knowledge.   Mme. Lallemand had commissioned
some of her friends to help in this detective work, but
their eager watchfulness had been equally unavailing.

One memorable evening Restif went with Boudard to the

Comédie-Française, and such was his enjoyment of play and acting that he formed the habit of frequent attendance there and at the "Italiens" and the Opéra-Comique, especially after he had made friends among actresses and dancers of minor parts.

The year 1757 was marked by the death of Mme. Parangon and the marriage of Fanchette, who had heard enough of Restif. "Now that I had lost my dearest friends, I made others who were anything but dear to me, and who occupied the emptiness of my life. I could aspire no higher than the danseuses of the Foire," a vaudeville theatre the history of which had been long and the fortunes, at that time, precarious. He sank lower and lower. One night, returning from dissipation which preyed upon his conscience as soon as it was over, he cried aloud so grievously that a gendarme, thinking these lamentations must come from one who had committed a crime, arrested him and took him before a chief of police. He was ordered to explain his disturbance of the peace, and he said that he had been unable to control the clamour of self-condemnation that oppressed him as he thought of the debauchery into which his loneliness had dragged him. The judge heard him as patiently as possible and let him go, suggesting that he had better think of his feelings before he hurt them.

Restif thought he would give anything to be an actor, especially a tragedian. He had been very often to the theatres,[1] and one day he called on the director of the Opéra-Comique, who looked at him as if he were a "negro

---

[1] At the Opéra he was interested in the quarrels between the followers of Glück and of Piccini.

slave," and gave him an extremely minor part which Restif considered beneath his dignity. He was told to go into the country where his abilities as an actor might be appreciated and where he could learn experience. This good advice he regarded as an insult, and he gave up the stage for which, he had persuaded himself, he was admirably fitted.

For some time he had been infatuated with Mlle. Guéant, one of the leading actresses of the Comédie-Française, and his custom was to watch her performance, and then station himself at the stage entrance to see her leave the theatre. She got into her carriage or chair, and he followed her to her doorway, and saw her enter the house. One evening in July, 1757, she went further than usual, and stopped at the Hôtel de Hollande where a *fête* was being given. "While I was eagerly watching her as she emerged from her chair, in the courtyard of the building, I heard behind me a voice which I at once recognized." He had known Mlle. Junie Prudhomme as a dancer at the Opéra-Comique. She asked him if he would like to go in, and he replied by raising her hand to his lips, in a most courtly manner. They joined Mlle. Guéant and went upstairs. Restif asked his friend if she did not admire the beautiful Guéant, and she replied that the lady in question was not only lovely, but very intelligent, whereupon Restif stooped and kissed the hem of her dress. A colonel of dragoons, arriving at the party, noticed this performance of Restif, and told Mlle. Guéant that one of her admirers was following her. She turned, remembered having seen Restif in the theatre, and gave him an encouraging smile. "You must belong to our world, Monsieur, for I see you with Mlle. Prudhomme."

Nic. Ed. RESTIF, Fils-EdME.
1785

RESTIF DE LA BRETONNE

Restif replied that she had very kindly introduced him, and that he appreciated the honour of remaining longer in the presence of Mlle. Guéant than he had ever been before.

Fortunately Restif had attended Mlle. Guéant's performance that evening, and consequently wore his best clothes, a suit of silk which, in later years, he still wore, or so it appeared, for he habitually neglected his appearance. Sometimes, however, he "put on a closely fitting rateen coat, with black drugget breeches and white cotton hose, carried a cocked hat under his arm, and a small, steel-hilted sword at his side, and, with his hair perfumed and curled, walking on tiptoe, so as not to soil his buckled shoes, strolled through the dirty streets, where he was taken for a chevalier or a marquis."

At the Hôtel de Hollande he wore no such rig as this, and, if he had, he would not have been mistaken for a nobleman. He entered the salon which was later turned into a billiard-room for Beaumarchais, who bought the house, and is said to have written the *Marriage of Figaro* while he lived there.

Restif saw many famous persons in the room, among them Sophie Arnould, whose wit and beauty and acting more than compensated for the mediocrity of her voice;[2] Mlle. Levasseur, the hated rival of Arnould; Mlle. Guimard, the leading dancer of her day; Mme. Favert, an actress of the Comédie-Italienne, of whom Grimm wrote that she could make a failure of any play. "I was amazed," says Restif, "at the unexpected proportions of

---

[2] Abbé Galiani called her voice the loveliest asthma he had ever heard. One day Mlle. Arnould told Champcenetz that she had bitten her tongue. "How did you escape being poisoned?" he asked.

this gathering, but Junie's flattering attention made me feel
at ease. Conversation at supper was very gay, but I could
not find out what the jokes were all about, though some of
them reached my ears. I should have more thoroughly
enjoyed the delicious supper if I had not sat at a great
distance from Mlle. Guéant; she occupied my thoughts, and
eclipsed everyone else in the room. After eating and drinking, came the entertainment. Everyone sang or recited or
did something for the amusement of the others. Mlle.
Guéant acted a scene from one of her plays, and Mlle.
Guimard danced. We were deeply stirred by Piron's [3]
recitation of his *Ode à Priape*. This was the ill-fated
"licentious" poem which Piron's enemies showed to Louis
XV, who consequently vetoed his election to the Academy.
Restif continues: "At last came my turn. I was asked
what I could do. Junie embarrassed me by laughing, and
by telling me to hurry, to do anything. Then Mlle. Guéant
said to me very kindly: 'Will you not do something for
us?' Her words were a command I could no longer resist." He rose, and begged his audience to excuse his lack
of talent. Everyone applauded him, and he began to tell
them about himself: "I am young, without experience,
without talent, and you have just listened to the foremost
actors and actresses of Europe, and to the leading literary
lights of France. I am too insignificant to be noticed in
such a gathering. (Applause from everybody, even the
Venetian ambassador, who had made fun of me before.)
I owe to Mlle. Prudhomme my introduction to the illus-

---

[3] Grimm says of Piron: "He was a machine for making epigrams. No
one could defeat him in repartee. Even Voltaire feared his wit."

trious persons here assembled. (I pointed to Junie; everyone applauded; the Venetian made a grimace.) For my
own part, I can only assert that I have a warm heart, and
have had a few adventures which, perhaps, I had best not
describe in this company. (I told one or two stories of
my youth, and Junie described a supper-party in the Bois
de Boulogne at which I had been present.)"

At about four o'clock the older, more distinguished, and
more serious members of the company took their departure.
"The Venetian ambassador remained," Restif seems glad
to observe, though not because he liked the gentleman.
The lights were turned out, and an orgy began.

Restif describes an exceptional week's work at the
printing-house, but it appears that his ordinary tasks were
not light. He took no holidays during the week. "I went
to the shop on Monday at seven o'clock. This day was
given over to correcting the type, and I worked till four-
thirty. Tuesday I began at six o'clock, Wednesday at five,
Thursday and Friday at four and Saturday at three."
Such a program was rare; there was seldom such a rush of
work to be done. Very often he could leave early in the
afternoon, and on Sundays he never worked, except in
later years when writing his novels.

His best friend at Auxerre, and perhaps the best he ever
had, was Loiseau, an apprentice older than he, who had
liked him from the day they met, and who did what he could
to counteract the bad habits into which most of Restif's acquaintances had enjoyed leading him. When he left
Auxerre, Loiseau told him, without irony, that the girls
he had known there were so much more charming than
any he would meet in Paris, that he would probably be able

to avoid them.   He promised to come to Paris as soon as
he could, for Auxerre would be a wilderness to him without
Restif.   In September, 1756, Loiseau arrived in Paris,
sorrowing at having to leave behind him a Mlle. Lebègue—
a circumstance of importance for Restif, later on.   Restif
and Boudard found a job for Loiseau in a rich printing firm,
but at first Restif did not see him very often, for he was
ashamed of the life he had been leading.   It was not long,
however, before Loiseau's principles broke down, though
never to the extent of those of Restif.   "In spite of the
fact that friendship for Loiseau, not yet at its height, was
my most firm support, my life seemed void without the society of women.   That is why I have always sought to find
love and friendship in their company, and my misfortune
has ever been that my choice deceived me, or that I failed
when I had chosen well."

Restif asked Loiseau for advice when his dissipations resulted in sickness, and Loiseau's suggestions were useful.
Sometimes still, Restif allowed himself to be led astray by
certain of his friends whose names were odious to Loiseau.
Then, one day, as he was wandering about, near the Opéra,
he saw a charming young girl whom he had never seen before.   He followed her, and found that her manner of living obliged him to rescue her, for she retained a certain
modesty and sweetness.   "I felt the same respect for her
as for Fanchette *in Mme. Parangon's presence"*—an extraordinary qualification.

Restif worked hard all the week, thinking of his discovery.   On Sunday, Loiseau proposed some expedition or
other, but Restif mysteriously replied that he had something better to do.   Loiseau smiled pityingly, and remon-

strated in a friendly way.   After a couple of weeks, Restif
introduced Loiseau to Zéphire, for such was her name.   A
few days later, Restif came down with fever which confined
him to his bed.   Loiseau took care of him, but, on account
of their poverty, very few comforts were available, though
Loiseau sold most of his clothes to buy essentials.   Restif
had not told Zéphire where he lived, and when she found
him after a long search, she was horrified at the untidiness
and want which Loiseau had not been able to abolish.   She
began at once to transform the room to make it livable,
and to give Restif a variety of attention to which he tear-
fully and gratefully responded.   Loiseau had not been there
on the occasion of her first visit, and, when he returned, he
found a sum of money which Restif said she must have left.
Zéphire came back with her sister Marion, and all four ate
their supper together.   Zéphire and Restif had one plate
between them, and Loiseau and Marion shared the only
other that the place afforded.   Restif learned that Zéphire,
who was seventeen, had practised her regrettable calling
since the age of ten.   She had been launched upon this
career by her mother, who told her that her prostitution
was useful, that she thereby saved many a good woman,
and that aside from the foolish prejudices of many people,
there was nothing objectionable in such a life.   Zéphire
had never been in love before she met Restif, nor had she
been so happy at any time in her life.   Restif could not
marry her at once, for all his savings had been spent in his
illness, so he promised to marry her as soon as he could.
It seemed good to him that she should be established as
assistant to the proprietress of a hat shop, for this sober
occupation would fit her for the duties of a wife, and ab-

solve her from the taint of her erstwhile profession, the
horrors of which were enlarged upon, for her benefit, by
Restif and Loiseau. Her betrothed could not avoid a
slight feeling of condescension in regard to Zéphire, in
spite of the fact that his own life had been far worse than
hers, for she had not had his bringing up. Zéphire and
Marion thought that Restif and Loiseau were most admirable young men.

When Restif's health returned, he determined to work as
he had never worked before, on account of Zéphire. They
went on picnics with Loiseau and his friend Zoé and
Marion, who had married another man after the failure of
an attempt to replace Zoé in Loiseau's affection. These
Sunday excursions were habitual, and for eighteen months
nothing marred the pleasant routine of their lives. "I had
been happy with Mme. Parangon, as one protected. Now
I found equal content in protecting Zéphire. Of course I
could not give my parents the joy that my marriage with
Fanchette would have been to them, for if I had told them
of the circumstances in which I had found Zéphire, they
would never have believed in all her good qualities. Consequently I was forced to invent a story about her. Meanwhile I was happy as in old age, when one feels that an
established condition of bliss will last till the end of one's
days. My greatest ambition was to marry Zéphire, who
should continue to sell hats while I worked in the printing-
house, so that our united efforts should provide a comfortable means of livelihood."

Nothing shows more completely than Restif's life with
Zéphire how hopelessly his evasions and errors had reduced
him to weakness. He loved Zéphire, but she must help him

make money. He swore to be true to her, yet he promptly failed and continued to fail in this regard. He blamed these infidelities on his friends, who had given him immoral books which affected him too strongly. Zéphire had proved and maintained a devotion to him which he deserved in no way whatsoever, and of which he had become absolutely and forever incapable toward her or anyone else. A kind of magnetism in him retained his friends long after a host of reasons would have carried them off. His excuses became more and more futile. Why did he read books that were harmful to him? "Well, so did Danton," he replies.

A strange adventure overtook him one night in December, 1758. He was walking along one of the main streets of Paris when he passed two well-dressed men who "seemed to be gentlemen." In accordance with his habitual detachment, he had been talking aloud to himself, forgetting his experience with the policeman. He heard one of the two men remark to the other: "What sort of eccentric do you suppose that is?" Restif turned and stared at them, and was thus addressed: "Are you angry at us?"—"Yes and no," replied Restif, and walked on. The man continued what Restif calls his insolence, so he promptly walked back and knocked him down. Unfortunately, however, he had forgotten to bring his sword with him. In those days no one went about in Paris without a weapon, and gentlemen of wealth or position further protected themselves by ordering their servants to follow them. Restif was at once attacked by the two valets of these men, from whom he fled and almost escaped, but they were too quick for him. "What a country," says Restif, "in which two coxcombs can attack and arrest a man who has asked nothing of them but to be let alone! How I detest these insolent nobles who take advantage of the fact that they were born in a family worthy or powerful in the past—a trivial circumstance, since their names are otherwise undistinguished to-day! They oppress useful men who are far more valuable than they." Restif wrote this in 1795, when the progress of the Revolution gave him the courage to add: "All tyranny is insufferable, and the oppressions of the sansculottes were even worse than the tyranny of the princes who did not persecute everyone, for they did not know everyone! But the sansculottes penetrated into every corner of Paris, and no one escaped their vigilance. They were wicked, jealous of their equals, drunk with the will-to-all-power, insolent and unjust like all ignorant men, cruel as only they can be who have become accustomed to degradation."

How did Restif dare to say these things in 1795? Because the power of the sansculottes ceased with the reaction that followed the fall of Robespierre in 1794. This guarded manner of speaking will be seen to be typical of Restif during the Revolution, which he described in *Les Nuits*.

The adventure with the valeted gentlemen continued. Restif was escorted to the prison of Chaillot,[4] on the outskirts of Paris. He refused to tell his name, for he would have had to sign the book containing the list of prisoners, and from this disgrace he wished to save his parents. The

---

[4] *À chaillot* became a slang phrase meaning "get out." *Un ahuri de chaillot*—an imbecile or simpleton.

prison authorities addressed his captors as "Monseigneur," and Restif found out later that they belonged to the family of Orléans. They advised the jailer to guard him very closely, but he was allowed to write a note which a messenger carried to Zéphire. This seems to have interested Messieurs, for they waited an hour, till she arrived. "They were touched by her beauty, and for her sake they set me free." To this improbable tale Restif adds: "If they had been Jacobins, I should never have regained my liberty," another thrust at the Revolution which he felt safe in making. The Jacobins, like the sansculottes, had ceased to be dangerous.

Even such a short stay at Chaillot involved certain expenses which, Restif says, were paid by Messieurs. "They whispered praise of Zéphire as we walked away."

Restif and Zéphire struggled along, as fast as they could, but Zéphire, weakened by fever, had nearly exhausted her strength when she reached Chaillot. Restif was obliged to carry her. At the Tuileries they took a cab, and when they came to her lodgings, Zéphire, pale and trembling, was put to bed at once. Restif did what he could for her, and did not know that her recovery was impossible. Loiseau helped at night, and Zoé stayed with her during the day when Restif and Loiseau were at the printing-house. Restif's friends decided to spare him the knowledge that Zéphire's death was inevitable, and on the evening of the second day, he felt encouraged by her smile. He gave her what food she could take, and the doctor told him to stay with her, hoping that his presence might keep her alive a few hours. Zoé stayed in the room all night. Zéphire said that she could breathe more easily with her head on

Restif's heart, and he held her thus till morning. She could not eat or drink. Her last effort was to open her eyes, to kiss his hand, to beg him to rest. Finally he laid her head on the pillow and sat in a chair beside the bed, thinking her asleep. She was dead. Zoé called him to the door, asked him to find Loiseau and bring him back. He went out weeping, humming a tune that made him weep still more. He told Loiseau to come, not knowing that this signal had been pre-arranged, but noticing that Loiseau was deeply moved. Loiseau urged him to go to the shop. "You are too tired to rest," he said. They worked together for an hour. "Now let us go," said Restif. "A little later," Loiseau said, and Restif agreed, in a wondering state of helplessness. At last Loiseau led him out, taking an indirect route. "Why are we going down this street?" Restif asked. Loiseau answered: "When one goes to a great sorrow, the way is always too short."— "What do you mean?"—"We have come to deep grief, my friend, you through love, and I through friendship."— "Zéphire is dead," cried Restif, "why did I leave her?"— "She died in your arms."—"Great God." Restif's voice was strange. They sat down silently on a stone bench. Loiseau wept, Restif's eyes were dry and staring. Suddenly he rushed to Zéphire's room, threw himself on the bed and kissed her cold lips. "She is not dead—she breathes."—Loiseau came in, and drew him gently aside.

Restif followed the funeral at a distance, his eyes fixed upon the coffin. When the earth closed over her he felt the deepest depths of his despair, and resolved to leave an empty world. Perhaps he would have thrown himself into the Seine if this had not seemed to him a shameful way to die. He went to Loiseau's room and found his pistol; but Loiseau caught his hand in time, and led him to his lodging, where, for days and nights, he or Zoé or one of their friends watched Restif constantly, till, by degrees, he recovered. Before long he heard that Mlle. Guéant had died, and that the cause of her death had been a disease which she had caught from him. Was there a curse upon him that separated him from everyone for whom he cared? "Ah, if I had known, when Zéphire died, that she was the last of all those who had really loved me, what would have become of me?"

The hope that he might find someone to take Zéphire's place seemed to him the one thing that saved him from utter despair during the agonizing days that followed her death. There was not enough consolation in the discovery, made early in 1759, that his daughter by Marguerite Paris had been well taken care of by an aristocratic lady who had undertaken to educate her and to provide for her in every possible way. Nor could he find interest in his small daughter whose mother had been Zéphire. He must have recreation. Nothing else could cure his misery. Amusement restored him, and yet the comparative rapidity of the convalescence cannot stand as the measure of the affliction at the time of its descent upon him.

In 1759, Restif had the misfortune to meet Henriette Kircher, an English girl, fairly well off, whose unscrupulous aunt plotted darkly against her. This undercurrent of intrigue escaped Restif's knowledge, and he found Henriette a desirable young person whom he asserts that he married. No legal or religious knot ever united them but the speed with which they separated would almost seem to indicate that marriage had bound them together. Restif's father heard that Henriette was a Protestant. On the contrary, she entirely lacked any formal or informal religion whatsoever, though her character did not resemble that of her aunt. For a Catholic, even of Restif's type, to marry a Protestant, even of hers, would have been a sin of the blackest dye, in the eyes of Edmé, and he wrote Restif a terrific epistle, full of every kind of "righteous" anger. Hardly had this letter arrived, when another came from Henriette, who had deserted Restif that morning, and who now bid him an eternal farewell, confessing that she had robbed the house, at her aunt's bidding, and that she would send back to him all that she could manage surreptitiously to extract from her aunt's clutches. She had not wished to go, but her aunt had always laid down the law, and she knew not how to escape. She further explained that this dreadful relative had raked up a most disreputable, though titled, person to whose mercies she intended to deliver her niece. Restif could think of nothing to do, for Henriette had not given him her address. "Thus ended my *second* marriage," says Restif, who always regarded the girl whose death he had bewailed in Auxerre, as his first wife. Bad as these two "marriages" were, they were admirable in comparison with his third *and only* matrimonial alliance.

Later in the year he left Paris for no particular reason except that he vaguely felt the need of a change. Not even his friendship for Loiseau could keep him at the work which had begun to pall upon him. He friends gave him an affectionate farewell as he took the great rumbling coach, a mammoth "sea-going hack," for Auxerre. At

Sens he started to walk, for the motion of the coach, as in his childhood, had been too much for him. Memories of his life at Auxerre aroused his usual outbursts of melodramatic sentimentality, when he entered that city. At Courgis he imagined he saw "Jeannette Rousseau guarded by two dragons with flaming eyes." He moved on to Sacy. "Reader, in following the course of my life, you will see that I have sometimes pictured *you* in my accounts of myself. Have you not often thought of doing many of those things which I have done?" How hard he sometimes found it to draw a parallel between his life and those of other people, even those whom he knew best!

When he reached the farmhouse of la Bretonne, one of his father's dogs remembered him, "and drove away the others who regarded him as a stranger." Restif's parents and their friends received him warmly, and they forgot unpleasant rumours of his life in Paris in their satisfaction at his return. He told them much of what he had heard and seen, and his powers of description and narration were highly praised. He omitted his most grievous faults, but he told practically everything about Zéphire, and his audience understood her tragedy. No one blamed him for the affair with Henriette Kircher. The pleasantest part of his story concerned Loiseau, for whose kindness Edmé felt especially grateful. If it had not been for Loiseau, he thought, Restif would have come back from Paris no better off than most of the country boys who went there. And then, in a day or so, a letter came from Zoé, telling of Loiseau's death. Restif had read the letter in a field, where he was found unconscious. He had not outgrown his fainting spells.

Edmé had set his heart on a plan for Restif to marry a girl whom he knew in the village, now that Fanchette had married someone else.   In consideration of the grief which Loiseau's death occasioned he let the subject drop, and suggested a trip to Dijon (the capital of their province) which he thought would interest Restif.   Evidently Edmé would never grasp the fact that the worst place in the world for Restif was any city.   It was particularly foolish to send him to Dijon, for Restif had begun to read and study again and would have been quite happy to remain at Sacy, at any rate for the time being, until something else occurred to him.

Naturally, at Dijon, Restif continued to indulge and to excuse himself with consistent inconsistency.   He worked in a printing-house and amused himself as he pleased.   He had almost made up his mind to marry an attractive girl whose mother proved to be she who had adopted his daughter by Mme. Parangon, when it occurred to him to return to Paris.   The alleged reason for this sudden departure was that he felt he ought to see Zoé.   She had asked him to come, in her letter telling of Loiseau's death, and, at that time, Restif had not been inclined to go. Now it seemed to him a pressing duty.   He urged the Dijon girl to write to him, and, strangely enough, to address her letters not to Paris, but to Sacy.   His parents had heard only of his indiscriminate love affairs in Dijon, and, when letters began to arrive, they determined to keep them, hoping that Restif would forget everyone he had known in the Burgundian capital.   Restif did not forget; he imagined that he had been forgotten.

On his arrival in Paris, he went at once to see Zoé,

whom he found ill and in bed. Her joy at seeing him increased her sickness, and in a few days she died. In her will she had left him everything, partly because he had been Loiseau's closest friend, and partly because she cared more for him, now that Loiseau had died, than for anyone she knew. Restif gave to her relatives all that had come to him through her; this left him practically destitute, and there were no vacancies in the printing-houses in which he had formerly worked. If it had not been for an old friend of Loiseau, who gave him board and lodging, Restif would have been without resource. Through this friend, Restif met a rich woman who agreed to marry him, but just before the wedding she was robbed and murdered. If he had had a deeper knowledge of her character, a knowledge which he did not gain in the perfectly free intimacy of her company—he would have congratulated himself upon such an escape. However, he was at once to fall into a much deeper trap.

Early in November he received a surprising letter from M. Parangon, for he had never been in favour with that gentleman, nor had he expected to see or hear from him again. M. Parangon offered him a job at Auxerre. Restif would not have accepted the offer if he had found means of self-support in Paris, for Mme. Parangon's death and Fanchette's marriage had deprived Auxerre of any attraction for him. When he reached Auxerre, he found that a man named Ruttot had been persuaded by M. Parangon to take Restif into his home, and there, accordingly, Restif agreed to live. For some time, he suspected nothing, and occupied himself in trying, with insufficient deliberation but without economy of mental effort, to de-

cide whether or not he wished to be in love, could be in
love, and, if so, would marry any one of several girls whom
he knew in Auxerre.   His family had a complete trust in
M. Parangon, whose plans for Restif's ruin were the exact
reverse of those for which the Restifs gave him credit,
and they were delighted to know that their son had returned to Auxerre.   When Loiseau lived there, he had
fallen in love with a Mlle. Lebègue and when he came to
Paris he had expatiated on her virtues and charms, and on
those of her cousin Agnès.   Finding that Agnès's mother,
Mme. Lebègue, was a close friend of his landlord, M.
Ruttot, Restif was at once disposed in Ruttot's favour, for
he would have doubted Loiseau himself before questioning
his opinion of the Lebègues.   The whole purpose of
Parangon in persuading Restif to return to Auxerre was to
entangle him in the meshes of these Lebègues, whom he
knew to be dishonest, immoral, common, and yet rich
enough to appear desirable to a young man who altogether lacked discrimination and money.   His reason for
this ill-will toward his deceased wife's friend was this very
friendship, the extent of which he had learned after Restif's
departure for Paris.

Meanwhile, Restif worked well and imagined himself to
be growing steadily in Parangon's favour.   Mme. Lebègue
and Agnès disappointed him at first, but he felt sure there
must be many fine qualities beneath their uninspiring sur-
faces.   Agnès was neither beautiful nor brilliant, therefore
Restif decided that she must be shy, though there was
nothing whatever in the manners of either Agnès or her
mother to indicate this quality as a family trait.

He quarrelled with his favourite among the other girls

of Auxerre, for her wit had offended his pride, and this contributed to his attendance upon the charming Agnès. Mlle. Lebègue's opportunity was not obstructed by Restif's memories of the marriageable girl in Dijon who continued to write to him, for his father had persisted in concealing the letters, not only on account of his distrust of the girl, but also because of another one, not Agnès, whom he had selected for Restif. To add to the misunderstanding, Parangon discovered this Dijon girl's affection for Restif, and informed her that Restif had ceased to love her, had become interested in someone else, and that it would be useless for her to hope to see him again. She accepted Parangon's advice and wrote no more. As for Restif, he had long ago decided that she had completely forgotten his existence.

Although everything that Restif saw or heard of Agnès and her mother served to strengthen his first impression of them, he clung to Loiseau's words; faith triumphed over experience. He went again to Sacy, and told his parents that the character of Agnès and her family connections were admirable. When he returned to Auxerre he discovered such an abyss of immorality and callousness in the Lebègues that it seemed, even to him, sheer madness to regard them as better than hopelessly corrupt. A numbness, dumbness, indifference or madness, if not all four, prevented Restif from calling off this ludicrous farce. The influence of her physical charm cannot explain his stupidity. Though her face lacked beauty, the proportions of her body seemed to him quite faultless. But, for the observation and enjoyment of these, neither he nor Agnès scrupled to waive a legal or religious sanction.

Restif writes: "I continued to blind myself. All my previous marriage plans had foundered miserably. Fate had ordained that no marriage could be better or worse for me than any other." In such a case, why marry at all? Restif had neither the simplicity of greatness nor of common sense. Only one thing can be said for the alliance. If Agnès had one redeeming virtue, Restif would have given her more pain than he actually did.

In April, 1760, Restif's parents joyfully came to Auxerre for the wedding. A large crowd assembled outside the church to see the happy pair. "I was very handsome that day," says Restif, "and I heard many whispering feminine voices praising me and saying: 'Agnès is not worthy of him.' I left the church, after the ceremony, with the depressing conviction of being lost. And so I was." And so he was.

Mme. Lebègue celebrated the day in a state of complete intoxication. "Alas!" cried Restif, "I could have been such a good husband! I should have loved to depend upon the prudence and intelligence of a devoted wife, who would take care of all the household affairs, so that I might occupy myself solely with my business."

Restif took Agnès to Sacy. His parents found no fault in her. How long they had dreamed of such felicity for their dear son! She remained, for a day or so, while Restif went back to Auxerre to attend to his work.

The little vagaries of Mme. Lebègue rapidly assumed the proportions of intolerable abominations. Her taste for a frequent sip became a habit of more constant and of greater intemperance, and what could, at best, be the pardonable frailties of an exuberant nature dragged her into noisy orgies which disturbed the peace of the house of M. and Mme. Restif. Agnès told her husband that they must leave her mother, since they could not reform her; and she advised him to look for a job in Paris. Suddenly she decided to do this for him. Parangon was about to cap the climax of his vengeance by doing unto Restif as he had been done by him. Agnès had no intention of permitting this, not through faithfulness to Restif, but through dislike of Parangon. And Parangon could not see that even if he had succeeded in his plan, he would in no way have upset the composure of Restif, for, in the absence of Agnès, Restif at once sought solace elsewhere, and Agnès no less promptly alleviated the cruelty of a temporary separation by blighting her troth. This mutual understanding alone rendered their bondage to each other endurable. What arrangement could be more reasonable, under the circumstances? What illusions had they? They dared look life in the face, they thought.

Agnès had informed Restif that she expected him to remain in Auxerre until he had made more money. When he accomplished this, he went to Sacy to bid his parents another farewell; and now he discovered the letters which the Dijon girl had written him. His father explained that he had kept them because of the information that, at Dijon, Restif had known no respectable girls. Restif contradicted these reports, and added that the family of this girl had virtually adopted his daughter by Mme. Parangon, which had been an incentive to him to marry into this family that he might thereby establish a new bond between himself and his daughter, who could thus have become his sister. His father showed great grief at the

consequences of his action, but he found consolation in
the thought that Restif had married well, in spite of these
misunderstandings.   Restif forgave his father in affectionate consideration of his good intentions, and he had reason
to be glad he had done so, for he never saw Edmé again.
He left Sacy with a heavy heart.   On the way to Paris he
foolishly stopped at Auxerre, where his gracious mother-
in-law managed to get from him practically all his money,
and consequently he reached Paris with very few francs
for the hands of Agnès, which were hardly less grasping
than her mother's.

He promptly began his work in a printing-house in
which Agnès had found a position for him.   His earnings
were devoured by his wife, and, later, by his two daughters.   Agnès got into debt and decided to do dressmaking,
the profits of which, however, were meagre.   She treated
him "cruelly and contemptuously," and their lives drifted
further and further apart.   One of Restif's daughters
married a brutal drunkard who got Restif into trouble during the Revolution; but the usually undiscriminating knife
of the guillotine finally descended upon the creature's neck,
and thereby injustice gloriously miscarried.   Dumas' novel
Ingénue was derived from this story.

This separation from his son-in-law had been preceded
in 1784 by a divorce from his wife, and upon these two
events Restif is to be as heartily congratulated as upon almost any other occurrence in his extraordinary history.

CHAPTER XIII

Restif's Social Experiences

RESTIF took himself very seriously when he went out to dinner, in contrast to the amusement which he caused others. In 1784 he met a young man named Grimot de La Reynière who was famous for his supper-parties. During the carnival of 1783 he gave a dinner to twenty-two people, beginning with an extraordinary funeral ceremony which was the talk of Paris for several days. There were nine courses, each composed of one kind of meat cooked in twenty-two different ways. This must have been almost as tedious as the opening ceremony, but the guests felt that they had had a rare and wonderful experience. When Restif first went to Grimot's, he met Mercier, the writer, who became a warm friend. The guests were invited to come at noon, and during several hours of rapid conversation there were light refreshments and coffee in abundance to which the guests helped themselves. There were recitals of unpublished poems and readings of new plays by their authors. Criticism was frank and epigrams were numerous, and nobody's feelings were hurt, for everyone had come to laugh at his own or another's expense. People who were not found to be amusing at one of these gatherings were not invited to the next, but any person who had been invited could bring as many as four of his friends with him to be tried out. Conversation and reading occupied the time till eight o'clock, when dinner was served.

There were twenty-eight courses. Each course, carried in on a large platter, was preceded by a master of ceremonies who held a baton with which he kept time for two flute players who followed him. Boys wearing long tunics, like the choirboys at Bicêtre, walked at the side of the servant who brought in the platter. The carver was the chief personage of the group, taller than the servants who passed the slices of meat. The long procession marched three times round the table where sat the twenty-eight guests, responsible for the twenty-eight courses. It seemed to M. de La Reynière that the numbers of everything must be in accordance with something. The room was lighted by three hundred and sixty-five candles, in honour of the three hundred and sixty-five days of the year. "As in the days of the Romans," says Restif, "there were no napkins; one wiped one's hands on the hair of maidservants who were provided for this purpose." This elaborate dinner bored Restif, but he had enjoyed the preceding conversation. The parents of Grimot disapproved of such display, though they allowed their son the use of the heavy silver platters which had added so much to the dignity of the occasion. It seems that in 1786 young Grimot was imprisoned by his father, "to keep him out of trouble," like the young Duc de Richelieu who was locked up because he would not live with the girl whom his parents had compelled him to marry. One might assume that the sons of the lords of France would have welcomed the Revolution.

In 1785 the Duc de Gèvres invited Restif to a dinner at which, says M. Nicolas, "I shone brilliantly for the only time in my life. Rivarol was present, and I defeated him in repartee. I was looked up to as an Oracle of Taste, and the famous Goldoni applauded me." Restif had written a play which he read aloud "to everyone's delight." He tried later to induce the Comédie-Française to perform his piece but it was rejected. He had treated a questionable subject far too broadly, and, worst of all, he had not written in verse. Restif wrote several volumes of plays, none of which were ever seen upon a stage, for they were all insufferably boring. One, called *The Judgment of Paris,* represents Venus, Juno and Minerva talking in the manner of pretentiously refined laundresses.

In January, 1787, Restif dined at the expense of the Duc de Mailly and of the Comte de Gémonville. He read some of his "scientific" writings, which were "applauded by two academicians of Amiens, but found to be un-Biblical in the opinion of an Abbé." Restif quotes the *highly* flattering remarks of one of the guests: "What good sense this Restif shows in his behaviour, for surely his conduct at dinner cannot be the result of experience! I am amazed at his logic, for I had expected him to reveal the most romantically exalted imagination!" Restif reports that not long after this he dined with the Duchesse de Mailly, the Princesse de Chalais, and the Comtesse d'Argenson, with whom he was surprised to feel singularly at ease.

During the early days of the Revolution, Restif consented to dine at the house of Senac de Meilhan, an unimportant but agreeable author. Restif sat next to a woman called Mme. Denis, of masculine manner, disguised as an Amazon, whose high voice and steady gaze were not irresistibly charming. Restif was informed that she worked in a dressmaking establishment. Her remarks were flattering, and Restif found her interesting. The conversation turned on politics, and Mme. Denis asked Restif what "the people" were saying about the Revolution. His glass had been kept full of excellent wine; consequently his eloquence and fire, grace and vivacity, delighted everyone. At the right moment the subject of his book was introduced, and from this time until the party broke up, Restif's voice and gestures knew no rest. Mme. Denis asked if she might call on him; and so she did, more than once, in the same costume. Restif's daughter mistook her for a man; but though Restif had learned who she really was, she never impressed him except at the dinner on account of the wine. His information had arrived, the day after, in a letter from Meilhan: "Mme. Denis is the Duchesse de Luynes; the lame, sarcastic man is the Bishop of Autun (Talleyrand), the man in the white coat is Sieyès. The company assembled in disguise to put you at ease. I had been asked to invite you; and you pleased us all."

Restif says that the Abbé Sieyès sent him all his books on politics—"for which I have forgotten to thank him." He may have felt on the subject of Sieyès what Talleyrand said when he heard the Abbé referred to as profound: "He is not deep; he is hollow."

Mercier took Restif to call on Mme. de Staël, and brought him away full of enthusiasm for that lady, though he does not mention her in *Monsieur Nicolas*.

In 1787, Restif met the Comtesse Fanny de Beauharnais, wife of an uncle of Josephine. She wrote very badly, and entertained a great deal, priding herself upon her salon, which, however, had none of the distinction of the more famous of these institutions. Fanny de Beauharnais was the only literary woman whom Restif ever thoroughly liked, and he never forgot her kindness to him and to his daughter Marion. She invited him to her weekly gatherings. The shabbiness of his fifteen-year-old clothes annoyed a number of her guests, and amused others, especially Fanny herself, who could not be persuaded to ignore him. He could think of no higher praise than to compare her to Mme. Parangon, for Mme. de Beauharnais remembered him when all his other rich friends had deserted him. Her "evenings" consisted of conversation for several hours before supper at eleven-thirty, followed by reading and discussion till three. In this company, Restif read the first part of *Monsieur Nicolas*. Some of his listeners are said to have been lulled to sleep, while others were charmed by his pictures of Mme. Parangon and of Zéphire. Most of the guests departed at three, but Restif frequently stayed till five to listen to the gossip which flourished in a small circle whose centre was always the Countess herself.

Restif at a formal dinner usually remained silent or even morose for various reasons—his hard life, his lonely days spent in writing and thinking, and the childish shyness from which he never entirely freed himself. He has been described [1] as of medium height, walking with a slight stoop, having a reserved almost clerical air, for the former divinity student did not lose the manners so completely as the morals of his early education. His eyelashes were long, his eyes narrow, his nose aquiline, and his mouth finely shaped. The flash of the eye, the well-proportioned head, the athletic figure and the sobriety of manner were noticed by

---

[1] J. Soury, in *Le Temps*, 1876, Feb. 4, 15, 24, 29. For Cubières-Palmézeaux's account, see Lacroix's *Bibliography*.

his friend Palmézeaux, who, however, resorted to fancy in depicting his character. Restif rather prided himself on his peculiar disregard for appearances, and frequently went directly from his work to a formal dinner. On one of these occasions something was said which Restif took as an insult—an impersonal allusion to novel-writing as not the highest form of literature. He rose, cried out that he was not appreciated, and left the room, much to everyone's amusement.

Cubières-Palmézeaux saw him one day in a bookstore, wearing a broad-brimmed hat which almost hid his face. His overcoat, of a heavy, coarse material, was strapped around the waist in a peculiar manner, giving him the appearance of a beast of burden. For some years he had neglected his wig-maker, and his hair was in disorder. He pulled from his pocket a broken candle which he lit and stuck in a lantern. Then he went upstairs to his room, without having paid the slightest attention to anyone, nor spoken a word. Palmézeaux asked the proprietor of the store who this strange creature might be. "Don't you know him?" replied the man. "He is Restif de la Bretonne." A few years later, Palmézeaux met Restif at Mme. de Beauharnais' and asked him to explain his manner in the bookstore, which had been observed on several other occasions. "I was working on one of my books," said Restif, "and I had sworn to speak to no one until I had finished it." Henceforth Restif cordially greeted Palmézeaux whenever he saw him. One day he appeared in the street, wearing a beard, contrary to precedent, and Palmézeaux expressed his surprise. "It shall not be cut," said Restif, "till I have finished my new novel, which will be published in fifteen volumes." Palmézeaux asked him how long this would keep him busy. "I have written three volumes, and I shall write half a volume each day, consequently I will shave in about three weeks."

At Mme. de Beauharnais', Restif had been introduced to the Comte de Tilly, a rake who eventually killed himself. This gentleman tells [2] of his surprise when Restif called on him, one morning: "I could not remember having seen him before, but he reminded me of the occasion, and I recalled having met him once or twice in the salon of the Countess. Her gatherings consisted of a crowd of fashionable and literary people of very unequal merit. The affectation of the many counterbalanced the *esprit* of the few, and I had ceased to attend. The author of the *Paysan Perverti* said that he had heard much of me, and that he had come to ask me to tell him of my most sensational love-affairs, which he would place advantageously in a book which he had planned to write for posterity; not for his contemporaries, whose attitude bored him. One could but laugh at the purpose of this visit. I told him that my life had been shockingly devoid of interest, but that I thanked him for his attention. I told him that I greatly appreciated this opportunity to appear before the eyes of posterity, and that I hoped in the future to be able to report an adventure worthy of the originality and colour of his style. My compliments charmed him; but he was still more charmed by the thought of his novels. He did not hesitate to affirm that the *Paysan Perverti* was a novel of the highest rank, which would last as long as the French language. He congratulated

---

[2] Comte de Tilly, *Mémoires*, II, pp. 264–8.

himself on being misunderstood by an epoch the dull satiety
and worthlessness of which were complete. The attacks
of the journalists and of academicians whose writings were
inferior to his, were his surest titles to immortality. To
all this I replied: 'You are right!' I bowed to him, and
he withdrew. Nevertheless it is difficult to judge Restif.
Criticism is compromised in praising him highly, yet it is
easy to be unjust to him. Some of his writings are those
of a man possessed; neither he nor his readers can explain
them. Elsewhere there is an originality and piquancy in
his style; and his lack of taste is, in itself, a kind of genius.
One feels no desire to read his books when one has merely
glanced at them, yet the reader who deliberately begins,
usually finishes Restif's novels. Some of his pages are so
remarkable that one continues to hope for others equally
so, and this hope is not always deceiving. The excuse for
his choice of subjects would be a masterful handling of
them, and in this he cannot always be said to have succeeded. If I have often shrugged my shoulders in pity for
him, he has sometimes caused me to laugh, to tremble and
to weep. In much of his work there is a vigorous though
disordered genius. He is the Teniers of novelists; his
Paysan Perverti is the *Liaisons Dangereuses* of the people."

It is clear that Tilly had not tried to read all of Restif's
books. There are some which, the more one determines
to read them, the more surely one fails, for their futility
and solemn nonsense increase with every page.

In 1788, M. Dumont failed to persuade Restif to offer
one of his books for the *prix d'utilité*, for he could not convince him that members of the Academy would ever be able

to appreciate his novels; nor is it likely that they would. The Academy of the *ancien régime* had ignored Restif. When, in 1795, it was reorganized by the Convention, and called the National Institute, Mercier, who was a member, thought that Restif might be admitted into this presumably more broad-minded society, and he proposed Restif's name. The President of the Academy replied: "Restif de la Bretonne has genius, but no taste." Mercier answered: "Sirs, which one of us has genius?" Restif's name was voted upon, and only Mercier favoured his admission. Restif did not know this, and stupidly assumed that Mercier had prevented his election. He had said that Mercier's kindness to him must be a mockery, for Mercier was a Parisian, and none of the critics of Paris had ever praised him.[3] For some time he treated Mercier very coldly, but at last he agreed to a renewal of friendship. In 1796 he wrote: "I wish to inform the public that there is a conspiracy afoot to keep me out of the Academy. This coalition embraces all the most vile of authors. Now, who says that I wish to be elected to the Academy? I have made no attempt to belong to that company whose members I am thankful not to resemble in any way." He had pasted up a large placard, in a conspicuous place in Paris, on which he had written:—"No doubt Restif has been forgotten in the formation of the Institut National, just as the article on Paris was forgotten in the printing of the Encyclopedia." He accomplished nothing by his protests, and, as usual, he was partly right, and mostly wrong. He did

---

[3] This reasoning is as false as the second premise.

well to question the judgments of the Academy. Wiser
men than he have done so, and greater men have been
excluded. None the less, his real feeling was of intense
desire to get in, for the Academy impressed him.

His bitterness in regard to academies was no less than
his hatred of censors, and he devised a means of evading
their decrees in regard to his books. When a censor
changed or erased his sentences, Restif printed a few copies
in accordance with their corrections. Then he would rear-
range the type, and print his book as he had written it.
This proved a dangerous game, for it would have been so
easy to give one of the wrong copies to the censor, and he
had to be specially careful that no one saw him reset the
type. It seems, however, that he managed to escape discovery, and a large number of his books were printed in
this way.

CHAPTER XIV

The Wanderer in the Revolution

IT has been said that Restif's habit was to walk about the
Île Saint-Louis, singing and reciting, or carving names on
the bridge-heads. Frequently he wandered through other
parts of Paris, in a general kind of curiosity, and sometimes
he spent a whole night in this way, in the most unhealthy
and dangerous parts of the city. He interfered in quarrels
on the side which seemed to him the weaker or the
worthier; often he consoled the sorrowful, gave them helpful advice, or found some means of doing them service.
In this way he gathered much material for his endless
stories. No sort of bad weather prevented these excursions. On the sixth of each October he visited every place
in Paris which he associated with the memory of Zéphire;
and other lost loves were celebrated on other days in a
similar manner. One of his books called *Mes Inscriptions:
journal intime* was found in the Bibliothéque de l'Arsenal,
after his death. No one knew how it got there, though
Restif had a strange habit of hiding his manuscripts in the
most unlikely places, fearing that his room might be robbed.
Fortunately, better copies of the *Inscriptions* and other records have been found, for the originals were practically
impossible to read. Restif economized paper to such a
degree that his microscopic writing became an indecipher-
able mass. "The fifth of November, 1779," he asserts,
"was the day on which I first carved names and dates on

the stone or wooden bridge-heads, parapets and railings of the Île Saint-Louis." He began on the Pont Rouge, which connected that island with the Île de la Cité. This bridge, built of wood in 1627, painted with red lead to preserve it, nevertheless rotted away, and a flood destroyed it and Restif's records in 1789. There were others on the Quai d'Orléans, and many different places all of which he remembered, and would visit from time to time to read the words he had carved in Latin, or in French; his tears would flow as he recalled the sorrows which had come to him, and the friends he had lost.

Not satisfied with *Les Inscriptions,* he wrote *Les Nuits de Paris,* or *Le Spectateur Nocturne,* in many volumes [1] recording his adventures just before, during, and after the Revolution. He imagined that, as he walked about, he resembled a distinguished officer, employed by the government, when in fact, he looked more like a tramp, or a lunatic who had escaped from Bicêtre.

In 1785 he had met the Marquise de Montalembert. Often, at night, he stopped at her window, in the course of his walks, and told her what he had seen, and she told him her misfortunes. [2] Her marriage to the Marquis de Montalembert had been unhappy. In 1792 he took her to London, and left her there while he returned to Paris and divorced her. She remained in London till he died, and settled again in Paris in 1800. After having been a charming hostess, and a talented actress in private theatricals, she was to become a novelist of no importance.

---

[1] Published between 1788 and 1794.
[2] According to Lacroix, Restif saw the Marquise only once. Lacroix, *Bibliographie,* p. 266.

One night, in a place called *le Cagnard,* at the corner of the rue de la Huchette, near a chemist's, Restif found the mutilated body of a dead child.   He went next day to tell the chemist, who said: "Students of surgery in Paris are not given bodies to dissect, and they are obliged to buy or steal them.   When they have finished their examinations they take great pains to dispose of the body in such a way that their theft cannot be traced.   At night they often come to a lonely place like this, and if they hear someone coming they drop the body and run.   Otherwise they carry it to the river or bury it."   The apothecary became eloquent on the subject of the absurdity of not giving the bodies of criminals who had been executed to the medical schools, "but," he added, "when I say these things, people look at me in horror."   Another night, in the cemetery of Saint-Séverin, Restif saw men digging up a body which had been buried the day before.   He followed them, and was able, later on, to recognize the face of a girl whom he had known.

Early in 1789 Restif went to Switzerland.   He had thought that his European vogue justified an effort to have his books printed in a foreign country; and he could thus free himself from the intolerable persecutions of the French censors.   When he returned to Paris the Revolution hung like a cloud over the city, and Restif was astonished at the agitation shown by the people.   He hoped this excitement would calm down, but on the contrary it increased daily. On the evening of his arrival, Restif saw a large crowd gathered around a table on which stood a man delivering a violent harangue with an accompaniment of extravagant gestures.   The crowd pushed closer and closer till the table was overturned.   The speaker hurt his leg in falling and told his friends to carry him to a café where he would make another speech. As he was borne along he passed Restif, and called out to him: "Are you a stranger here?" Evidently Restif's eccentric appearance suggested anything but a Parisian. "No," replied Restif, "I have just returned from Switzerland." "All right," cried the orator, "come along—I have something to tell you." Restif followed him and heard him describe the discontent of the people, the great events which were sure to happen, and he said: "Everyone must watch and be ready." Restif was not greatly impressed.

He had often spent his evenings in the garden of the Palais-Royal, listening to the laughter of the children, watching their games, and enjoying the spectacle of young lovers walking down the tree-lined paths, across the open spaces, by the pool where the fountain played, and lingering in secluded spots. On the night of July twelfth, soldiers charged into this peaceful place and frightened the children, whose mothers rushed shrieking to their rescue. The cause of this disturbance had been an imagined insult to an officer. At the Café de Foy, near the entrance to the garden, Camille Desmoulins made his famous speech, and so thrilled a large crowd that the taking of the Bastille became a certainty. Restif heard him—and fled. "I hated him already. I belonged to no club or party; I knew not which to choose, so I held back from all. In Desmoulins' audience I saw only gross men with flaming eyes who were preparing themselves for plunder, rather than for liberty."

Restif tells of the confusion of the next day, the long search for powder and ammunition. On the fourteenth, he remained in his room till the middle of the afternoon.

When he went out, he saw the heads of two men on pikes, carried like banners through the streets. Another pike had been decorated with intestines, and was held aloft by a "cannibal who uttered fearful oaths." No one seemed to be moved by these sights. Already they took them for granted. Restif walked toward the Bastille. The fortress had fallen. "Madmen were throwing precious historical documents from the towers into the moat." Restif approved of the fall of the Bastille,[3] but was greatly terrified at the destruction of that prison which he had feared and hated so long. He pitied the governor, whose headless body lay in the Place de Grève.

His own inconveniences, even more than the cruelties of the Revolution, were uppermost in Restif's mind. "For twenty-five years I had lived in Paris, free as air. For this liberty, only two things had been necessary: to be honest, and to write no articles against ministers of state. I had never been arrested before the Revolution." Now he began to be frequently stopped and questioned in his favourite haunts, especially on the Île Saint-Louis. The Fourteenth of July, 1789, is not, to Restif, the day of the fall of the Bastille, but the last day on which he inscribed a memorandum on "his" île. The joy of his sad wanderings had been stolen from him, and henceforth he associated the island with the valley-kingdom of his youth, for it had also been the Fourteenth of July, he wails, when he ended his days as shepherd.

---

[3] Historians have recently maintained that the conditions at Bicêtre were worse than at the Bastille when the Revolution began. It appears that after the taking of the Bastille, the revolutionists established prisons still more barbarous than any for which the old régime was responsible.

Palmézeaux says that, in spite of Restif's timidity, he saw him station himself in front of the Tuileries, as one of the King's guard, at a very dangerous time. If this be true, it was probably an effort on Restif's part to show himself loyal to Louis XVI at a time when he feared the king's anger, for at first he could not believe that the monarchy would fall. Palmézeaux also reports that Restif had a friend in the National Convention whom he had liked and respected for a long time. On the day when Louis XVI was condemned, Restif stood outside the building in which the trial was proceeding, with a pistol in his pocket. When his friend appeared, Restif asked him if he had voted for the death of the king.—"No."—"So much the better," said Restif, "for if you had, I would have blown your brains out."

It appears that, early in the Revolution, at the instigation of Mirabeau, Restif wrote pamphlets against the Abbé Maury,[4] Mirabeau's enemy, and, according to some, a rival in politics as well as in wit and immoral living. Mirabeau once threatened to "close a vicious circle around him." The Abbé replied: "Are you going to embrace me?" Mirabeau sought the aid of all sorts of people in his political campaigns, and it occurred to him that Restif might have some influence among the people of the lower classes. Of the libels (or just criticisms) aimed at Maury during the Revolution which he survived, three have been attributed to Restif without sufficient testimony. It appears,

---

[4] This Abbé inspired almost the only witty remark ever attributed to Louis XVI, who had listened to one of his sermons: "He would have preached on every subject, if he had mentioned religion."

however, that Restif greatly admired Mirabeau, who would have known how to lead him by flattery; and Restif remarks in *Les Nuits* that Mirabeau alone could have saved the monarchy, had he lived.

He witnessed several executions, but his horror at the trivial and mocking references which were made to the victims as soon as the ax had fallen, kept him from frequent attendance on such occasions. "I am an excellent patriot, and yet I said to myself, when I heard the jibes of the mob: 'If human beings must be sacrificed to the public good, why may they not be treated with dignity?'"

"On the fourth of October, a dull rumble preceded the outbreak of new terrors. On the fifth, the roar resembled an eruption of Vesuvius. This hideous commotion was caused by the women, protesting against the high price of bread. The market-women added to their forces a collection of men of the most base depravity, disguised as women, and out-going them in atrocity. If they met along the road to Versailles a well-dressed lady whom they assumed to be a countess, or, worse than that, of higher rank, they tripped her up and covered her with mud. There was a baroness who seemed to find less than her usual pleasure in this contact with the mire." Had the Revolution taught Restif the use of irony?

In spite of these disturbances, the theatres of Paris were open every evening, and there were the usual performances of very bad and very good plays, both kinds as popular as before.

The twenty-sixth of October was a fearful night for poor Restif. His wicked son-in-law Augé denounced him, telling the authorities that his printed and spoken words had been constantly disloyal to the "principles" of the Revolution. Restif, ill and in bed, was routed out by fusiliers who had been summoned by the soldiers of the guard stationed near the street where he lived, and who took him to a police station. In the trial which followed, Restif and Augé accused each other of objectionable authorship. Both were searched, and their papers examined. For once, injustice miscarried; Augé was permanently locked up and Restif gained his freedom. In this frame-up, Augé had been energetically aided by Agnès Lebègue, whose hatred of Restif had not been appeased by divorce. She confirmed all of Augé's charges; her ingenuity had been perfected by long practice in false accusations, the devising of which had been the joy of her marriage.

Restif describes the great "Feast of Federation," July 13–14, 1790. "I walked about the Champ de Mars, watching the assembling of various bodies of troops and the arrival of deputies from every part of France. Finally the king himself appeared. This was the last happy occasion of his life. The ceremony was beautiful and impressive, and the king seemed to be moved by the demonstration, for I think I saw tears in his eyes. This was the most magnificent day of the Revolution. La Fayette graced the festival with all his glory which has since passed away like a dream." Restif was ready to lose his former confidence in Louis XVI (who somehow failed to say the word which would have inspired the trust of the populace) and to criticize the political intrigues of Marie-Antoinette, the royal flight to Varennes, and the emigration of the nobles.

He says of Marat: "It was this infamous man whose theory of administration ignored intelligence, culture, and education." He calls the revolutionary committees "good in themselves, but dominated by the ignorant and immoral sansculottes."

"The massacres of September cast a sombre horror over Paris. The writer who describes them should write calmly and without passion, in order to be a true historian." One night Restif was watching the dancing through the open windows of a large restaurant, when a passerby called out: "Will you stop your dancing? There is another kind of dance going on elsewhere." The massacres in the prisons had begun. Restif saw the murder of the Princesse de Lamballe, who had refused to cry: "Down with the nobles!" Her robe was torn off, and her body was cut open. Restif fainted. When he regained consciousness, he saw her head carried on a pike.

On Christmas night, 1792, Restif again broke his vows, and visited the Île Saint-Louis. Little boys threw stones at him, and he sorrowfully ran away.

Restif came to the point of calling Louis XVI blind, not criminal. Then terror got the better of his judgment, and when the royal execution had taken place, Restif wrote: "Louis, justly condemned by the nation, was worthy of death. Now it is necessary to call him tyrant." He follows this with another change of attitude, while watching the street-fighting of February, 1793: "Paris is peopled with worse subjects than under the old régime." Then, hastily: "I do not regret the monarchy, for it caused too much suffering." Restif made these remarks in a street where a battle was raging. A young soldier of the national guard said to him: "You did well, old man, to add that last sentence. Otherwise I would have taken you for an aristocrat." Restif explained that he was not a socialist; that he believed some men had a right to be rich, but that no one should be allowed to own too much land, for it would be kept idle and uncultivated.

Now he is converted to revolutionary principles: "Marie-Antoinette's death is the result of not following in the footsteps of the revolutionists. . . . When a society, or its majority, desires something, it should have it. The minority is always wrong, even when morally right. . . . !" He closes his *Nuits* with this profession of political *faith*: "I believe the true representative of the Republic is the Mountain; that the Jacobins and the members of patriotic clubs and those who think as they do, are the true patriots of France; that Marat and Robespierre have saved the nation; that the September massacres were just and necessary, especially the execution of all reactionary priests and laymen. *Vive la Republique et la Montaigne!*"

The worst element in this shifting about, is Restif's toleration of cruelty, the crime which had always seemed to him supreme, although he had always thought of government as a despotism. "In my childhood I did not doubt that the king had a right to oblige a man to give up his wife or his daughter, no matter for what reason. This was also the opinion of everyone in Sacy." Just as he had believed in the divine right of the Bourbons, so he persuaded himself that the revolutionists were the unquestionable oracles of the destinies of the state.

According to Quérard,[5] "Restif boasted of having prepared the way for the Revolution by his writings. In 1795

---

[5] Quérard, *La France Littéraire*, VII, p. 551.

he flattered himself that he would be elected deputy to the
Convention by the Department of the Indre, and when he
failed to be chosen, he laid the blame on the jealousy and
malice of his enemies. When, in 1795, the Convention announced the distribution of prizes to men of letters, Restif
applied for and obtained a reward of two thousand francs
for having written 'several moral books.' "

CHAPTER XV

The Last Years

As early as 1794 Restif reports the beginning of a conviction that he had not long to live. He withdrew more and
more within himself, in daily life, and at the same time began to write the most confidential of autobiographies. He
admitted that *Monsieur Nicolas* was too intimate to warrant
its publication during his life, but his need for money would
not spare him the pain of self-revealment, and he became
the historian of his life for the next three years. From
time to time his friends gave him certain sums which resulted in very little material good, for his expenditures were
foolish. Several of his grandchildren were orphans, and
none of his relatives were well off.

He still continued his absurd flirtations, but gradually he
realized that they were too undignified. Girls who were
pretty enough to attract his attention, began to mock him
in the streets. He discovered, he says, that one of his
mistresses had proved to be one of his illegitimate daughters. Formerly he had persuaded himself that his "affairs"
were good for him. He would otherwise have satisfied his
desires in unnatural ways. Now he had no excuse that
could convince even his own ready credulity, and he became
a superannuated figure that often aroused pity. He put the
story of Sara chronologically out of place because he did
not wish to end his book with an old man's last sad years.
"I desired to close my chapters with a story of passion, in
defiance of the laws of nature."

He set up a little printing-press, and hired a few assistants, but this experiment only added to his poverty. His workers cheated him, his publishers continued to rob and then to ignore him. During the last ten years of his life he sold no books except at a loss, and even *Monsieur Nicolas* was a financial disappointment. "I am ending my life as Mme. Parangon said I would end it. I have lost most of my friends, and most of my children. What a comfort they would have been to me!"

Thus, on the last page of *Monsieur Nicolas:* "At the close of my career I have nothing left but despair. Someone else, not I, will commemorate my death. Reader, I know not whether I now bid you a final farewell—1797."

The thirteenth volume of *Monsieur Nicolas* is a calendar in which each day of the year is devoted to the memory of one or more of the names that stood, in his experience, for the landmarks along the road of love. The year groans with the burden; December's task is no lighter than January's. The fourteenth and last volume is a set of notes on his books—*l'histoire de mon esprit*—as the others had been the history of his body, soul, and heart.

He lived with his daughter, Marion, whose husband had died, leaving her to provide for three children. She bore the burden of her father's peculiarities courageously and devotedly till he died. For a month it was necessary for him to go to a hospital from which he returned in better health than he had enjoyed for some years. "Like most hypochondriacs," says Soury,[1] "Restif worried constantly about his health; he often mistook a slight ache or pain

---

[1] *Le Temps,* Feb. 29, 1876.

for a serious illness, and rushed in a panic to a doctor."
Restif asserts that after 1764 he suffered from frequent
attacks of indigestion.   Often he can recall a year, a month,
or a day, when some slight physical annoyance had upset
him, and medical science in the eighteenth century was not
always equal to the task of providing adequate remedies.
Restif's favourite doctor was Guillebert de Préval, persecuted by his colleagues for a water-cure which he put on
the market.   Préval considered himself a specialist in vene-
real diseases, and his public demonstrations of special cures
had become notorious.   For these experiments he had been
ejected from the Faculty of Medicine in Paris, and his reputation became that of a quack.   None the less, Restif's confidence in him could not be shaken; he called him friend and
brother, and when Préval died his patient wrote an epitaph,
which had become his favourite mode of honouring the
dear departed.   Restif despaired of finding another doctor
to take Préval's place, and he went occasionally to Mme.
Préval, who gave him the medicine which her husband had
used, and probably told Restif, as her deceased spouse had
sometimes impatiently done, that his troubles were largely
the work of imagination.

Restif read a medical book, one day, when he thought
himself sick: "Never do this," he warns; "it does more
harm than good, and one begins to feel the symptoms
which one has studied.   I would no doubt have died of
such effects, if it had not been for my friend Préval."

Restif's constant work at his books and printing-press had
weakened his nerves, and after 1795 he expected to die
at any time.   "My heart has vanished with my senses, and
when I feel a tender emotion I know it is an illusion.   The

one real joy of my life was physical passion. When this power left me, my life seemed without meaning, and my sorrow has grown heavier and more profound." This unbalanced condition explains the story and the history of Restif. "I have written freely, like Rabelais and Montaigne. It is the abomination of censorship which has kept others from writing as they wrote."

In 1796 appeared *The Philosophy of M. Nicolas,* a confused rhapsody, an attempt to be scientific which is, at best, amusing. Everything on earth and in the sky, from plants to planets, he explains in terms of sex. Then he jumps to religion: "How do I know that God is good, and intelligent? Because I am." Then back to scientific discoveries: "The comets are males, the planets are females. Their off-spring are satellites." There are volumes devoted to the explanation of these great truths. The *Philosophy* recalls the last effort of Nietzsche to explain himself, after he had become insane, under the title: "Why I write such great books."

In 1798 appeared *L'Anti-Justine,* which Restif hoped would combat the influence of the Marquis de Sade, whom he scorned, and whose *Justine* seemed to Restif a dangerous book against which it was his duty to warn the public, and to tell them that his (Restif's) two *bêtes noires* were perversion and cruelty. In this case Restif's influence was less than it deserved to be.

In 1802 appeared *Les Posthumes,* or *Letters du Tombeau,* inspired by Mme. de Beauharnais, who gave Restif the general idea which he developed into erotomania. There is an extraordinary character, the Duc de Multiplitandre, whose adventures, wanderings, mysterious transformations are not without a certain power of imaginative description, and when one wonders at this quality in Restif, one is not surprised to discover that the book was partly written by Cazotte,[2] who, it seems, had asked Restif to finish and publish it.   Cazotte's reputation for licentiousness had often got him into difficulties, and Restif determined to publish the book under Cazotte's name to save his own from the censor's inevitable objections.   Why should he not?   Cazotte had been dead for six years, and though he might have had, during that time, infinite trouble with other censors, surely those of Paris could do him no harm.   In *Les Posthumes* there is much hocus-pocus, but even the greatest feats of hypnotism cannot dispose of the essential boredom of the book.

When Restif died, he left many plans for more novels, and some that he had begun.   In *L'Enclos et les Oiseaux* the influence of Cazotte is still apparent.   In *Les Rêvies,* Restif planned to write his life as it would have been if it had been happy.   His idea of perfect bliss was to recover (perhaps by a new magic) his youth, to go back to Sacy and buy acres of land which he would donate to his family, and then, with a mysterious income of fifty thousand f~ancs a year, he would return to Paris and conquer the city with his books.

His last years dragged themselves out, and only one amusing incident relieves their monotony.   In 1798 [3] he

---

[2] Cazotte was a popular writer, executed in 1792. Among other vagaries, he believed himself to have the power of prophecy. In his *Diable Amoureux* the hero succeeds in conjuring up the devil.

[3] See Funck-Brentano's article in *Revue des Études Historiques,* LXXVII, pp. 589–594.

wrote an historical essay which won for him a position in Moulins. He was to teach history in a high school, and Moulins congratulated itself that it had found a distinguished scholar who would stimulate the young students in that part of France. A formal invitation was sent to him, and his arrival was expected to be prompt; but Restif never arrived. The city of Moulins waited "for seventeen months," and at the expiration of this generously long period it was decided to find someone else to take his place. Restif had been in great need; he should have jumped at the chance, and, in fact, he did accept, and then forgot to go. Several minor jobs were given to him in Paris, and he drew the small salaries thereby accruing without bothering to fulfil the duties thus undertaken.

He wrote to a friend: "Help me to print at least four or five of my manuscripts, and I will mortgage my share of the proceeds." There was no reply. An edition of a part of his later productions which he printed himself, is said to have been seized by Napoleon; [4] but this is unlikely. Napoleon attempted to help him by assigning him to a small job in connection with tax-collecting. This came too near his death to be of use.

After the Revolution, Restif's capital consisted entirely of paper money (issued during the political upheaval) which proved to be almost worthless by the time Napoleon had established his government. A hundred francs in this currency was worth about thirty centimes. The result had been widespread bankruptcy, which fell most heavily on the bourgeoisie. The Director Carnot had come to Restif's

---

[4] *Révue des Livres Anciens*, I, p. 87.

rescue and that of his family, and, as usual, they had promptly sunk again into poverty. Fontanes,[5] who seems to have known every writer in Paris (even Agnès Lebègue, whose qualities as authoress were closely akin to her other attributes), did what he could for Restif, but in vain; for his irresponsibility grew with his declining health, and it had become more and more difficult for his daughter Marion to restrain his whims and to quiet his nerves. She nursed him throughout his illness, which grew steadily worse. He died on February 8, 1806. Fontanes went to his funeral and saw him buried in the cemetery of Sainte-Catherine. It was written of Restif:—

Son esprit, libre et fier, sans guide, sans modèle,
Même alors qu'il s'égare, étonne ses rivaux;
Amant de la nature, il lui dut ses pinceaux,
Et fut simple, inégal et sublime comme elle.

---

[5] *Le Temps,* Feb. 29, 1876.

Bibliography

Bibliography

This bibliography gives the principal works of the four authors under consideration. A complete list would include many unpublished, unfinished and unrevised writings, with the various translations, especially into German, of a large number of Restif's novels.

WORKS OF C. P. J. DE CRÉBILLON

Œuvres, 7 vols., Londres, 1777
Ah! Quel Conte, Paris, 1754
Atalzaïde, Paris, 1745 '
L'Écumoire, Bruxelles, 1733
Les Égarements du Cœur et de l'Esprit, Paris, 1736
Le Hazard du Coin du Feu, Bruxelles (Charles Gilliet, éditeur, Paris), 1880
Lettres de Mme. la Marquise de Pompadour, Paris, 1753
Lettres de Ninon de Lenclos au Marquis de Seirgné, Paris, 1806
La Nuit et le Moment, Bruxelles, 1881
The Skimmer (L'Écumoire), London, 1742
Le Sopha, Paris, 1740
Le Sylphe, Paris, 1730

WORKS OF DENIS DIDEROT

Œuvres Complètes, 20 vols., Paris, Garnier *frères*, 1875–7
Le Neveu de Rameau, Paris, Plon-Nourrit et Cie., Monval et Thoinan, éditeurs (on basis of original document), 1891

WORKS OF C. A. F. CHODERLOS DE LACLOS

Les Liaisons Dangereuses, ou Lettres recueillies dans une Société et publiées pour l'Instruction de quelques autres, par M. C—— de L—— à Amsterdam, et se trouve à Paris chez Durand *neveu,* Libraire à la Sagesse, rue Galande, 4 vols., en 4 parties, 1782. (The original MS. given to the Bibliothèque Nationale, 1849, by Mme. Charles de Laclos [MS. Français, 12845], entitled *Le Danger des Liaisons,* was altered as to title in first edition because of a novel by Mme. de Saint-Aubin, *Le Danger des Liaisons, ou Mémoires de la Baronne de Blémon,* Paris, 1763.)

Dangerous Connections or Letters collected in a Society and published for the Instruction of other Societies, by M. C—— de L——, London, printed for T. Hookham, 1784, 4 vols. in—8°

Les Liaisons Dangereuses, 2 vols., Paris, G. Crès et Cie., 1920

Vœux d'un Gallophile, Paris, 1786

De l'Education des Femmes, avec notes par Baudelaire, Paris, 1903

Lettres Inédites, Paris, 1904

Poésies, Paris, 1908

WORKS OF N. A. E. RESTIF DE LA BRETONNE

La Famille Vertueuse, 4 vols., Paris, 1767

Le Pied de Fanchette, 3 vols., Paris, 1769

La Fille Naturelle, 2 vols., Paris, 1769

La Femme dans les trois états de Fille, d'Épouse et de Mère, histoire morale, comique et véritable, Londres et Paris, 1773

Le Ménage Parisien, 2 vols., La Haie, 1773

Le Paysan Perverti ou Les Dangers de la Ville, 4 vols., Paris, 1775

L'École des Pères, 3 vols., Paris, 1776

Le Nouvel Abeilard, ou Lettres de deux amants qui ne se sont jamais vus, 4 vols., Paris, 1778

La Vie de Mon Père, 2 vols., Paris, 1779 (Published also in the series *Les Mœurs légères au 18ᵉ Siècle,* with introduction by H. d'Almeras, Paris, Louis-Michaud)

Les Contemporaines
   1. *Les Contemporaines, ou Aventures des plus jolies femmes de l'âge présent,* 17 vols., Lyon, 1780–2
   2. *Les Contemporaines du Commun,* 13 vols., Paris, 1782–3
   3. *Les Contemporaines par Gradation,* 12 vols., Paris, 1783
La Découverte Australe, 4 vols., Paris, 1781
La Dernière Aventure d'un Homme de 45 Ans, Paris, 1783
La Prévention Nationale, 3 vols., Paris, 1784
La Paysanne Pervertie, 4 vols., Paris, 1784
Les Veillées du Marais, 2 vols., Waterford, capitale de Mommonie, 1785
Les Parisiennes, 4 vols., Paris, 1787
Le Paysan et la Paysanne Pervertis, 4 vols., La Haie, 1787
Les Nuits de Paris, ou Le Spectateur Nocturne, 8 vols., Londres et Paris, 1788–94
Ingénue Saxancour, 3 vols., Paris, 1789
Le Palais-Royal, 3 vols., Paris, 1790
L'Année des Dames Nationales, 12 vols., Paris, 1791–4
Théâtre, 5 vols., Paris, 1793
Le Drame de la Vie, 5 vols., Paris, 1793
M. Nicolas, ou Le Cœur Humain Dévoilé, 16 vols., Paris, 1794–7
(Published also by Isadore Liseux, 5 Quai Malaquais, Paris, in 14 vols., 1883)
La Philosophie de M. Nicolas, 3 vols., Paris, 1796
L'Anti-Justine, Paris, 1798
Les Posthumes ou Lettres du Tombeau, reçues après la mort du mari par sa femme qui le croit à Florence, 4 vols., Paris, 1802

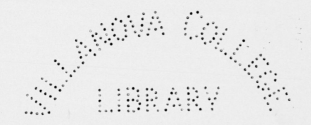

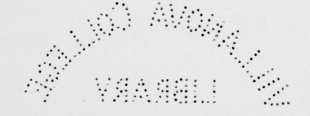